Software Engineering with B

INTERNATIONAL COMPUTER SCIENCE SERIES

Consulting Editor **A D McGettrick** University of Strathclyde

SELECTED TITLES IN THE SERIES

Software Development with Z *J B Wordsworth*

Program Verification *N Francez*

Concurrent Systems: An Integrated Approach to Operating Systems, Database, and Distributed Systems *J Bacon*

Introduction to Parallel Processing *B Codenotti and M Leoncini*

Concurrent Programming *A Burns and G Davies*

Comparative Programming Languages (2nd Edn) *L B Wilson and R G Clark*

Functional Programming and Parallel Graph Rewriting *R Plasmeijer and M van Eekelen*

Object-Oriented Database Systems: Concepts and Architectures *E Bertino and L D Martino*

Programming in Ada (4th Edn) *J G P Barnes*

Software Design *D Budgen*

Ada from the Beginning (2nd Edn) *J Skansholm*

Programming Language Essentials *H E Bal and D Grune*

Human-Computer Interaction *J Preece et al.*

Distributed Systems: Concepts and Design (2nd Edn) *G Coulouris, J Dollimore and T Kindberg*

Fortran 90 Programming *T M R Ellis, I R Philips and T M Lahey*

Foundations of Computing: System Development with Set Theory and Logic *T Scheurer*

Principles of Object-Oriented Software Development *A Eliëns*

Object-Oriented Programming in Eiffel *Pete Thomas and Ray Weedon*

Compiler Design *R Wilhelm and D Maurer*

Miranda: The Craft of Functional Programming *Simon Thompson*

Software Engineering (5th edn) *Ian Sommerville*

Haskell: The Craft of Functional Programming *Simon Thompson*

Software Engineering with B

J.B. WORDSWORTH
IBM United Kingdom Laboratories

ADDISON-WESLEY

Harlow, England ■ Reading, Massachusetts ■ Menlo Park, California
New York ■ Don Mills, Ontario ■ Amsterdam ■ Bonn ■ Sydney ■ Singapore
Tokyo ■ Madrid ■ San Juan ■ Milan ■ Mexico City ■ Seoul ■ Taipei

Addison Wesley Longman Limited
Edinburgh Gate
Harlow
Essex
CM20 2JE
England

and Associated Companies throughout the world.

The programs in this book have been included for their instructional value.
They have been tested with care but are not guaranteed for any particular
purpose. The publisher does not offer any warranties or representations
nor does it accept any liabilities with respect to the programs.

Many of the designations used by manufacturers and sellers to distinguish
their products are claimed as trademarks. Addison Wesley Longman has
made every attempt to supply trademark information about manufacturers
and their products mentioned in this book. A list of the trademark
designations and their owners appears on page xv.

Cover designed by TGC Ltd and
printed by The Riverside Printing Co. (Reading) Ltd.
Typeset using BookMaster™ and the IBM 3116 Page Printer.
Printed and bound in Great Britain by T. J. Press (Padstow) Ltd, Cornwall.

First printed 1996

ISBN 0−201−40356−0

British Library Cataloguing in Publication Data
A catalogue record for this book is available from the British Library.

Library of Congress Cataloging in Publication Data is available.

Preface

Software engineering with B has three aspects, and in this book I hope to show that the interaction of these can be used in two ways: first as an aid to practical software development in a competitive environment, and second as a subject of study for potential software engineers. The dual nature of the book means that it caters for two distinct audiences. For the industrial user it is a complete account of the B-Method, with examples and exercises, for many of which solutions are provided. For the academic user it is a source book of applications of a simple but far-reaching mathematical theory, and can serve as a text for an undergraduate or post-graduate software engineering course.

The first aspect of B is the B-Method, a method for the systematic development of large software systems from reusable fragments, which is an essential part of software engineering. It is important that the approach should be systematic, and not piecemeal, or software development could hardly qualify as an engineering discipline. It is also important that we should be able to develop large software systems, since today's software purchasers demand a lot of function. Lastly it is important to have a way of reusing software components, or software development projects will inevitably have low productivity and take a long time to market.

The second aspect of B is the abstract machine notation (AMN), a well-tried body of mathematics to support the systematic method just mentioned. The abstraction and precision that come from using set theory and predicate calculus in software development give the software developer a power that is not available to those using informal methods. This power is required by some software procurers, especially for defence and safety-critical systems, but its use to gain commercial advantage in industrial software development, particularly in high-integrity, high-availability systems, is becoming more common.

The third aspect of B is the B-Toolkit, a collection of computer-based tools to automate many of the procedures of a mathematically based software development method. The toolkit supports most of the activities of software engineering: specification, animation, consistency proofs, design, proof obligation generation, correctness verification, code generation from designs, test application generation, and the production of well-indexed documentation to record the development.

The subject of this book is the ideal combination of these three. The systematic method makes the software engineer's efforts profitable, the mathematics makes them dependable, and the toolkit makes them possible.

The contents of the book are as follows:

- Chapter 1 introduces the ideas of software engineering supported by the B-Method, particularly the notion of a layered structure for software.

- Chapter 2 introduces the idea of a machine as a specification for software, discusses the nature of the proof obligations for consistency of a machine, and describes ways of using machines in various layers of a software structure.

- Chapter 3 shows how a component-layer machine is built, and introduces more substitutions for machines.

- Chapter 4 introduces the ideas of deferred sets, and introduces some substitutions for specifying non-determinism in operations.

- Chapter 5 shows how large machines can be constructed from smaller machines.

- Chapter 6 completes the repertoire of substitutions that can be used in machines.

- Chapter 7 introduces the idea of software design as the process of producing a software object from a specification expressed as a machine. It explores the idea of correctness of designs.

- Chapter 8 introduces the idea of an implementation as the software developer's view of a software system, and describes ways of reusing machines from lower layers of the software structure.

- Chapter 9 concentrates on machines for the application programming interface (API) layer, and on their implementations. This chapter also shows how data types more complex than numbers can be introduced into a development.

- Chapter 10 introduces the idea of a refinement as an intermediary between a machine and its implementation.

- Appendices review the relevant discrete mathematics, and summarize the notation used in the book. There are definitions of the B-Toolkit library machines used in the book, sample solutions to many of the exercises, a bibliography, a glossary of technical terms and a comprehensive index.

Supplementary material on the World Wide Web

Readers of the book who do not have a copy of the B-Toolkit are invited to access the following FTP site

ftp://ftp.aw.com/cseng/authors/wordsworth/softeng-b/

where they will find a demonstration copy of the B-Toolkit. The **README.softeng-b** file gives instructions for down-loading the toolkit and for operating it using some of the material from this book.

Readers of the book who have access to a full-function copy of the B-Toolkit can use the diskette provided with the book for working through the demonstrations and exercises. Full operating instructions for using the diskette with the B-Toolkit are available on the World Wide Web. Use your web browser to find

http://www.aw.com/cseng/authors/wordsworth/softeng-b/

and follow the link to the book supplements page.

If you have questions or comments about this book, please send e-mail to aw.cse@awl.com.

Acknowledgements

The B-Method and the abstract machine notation were invented by Jean-Raymond Abrial, and developed by him and others over several years at BP Research, Sunbury on Thames. As Abrial is also the inventor of Z, everyone interested in formal methods of software development owes him a considerable intellectual debt.

An early draft of this book was reviewed by several people who made useful comments, and I list them here: Juan Bicarregui, Rutherford-Appleton Laboratory; Jeremy Jacob, University of York; Michel Lemoine, CERT-ONERA; Ken Robinson, University of New South Wales; Arthur Ryman, IBM Canada; Shin'ichi Sano, Fujitsu Co.; Bill Stoddart, University of Teesside; Takeji Tanaka, International Christian University, Tokyo; Eoin Woods, LBMS. Several anonymous reviewers made comments on behalf of publishers, but they must remain anonymous.

IBM has always encouraged its employees to publish books that might enhance the corporation's technical reputation in the industrial and academic worlds. I am pleased to say that they have supported the preparation of this book by allowing me to use a B-Toolkit system at the Hursley Park laboratory, by giving me facilities for text preparation and storage, and by allowing me to print drafts, of which the last is the one now published. The figures and some of the text relating to the Resource Manager example have appeared before in tutorial material prepared for IBM, and this material is reproduced here with IBM's permission.

During most of the fourteen years that I have been studying and using formal methods, I have been fortunate to know Ib Sørensen, first at the University of Oxford, where he worked on the IBM CICS project, then at BP Research, and finally at B-Core (UK) Ltd. His help with this book has been invaluable, and he has acted as teacher, critic, and as an inexhaustible source of information.

Finally I should like to thank my wife and family for putting up yet again with the disruption to family life caused by the writing process.

John Wordsworth
June 1996

Contents

Chapter 1
Introduction

Summary: Software engineering education — mathematics in software engineering — industrial and academic users — function model — state machine model — abstract machines — encapsulation — implementations — refinements — the component layer — the library layer — the application programming interface layer — the application layer.

1.1 Why this book was written

The development of software engineering education and software
engineering practice over the past few years has been marked by the
improved position given to mathematics. Not many years ago, in
spite of the efforts of such eminent teachers as Dijkstra, Hoare and
Gries, mathematics was still regarded as being connected more with
the design of the electronic hardware of computing than with the
software that breathed life into it. The increased popularity of software development notations like Z and VDM suggests that an engineering approach to programming has begun to displace the arcane
practices of the traditional craft.

The software development method presented in this book has a
contribution to make to practice and to education that is at least as
significant as that of the other methods mentioned above. It is almost
unique among software development methods in that it uses a
unified notation for specification, design and programming. The
problems of changing notation from specification to design, or from
design to program, are removed, and a single notation serves for all.
The abstract machine notation, and the development method based
on it, are supported by the B-Toolkit. The toolkit provides a
computer-aided software engineering (CASE) environment that is
firmly based in mathematics, with facilities for specification, animation, design, proof obligation generation, automatic and interactive proof, and code generation.

Although the method has industrial users, and although its characteristics make it attractive as an education vehicle for software engineering, there are so far no textbooks that provide a step-by-step
guide to the fundamental ideas of the method or their application to
software development. I hope this book will be found to fill both
rôles.

1.2 Who should read this book

This book is intended for two classes of readers:

- Students of software engineering at undergraduate or graduate
  level can use the book as an introduction to formal methods of
  software specification and design.

- Analysts, programmers and software design specialists in the software development industry can use the book to learn the
  B-Method and its application to practical problems.

In either case, readers are expected to have some prior knowledge
of discrete mathematics: arithmetic of the natural numbers; algebra
of sets, relations, functions and sequences; propositional algebra;

predicate calculus; informal proofs using formal notations. Appendix A sets out the scope of this prior knowledge, but is intended as a primer rather than as a tutorial text.

1.3 Subjects covered

The book covers a complete software development process from specification through to the production of program materials. The activities in such a process, as envisaged in the B-Method, are discussed later in this introductory chapter. The use of mathematics as a vehicle for software development means that a certain amount of mathematical notation has to be presented. Appendix A reviews the necessary discrete mathematics, and readers should, in the first instance, skim this appendix to see what parts of mathematics they are going to need, and to check on the technical vocabulary that is used to talk about it.

At the end of the book, readers should be able to:

- Write informal descriptions of software components as state machines.

- Formalize simple state machines using abstract machine notation.

- Outline the different characteristics of component machines and API-layer machines, and their rôles in software development.

- Write informal descriptions of state machines that are formally specified.

- Understand the use of the B-Toolkit for entering, committing, analysing and animating machines.

- State the consistency conditions for a machine, and do simple informal proofs of consistency.

- Construct large machines from smaller machines.

- Use an implementation to record design decisions for a machine.

- State the correctness conditions for an implementation of a machine, and do simple proofs of correctness.

- Use a refinement to record data design decisions for a machine.

- Use an implementation to record algorithm design decisions for a refinement.

- Write system definitions for complex data structures.

- Understand the use of the B-Toolkit for generating machines from system definitions.

- Understand the role of the B-Toolkit for translating implementations into C language statements, and for generating sample applications for machines.

1.4 How to use this book

The book can be read as a tutorial in the B-Method. It contains a full account of the method and the notation, illustrated with examples of varying degrees of complexity, and there are numerous exercises, many with solutions supplied. The book can also be used for reference by those using the method in a real software development environment. For the academic community it provides a text that can be used to support a course in formal methods and computer-aided software engineering. It contains many examples and exercises on the application of mathematics to software development. Students are recommended to work in groups to solve some of the longer problems, as one of the aims of formal methods is to make possible precise communication between different interest groups — users, designers, programmers, testers, and so on.

The book will serve both of its intended audiences best if it is used in conjunction with the B-Toolkit. Although it is possible to work the exercises using only pencil and paper, it is much better, and more fun, to do them with the toolkit. A diskette containing the examples used in the text is supplied with the book, and instructions for using it with the B-Toolkit are given on page 31.

1.5 Models of software objects

When software engineers wish to understand the nature of a computer system that they are required to build, they will usually make models of it, like engineers in other disciplines. An important question in software engineering is 'what are the appropriate models for software objects?' Models of software objects can be used for different purposes, and are expressed in different languages. Software engineers, believing that programming is an engineering profession, use models and languages that have a precise basis in mathematics. Some models can be used to express concurrency of operation of the different parts of a software system, and the interaction between the parts. Other models are used to study the performance of systems where many external users are contending for the system's resources. Another class of models is used to study the function of the system independent of its performance characteristics or how its parts will interact, and it is with this last class that we shall be concerned in this book. A model of a software system that expresses its function, that is, *what* it does rather than *how* it does it, is called a **functional**

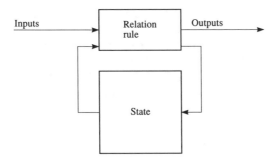

Figure 1.1 Defining an operation in the state machine model.

specification. In this book we shall use **specification** to mean functional specification.

The behaviour of all but the simplest software systems is influenced by the previous history of the system's use. For example, the behaviour of the storage manager of an operating system depends on what storage allocations it has made already, and part of the storage manager's internal state is a record of what storage has been allocated, or what is still free, and this information is updated with each request to allocate or free storage that it processes. There are different ways of modelling such systems. The black boxes of the software engineering methods described in Mills *et al.* (1986) model these systems by specifying the next system response in terms of the history of stimuli to which the system has already been subjected. In the B-Method we prefer the **state machine model**, in which we give an explicit model of the state of the system being described. In a specification, the model is an abstract one, that is to say the essential properties of the internal data are recorded, but not the implementation details. These models are built not from arrays, pointers, database table entries, and so on, but from mathematical values, sets and relations. The state components are usually related in a fixed way, and this relation is expressed in an **invariant**, a property of the state that is always true. The model contains a statement of the **initialization** of the state components, and of course these values must satisfy the invariant. There is also a rule for each of the permissible **operations** that relates the inputs and starting values of the state components to the outputs and ending values of the state components, and it is these ending values that persist until they are modified by the next operation. The interaction between inputs, outputs and state is illustrated in Figure 1.1.

In this model an operation is defined by first presenting a **precondition** that the user of the program must guarantee before the program is executed. A typical precondition might insist that users of storage should free only the storage allocated to them. The general idea of a precondition is that anything that might happen if the precondition is not true when the program runs is the user's responsibility, not the programmer's. Preconditions are often skimped in informal statements of specifications, and this leads user and programmer into frustration and mutual recriminations. The rule relating inputs and starting values to outputs and ending values might be functional – given the inputs, the outputs are uniquely determined, or it might be a more general relation, stating only essential properties that the outputs will possess. In the storage manager, the user asking for storage is guaranteed that the requested amount of storage will be provided for the user's use, but no promise is given about how it will be chosen from the storage available for allocation. Situations that appear to the user to be identical will sometimes yield one address, sometimes another, depending on the storage allocation algorithm chosen by the designer of the storage manager.

Each operation, though it might change the values of the state components, must respect the invariant, that is to say the invariant predicate must be true of the ending values of the state components. The aggregate of state, invariant, initialization and operations constitutes the state machine model of a software system.

1.6 Informal descriptions of state machines

State machines can be described in informal language, and informal descriptions can be used as a preliminary analysis of requirements before a formal specification is attempted. When the formal specification has been finished, the informal description can be improved in the light of the formal. The following informal description describes a state machine that will be used in some of the examples in the rest of the book. This example is based on one used in Wordsworth (1992), where it is formalized in Z.

An oil terminal has berths for five tankers, and the approaches to the terminal can be used to queue up to eight tankers. The owners of the terminal wish to emphasize that if there is a free berth, no tanker can be waiting in the queue. Once a tanker has joined the queue of waiting tankers, it is not allowed to leave until it has docked and has discharged its cargo. Table 1.1 gives the informal description for this oil terminal control system.

It is a state machine with four operations, and it is illustrated in Figure 1.2 on page 8.

Table 1.1 Informal state machine for an oil terminal control system.

Inputs	Processing	Outputs
When a tanker arrives		
tanker	If the input tanker is already docked in a berth or waiting in the queue, this is an operator error, and the response is 'Known tanker'. Otherwise, if there is a free berth, allocate it to the tanker, and output the berth and the response 'Tanker berthed'. If there is no free berth, but the queue is not full, the response is 'Tanker must wait', and the tanker is put at the end of the queue. If the queue is full, the response is 'Queue full'.	response berth
When a tanker leaves		
tanker	If the input tanker is not at a berth, this is an operator error, and the response is 'Tanker not berthed'. If the input tanker is at a berth, and there are no tankers waiting in the queue, the berth becomes free, and the response is 'Berth free'. If there is a tanker waiting, the first tanker in the queue is docked at the berth that is being vacated. The name of that tanker is output, the berth it is to occupy is output, and the response is 'Move tanker'.	berth tanker response
Enquire about a berth		
berth	If the berth is free, the response is 'Berth free'. If there is a tanker docked in the berth, the response is 'Berth occupied', and the tanker occupying the berth is output.	tanker response
Enquire about a tanker		
tanker	If the tanker is at a berth, the response is 'Tanker berthed', and the berth it occupies is output. If the tanker is waiting, the response is 'Tanker waiting', and the position of the tanker in the queue is output. If the tanker is neither docked nor waiting, the response is 'Unknown tanker'.	response berth number

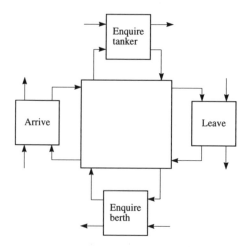

Figure 1.2 State machine with four operations.

1.7 The abstract machine as a state machine

The B-Method works with **abstract machines**, which are just state machines of the kind described in the previous section. The abstract machine has three forms that are used at different stages of the development process, but the nature of the abstract machine as a state machine persists through the stages. The first form of abstract machine is used to model the functional requirements, and it is called simply a **machine**. The machine is the specification construct of the B-Method. In the next chapters we shall look at some simple machines in detail, but for the moment it is sufficient to note that a machine has the essential ingredients described above for the state machine model. As a construct in software development, the machine is used to enforce the idea of **encapsulation**.

The machine provides facilities that might be useful to external users, or in implementing the operations of other machines, but the principle of encapsulation says that the only way to use these facilities is by means of the defined operations. Software developed from machines using the B-Method cannot break this encapsulation. The idea of encapsulation is not of course limited to the B-Method – it is a guiding principle of the engineering approach to software construction – but the B-Method and its supporting tools enforce it completely.

1.8 Implementations and refinements

Although software objects can be executed on computer systems, it is usually the case that specifications cannot be executed. The purpose

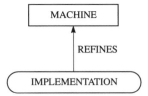

Figure 1.3 A simple development.

of the specification is to act as the basis of discussion about whether the requirements have been properly understood, and to illuminate the requirements and explore them. Specifications are built using mathematical constructs: sets and their members, and predicates about them. The skill of the specifier is to build a model that makes exploration possible. Unfortunately the mathematical constructs used in specifications are not usually good for efficient execution, so given a specification we have to find some way of implementing it using programming facilities like numbers (in a limited range), strings, arrays, pointers and algorithms. In a simple case this might be an easy step to make, and to believe correct. In B-Method terminology an **implementation** is said to refine a machine. A simple situation is illustrated in Figure 1.3.

Like the machine, the implementation has state variables, but as well as being a mathematical model, the state is something that a programmer might devise from program variables and data types. Like the machine, the implementation has an invariant, which says something about the values of the implementation's variables, but also something about the relation of those values to the machine's variables. Like the machine, the implementation has a state, an initial value and operations. The operations are identical in appearance, that is, number and types of inputs and outputs, to those of the machine being refined.

The user of the software is promised a machine, but supplied with an implementation, or rather with code generated by the B-Toolkit from the implementation. The idea of the 'refine' relation between machine and implementation is that the user is entirely deceived by this substitution. There is a limitation that the user must accept, namely that the exploration of what has been provided can only be done using the operations of the machine. Of course if the user is allowed to lift the lid of the implementation, then instead of an elegant mathematical model arranged for ease of understanding, there will appear various programming constructs arranged in a manner to make execution quick and easy.

The software engineer has to be satisfied that a proposed implementation is efficient in execution, able to be done in the time

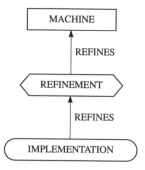

Figure 1.4 A larger development.

allowed and with the resources available, and that it really does refine the machine. Various mathematical tests can be applied to check the correctness of the implementation. These tests are expressed as proof obligations, mathematical theorems that have to be proved to ensure correctness. The B-Toolkit helps the software engineer by generating the proof obligations, and by helping to do the proofs. By omitting to do the proofs, the software engineer is taking a risk. In all stages of software development such trade-offs have to be made, so the conscientious engineer will assess the risk of not doing the proofs.

If the step from machine to implementation is large, the proof obligations will be tedious to state and to prove, so the B-Method allows some easier steps to be inserted between the machine and its implementation. Such an intermediate abstract machine is called a **refinement**, and we say that the refinement refines the machine. The correctness of a refinement is also the subject of proof obligations. Figure 1.4 illustrates a situation where a machine has a refinement, and the refinement has an implementation.

In this case we say that the implementation refines the refinement. In more complex systems, several stages of refinement might be introduced.

1.9 Layered software

1.9.1 Software layers in current systems

The successful operation of most software systems depends on the cooperation of software modules produced by different writers with different skills and interests. The B-Method is aimed at a certain part of the software spectrum. We investigate the characteristics of software by looking at an example of part of a transaction processing system, illustrated in Figure 1.5.

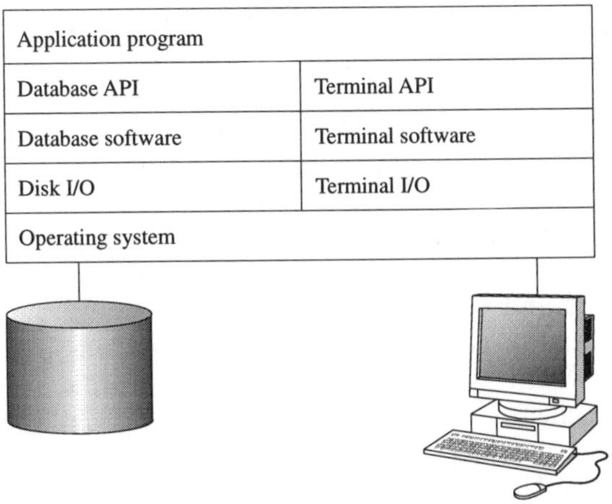

Application program	
Database API	Terminal API
Database software	Terminal software
Disk I/O	Terminal I/O
Operating system	

Figure 1.5 Software structure in a transaction processing system.

The application program, usually written in a high-level language like COBOL, embodies knowledge about the business objectives that the transaction is trying to meet. The designer of the transaction knows the business environment well, and can communicate the business requirements to the application programmer.

The transaction processing requirements are satisfied by using one or more application programming interfaces (APIs), each of which provides a high-level view of data or other facilities useful for constructing transaction processing applications. The left hand side of the diagram is concerned with the database API. The provider of this API is usually not the writer of the application program. Providing APIs is a different part of the software industry from providing applications. The APIs have no knowledge of the business requirements that the application embodies, but they embody concepts of transaction processing.

The implementer of the API uses lower-level components like the database software provided by database manufacturers. The provider of the database software is often not the provider of the API. The database software embodies database concepts, and knows nothing of the importance of databases in transaction processing, and nothing of the business requirements that the databases are meeting.

The database software is implemented using input/output (I/O) software, which knows nothing of databases. This software is usually provided by a hardware manufacturer, and is often part of the computer's operating system. It is however possible to make a distinction between the disk I/O software and the operating system's I/O supervisor. The disk I/O software embodies disk concepts like cylinder and sector, and these concepts are implemented using the device communication facilities of the operating system's I/O supervisor.

The right hand side of Figure 1.5 shows how the same analysis can be applied to an API for controlling the end user's terminal. The terminal API gives the application writer an abstract view of a terminal, while the software in the lower layers relates that abstract view to a data stream, and uses terminal I/O routines to transmit data streams to and from the terminal.

The same kind of structure is seen in other kinds of software. For instance, in a client − server environment the layered structure is replicated on the client system, where the client application might use an API for communicating with the server and an API for a graphical user interface (GUI) for communicating with the end user.

1.9.2 The B-Method and layered software

To understand the rôle of the B-Method in software development we begin by considering a layered model of software structure based on the foregoing discussion. The layered software model appropriate to software development with B is illustrated in Figure 1.6.

The B-Method is not intended for creating software in the application layer, since applications usually have informal requirements. It is however intended for producing software in the API layer and the component layer, since in these layers the requirement is often formally expressed. Part of a B development usually includes creating machines that specify an API. These machines are implemented by

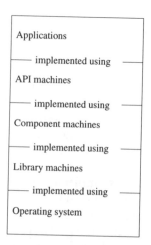

Figure 1.6 Software layers for the B-Method.

using machines from the component layer, which are also specified and developed as part of a B development. The component-layer machines are implemented using library machines, some of which are supplied as part of the B-Toolkit. Machines in the B-Toolkit's **system library** have machine definitions and executable code, but do not have implementations recorded as abstract machines. The toolkit provides a **team library** facility that allows you to create a library of machines to be shared by a team of software developers. The machines in a team library have implementations and executable objects generated from them.

In the rest of this book we study machines in the library, component and API layers, and learn how to implement API-layer machines using component-layer machines, and how to implement component-layer machines using library machines.

Chapter 2
Structure of a simple machine

Summary: A resource manager informally described − a model built from sets and predicates − types in set-theoretic models − the MACHINE clause − the rôle of parameters − the VARIABLES clause − the INVARIANT clause − the INITIALISATION clause − the assignment pseudo-program − the OPERATIONS clause − the PRE-THEN-END pseudo-program − the END clause − establishing the invariant − the substitution predicate − proof obligation for initialization − preserving the invariant − proof obligation for operations − the PRE-THEN-END rule − generalized substitutions − the B-Toolkit − editor − analyser − animator − proof obligation generator − autoprover − proof printer − interprover − markup generator.

In this chapter we construct a simple machine and examine some of its properties. If you have access to the B-Toolkit, you can use it to explore the properties of the machine by animating it, as explained in this chapter.

2.1 Using sets to make a model

The first machine that we study is the specification of a resource manager that will be embedded in a larger system. The resource manager's task is to keep track of a fixed pool of resources. When a user of the resource manager asks for a resource to be allocated, that resource is no longer available for allocation until the user asks for it to be freed. Depending on the system in which the resource manager is embedded, the resources might be hotel rooms, telephone circuits, time slots in a diary, hire cars, and so on.

We first describe the model informally. We introduce the set *RES* to represent the resources to be allocated, and then introduce a subset of it. The subset is called *rfree*, and it is the set of resources that are available to be allocated. We use familiar notations of set theory and predicate calculus to express the properties of parts of the model, so

$$rfree \subseteq RES$$

is used to express precisely what was just expressed informally. This is a simple predicate that says that *rfree* is a subset of *RES*.

The Venn diagram in Figure 2.1 shows a typical configuration of the model. In this diagram the rectangle represents the set *RES*, and the small circles represent individual members of *RES*. In this case there are seven resources to be controlled. The ellipse represents the set *rfree*, and in this case there are three free resources.

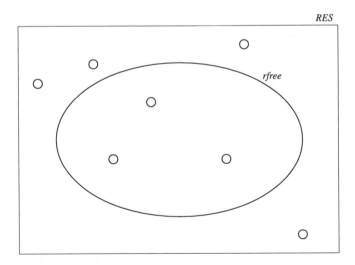

Figure 2.1 State of the resource manager.

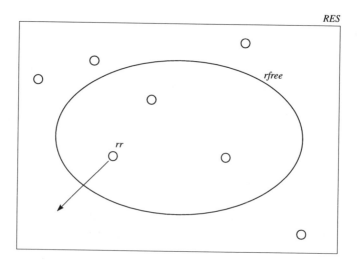

Figure 2.2 Allocating a resource.

Figure 2.2 illustrates the operation of allocating a resource. The user of the operation is expected to identify the resource to be allocated, here called *rr*, and that resource is removed from *rfree*. The resource must be in the set *rfree*, so the operation has a precondition that can be precisely expressed by the following predicate:

  rr ∈ *rfree*

This is a membership predicate. The value of *rfree* after the operation can be precisely expressed by the following notation:

  rfree − {*rr*}

This is the difference of two sets, *rfree* and the singleton set of *rr*, and it denotes *rfree* with the element *rr* removed.

Figure 2.3 illustrates the operation of freeing a resource. The user of the operation is expected to identify the resource to be freed, here called *rr*. That resource must not be in *rfree*, so this operation has a precondition that can be precisely expressed by the following predicate:

  rr ∈ *RES* ∧ *rr* ∉ *rfree*

This predicate is a conjunction of two conjuncts:

- The first conjunct says that *rr* must be a resource. It has the form of a membership predicate.

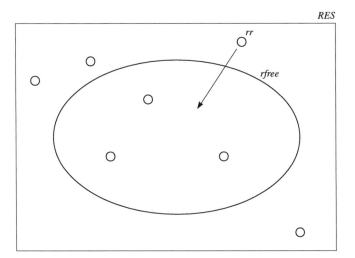

Figure 2.3 Freeing a resource.

- The second conjunct says that *rr* must not be in *rfree*. It has the form of the negation of a membership predicate.

The value of *rfree* after the operation can be precisely expressed by the following notation:

rfree ∪ {*rr*}

This is the union of two sets, *rfree* and the singleton set of *rr*, and it denotes *rfree* with the element *rr* added.

2.1.1 Types in the set-theoretic model

The set theory used in the abstract machine notation is a typed set theory. This means that in any specification that formalizes informal requirements there are certain sets that are used as the basis of the construction. These sets are called the **given sets** of the specification. (The set ℕ of natural numbers from 0 upwards is always considered to be a given set.) The **types** of a specification can be defined recursively as follows:

- Each given set is a type.

- If **T** is a type, so is ℙ (**T**), the powerset of **T**.

- If T_1 and T_2 are types, so is $T_1 \times T_2$, the Cartesian product of T_1 and T_2.

The type of an expression is the type of which it is a member.

The theoretical purpose of a type system is to avoid the paradoxes of set theory. The practical purpose of a type system is to allow us to check that the expressions we write have mathematical meaning.

For the resource manager specification we choose *RES* to be a given set. The predicate

$$rfree \subseteq RES$$

is equivalent to

$$rfree \in \mathbb{P} \ (RES)$$

and so establishes the type of *rfree* as $\mathbb{P} \ (RES)$. The predicate

$$rr \in rfree$$

implies that

$$rr \in RES$$

and so establishes the type of *rr* as *RES*.

Every expression must be built from components of appropriate type. The type rules for set difference, for instance, say that the types of the expressions must be the same, and they must both be of set type, that is, their common type must be of the form $\mathbb{P} \ (\mathbf{T})$. So

$$rfree - \{rr\}$$

is well-typed, since the type of the two expressions is $\mathbb{P} \ (RES)$. The expression

$$rfree - rr$$

is ill-typed, since the types of the two expressions are different.

Every simple predicate that is not establishing the type of one of the values in it must obey certain type rules. For instance, the type rules for the subset predicate say that both the expressions must be of the same type, and that type must be a set type.

2.2 The elements of a simple machine

In this section we look at how we use abstract machine notation to record the specification discussed informally above. In this section, the formal text of the machine is displayed indented, and the parts of it are interspersed with informal explanations and discussion.

We have a choice about how we introduce the set *RES* into the machine, and we consider that now.

- If we choose to make the set internal to the machine we are going to define, the implementer of the resource manager decides what the values in the set are.

- If we choose to make the set a **parameter** of the machine, the user of the machine decides what the values in the set are.

In the example that follows, we have chosen to make the set a parameter of the machine. When a machine is to be used as part of a larger machine, or as part of the implementation of a machine, values have to be supplied for the parameters. The process of supplying values for the parameters is called **instantiation**. A machine with parameters represents a class of machines, and a particular instance of that class is selected by instantiation. Machines with parameters are much harder to develop into software than machines without parameters, because the implementation must be able to cope with whatever sets are provided for the parameters.

2.2.1 The MACHINE clause

The machine begins with a **MACHINE clause**, in which we specify the name of the machine and the names of the parameters. The name is *RMan*, for resource manager. The machine has only one parameter, the set *RES*. It is a convention of abstract machine notation that parameters spelled in uppercase represent sets. Set parameters are given sets of the specification being recorded in the machine. We shall see later that we can use other sorts of values as parameters of a machine.

MACHINE

RMan (*RES*)

The form of the MACHINE clause is the name of the machine followed by a list of parameters, if there are any. The names of the parameters in the list are separated by commas, and the list is enclosed in parentheses. A name in abstract machine notation must be at least two characters, and the first must be alphabetic.

2.2.2 The VARIABLES clause

The next clause of this machine is the **VARIABLES clause**, in which we name the variables that are the components of the model. In this case we have only one, and we call it *rfree*.

VARIABLES

rfree

The form of the VARIABLES clause is a list of names separated by commas.

2.2.3 The INVARIANT clause

The next clause is the **INVARIANT clause**, and here we specify the types of the variables introduced in the VARIABLES clause, and any other constraints on the variables. The form of the invariant is always a predicate.

INVARIANT

$rfree \subseteq RES$

The VARIABLES and INVARIANT clauses together establish the state of the machine *RMan*.

2.2.4 The INITIALISATION clause

In the **INITIALISATION clause** we specify how the machine is to be initialized. We are going to start the machine with no resources in *rfree*. The INITIALISATION clause has the form of a very simple program that assigns the empty set to *rfree*. In this assignment statement, *rfree* is the **receiver**, the sign ':=' is the **assignment sign**, and Ø (the empty set) is the **source expression**.

INITIALISATION

$rfree := \emptyset$

Although the initialization looks like an assignment statement from a programming language, the receiver *rfree* and the source expression Ø are not the kinds of things to be found in most programming languages. We refer to a program-like notation used in such a context as a **pseudo-program**, and use the term **assignment pseudo-program** for the kind of assignment used above.

2.2.5 The OPERATIONS clause

In the **OPERATIONS clause** we specify what operations are available to manipulate the values of the variables in the state. The form of the OPERATIONS clause is the OPERATIONS keyword followed by a list of operation definitions separated by semicolons. For each operation we specify its inputs, its outputs and its effect on the state variables.

We deal first with operations that have inputs but no outputs. Here is an example of an operation definition.

```
alloc (rr) =
  PRE
    rr ∈ rfree
  THEN
    rfree := rfree − {rr}
  END
```

This operation is called *alloc*, and the informal intention is that it should allocate a free resource. It has one input, and the name used to refer to it in the definition of the operation, *rr*, appears in parentheses after the name of the operation. This operation has no outputs, but we shall see later how to specify operations with outputs. The pseudo-program that defines the operation follows the equals sign, and it is an instance of a **PRE-THEN-END pseudo-program**. A PRE-THEN-END pseudo-program has two parts. The **precondition** is the predicate following the PRE keyword, in this case *rr* ∈ *rfree*. Users of this machine are warned not to attempt this operation unless they are sure that the precondition is true. If the operation is used when the precondition is not true, the results are unpredictable. The precondition demands that the input must be a member of *rfree*, because only free resources can be inputs to this operation, and this establishes the type of *rr*, since the invariant says that all members of *rfree* are members of *RES*. The **then-part**, in this case the assignment pseudo-program *rfree* := *rfree* − {*rr*}, is separated from the precondition by the THEN keyword. The then-part specifies the effect of the operation when the precondition is true, and we can interpret it informally by saying that *rr* is removed from *rfree*.

The next operation is *free*. The precondition establishes the type of the input *rr*. It must be a member of *RES*, and it must not be a member of *rfree*. The then-part says that the input is added to *rfree*.

```
free (rr) =
  PRE
    rr ∈ RES ∧ rr ∉ rfree
  THEN
    rfree := rfree ∪ {rr}
  END
```

The last operation of this machine, an operation not discussed in the informal treatment at the beginning of this chapter, is *setfree*, which takes any subset of *RES* as input, and replaces *rfree* with it.

```
setfree (rrs) =
  PRE
    rrs ⊆ RES
```

```
THEN
    rfree := rrs
END
```

2.2.6 The END clause

The machine definition ends with the **END clause**, which consists simply of the END keyword.

2.2.7 Observations on the resource manager machine

We gather together the parts of the *RMan* machine, and display them as a connected whole in Figure 2.4.

Although *RMan* has served as an introduction to the ideas and notations of machines, as an interface for supplying function it is not much use. The *alloc* and *free* operations seem to be doing useful things, but each has a precondition that the user of the interface must guarantee. We must not use *alloc* unless we are sure that the input is already free, and we must not use *free* unless we are sure that the input is already allocated. There are two main ways in which we might improve this situation:

(1) We could add an enquiry operation to the machine to report whether a resource is free or allocated.

(2) We could make the operations robust by giving them outputs that report whether they worked, or why they did not.

We shall study examples of both these approaches in later chapters.

2.3 Proof obligations and substitution predicates

Because the machine is a mathematical construct, it expresses precisely the properties of its state and its operations. If the machine is to represent anything worthwhile, it must have certain properties of consistency:

• Consistency of initialization – the initialization must **establish** the invariant.

• Consistency of operation – each operation must **preserve** the invariant.

In this section we give a precise meaning to the informal notions of 'establish' and 'preserve', and are led to a new way of looking at programs as operators on predicates.

MACHINE

   RMan (RES)

VARIABLES

   rfree

INVARIANT

   rfree $\subseteq$ *RES*

INITIALISATION

   rfree := $\emptyset$

OPERATIONS

   alloc (rr) =
     PRE
      rr $\in$ *rfree*
     THEN
      rfree := *rfree* $-$ *{rr}*
     END
   ;
   free (rr) =
     PRE
      rr $\in$ *RES* $\wedge$ *rr* $\notin$ *rfree*
     THEN
      rfree := *rfree* $\cup$ *{rr}*
     END
   ;
   setfree (rrs) =
     PRE
      rrs $\subseteq$ *RES*
     THEN
      rfree := *rrs*
     END

END

Figure 2.4 The resource manager machine.

2.3.1 Establishing the invariant

The statement 'the pseudo-program *rfree* := Ø establishes the predicate *rfree* ⊆ *RES*' can itself be formalized in a predicate. We introduce a new notation to formalize it:

[*rfree* := Ø] *rfree* ⊆ *RES*

The notation introduced above has the form of a function application where the pseudo-program in square brackets is the function name and the invariant is the argument. We can think of the pseudo-program in square brackets as a function whose domain is predicates and whose range is predicates. The value of the function is found by replacing *rfree* in the argument with Ø, which corresponds to our intuition that the assignment establishes the invariant if and only if the empty set is a subset of *RES*. The result

Ø ⊆ *RES*

is a simple theorem of set theory. We therefore call the new form of predicate a **substitution predicate**, and add it to the list of forms that includes conjunction, existential quantification, and so on. Assignment pseudo-programs will in future be referred to as **simple substitutions**.

If **x** is a variable, **E** an expression of the same type as **x**, and **P** a predicate, the predicate

[**x** := **E**] **P**

is obtained by substituting **E** for all the free occurrences of **x** in **P**. In making this substitution only the free occurrences of **x** in **P** are to be replaced by **E**. If **E** contains a variable that would become bound when the substitution is made, bound variables of **P** might need to be renamed before the substitution is made.

The juxtaposition of substitution and predicate has a higher priority than any of the propositional functions, so if **G** is a substitution,

[**G**] **P** ∨ **Q**

is the disjunction of [**G**] **P** and **Q**, while

[**G**] (**P** ∨ **Q**)

is a substitution predicate that applies the substitution **G** to the disjunction of **P** and **Q**.

We can summarize the consistency condition for the initialization of a machine as follows: if **I** is the invariant of the machine, and **G** is the pseudo-program for the INITIALISATION clause, the proof obligation is

[**G**] **I**

We have seen how to simplify [**G**] **I** when **G** is a simple substitution. Much of the next few chapters is about more complex pseudo-programs, and for each we shall give a rule for simplifying its effect on a predicate.

2.3.2 Preserving the invariant

We must now make precise the idea that an operation preserves the invariant of the machine. An operation operates under two assumptions:

- The invariant is true when the user of the machine uses the operation.

- The precondition of the operation is true when the user of the machine uses the operation.

We formalize the idea that *alloc* preserves the invariant of the machine with the following predicate:

$rfree \subseteq RES \land rr \in rfree \Rightarrow$
$[rfree := rfree - \{rr\}] \, rfree \subseteq RES$

The antecedent formalizes the two assumptions stated above, and the consequent says that the then-part of the PRE-THEN-END pseudo-program establishes the invariant. We can make the substitution in the consequent to give the following consistency condition for *alloc*:

$rfree \subseteq RES \land rr \in rfree \Rightarrow rfree - \{rr\} \subseteq RES$

We should not be surprised to find that this is a theorem of set theory.

In *RMan*, all the operations are defined by PRE-THEN-END pseudo-programs, so in each operation the precondition is just the predicate between PRE and END. If the operation is defined by a pseudo-program that is not a PRE-THEN-END pseudo-program, the precondition is just true, and can be omitted from the proof obligation. For instance if we had defined an operation *freeall* to free all the resources, its definition would have been the assignment pseudo-program $rfree := RES$, and we should have to prove the following:

$rfree \subseteq RES \Rightarrow [rfree := RES] \, rfree \subseteq RES$

This simplifies to another theorem of set theory:

$$rfree \subseteq RES \Rightarrow RES \subseteq RES$$

We can summarize the consistency condition for an operation of a machine as follows: if **I** is the invariant of the machine, and **G** is the pseudo-program for the operation, not necessarily a PRE-THEN-END pseudo-program, and if **P** is the stated precondition of **G**, then the proof obligation is

$$\mathbf{I} \wedge \mathbf{P} \Rightarrow [\mathbf{G}]\,\mathbf{I}$$

If we apply this rule to the operation *alloc*, we have the following:

$$rfree \subseteq RES \wedge rr \in rfree \Rightarrow$$
$$[\text{PRE } rr \in rfree \text{ THEN } rfree := rfree - \{rr\} \text{ END}]\, rfree \subseteq RES$$

To simplify the consequent we need the **PRE-THEN-END rule**:

$$[\text{PRE } \mathbf{P} \text{ THEN } \mathbf{H} \text{ END}]\, \mathbf{I} \Leftrightarrow \mathbf{P} \wedge [\mathbf{H}]\, \mathbf{I}$$

The rule says that the PRE-THEN-END substitution establishes a predicate if and only if the precondition is true and the then-part establishes the predicate.

If we apply this to the above predicate we have:

$$rfree \subseteq RES \wedge rr \in rfree \Rightarrow$$
$$rr \in rfree \wedge [rfree := rfree - \{rr\}]\, rfree \subseteq RES$$

Since $rr \in rfree$ is in the antecedent we can simplify this by dropping it from the consequent.

$$rfree \subseteq RES \wedge rr \in rfree \Rightarrow$$
$$[rfree := rfree - \{rr\}]\, rfree \subseteq RES$$

Now we have the form that we derived by intuition earlier.

2.3.3 Generalized substitutions

The effect of a PRE-THEN-END pseudo-program on a predicate is rather more complicated than a simple substitution, and we shall soon meet other pseudo-programs that effect more elaborate transformations. Because the term 'substitution' is too narrow to describe their effects, these more elaborate transformations are referred to as **generalized substitutions**. From now on in this book, the term 'substitution', meaning 'generalized substitution', will be used in preference to 'pseudo-program'.

2.4 Using the B-Toolkit with machines

The machine definition given above was produced with the help of some of the facilities of the B-Toolkit, and we now look at these.

2.4.1 Editing and analysis

You use an editor to enter the machine definition into a template that is provided by the B-Toolkit. The template contains the most common clauses, and you add other clauses just by editing in the keywords that start them. The mathematical signs that appear in the examples in this book are not available on most computer keyboards, so the B-Toolkit has a representation of these signs that uses combinations of symbols in the ASCII symbol set. Thus the membership sign '∈' is represented by the colon ':', and the subset sign '⊆' by the combination '<:'. Appendix B shows the representation of all the mathematical signs used in this book. Figure 2.5 shows the *RMan* machine as entered into the specification editor.

After you have edited your machine, you can **commit** it, that is, subject it to some simple syntax checks and enter it into the B-Toolkit's configuration control system.

Once you have committed a machine, you can use the **analyser** to check the types of all the expressions, and to ensure that predicates have expressions of the correct type. When an error is found, you are invited to re-edit the machine, commit it and rerun the analysis.

2.4.2 The animator

The B-Toolkit provides an **animator**, which allows you to test the specification without having to construct an implementation and generate code from it. A machine must have been analysed before it can be animated. Animation is not a suitable way of using a machine in practice, since many, perhaps most, machines are used by programs rather than by humans, but animation does allow you to check that a machine behaves in accordance with the intuitive ideas that gave rise to it. It provides a simple prototype that gives a faithful representation of the specified behaviour.

If you use the B-Toolkit animator for *RMan*, you must provide a value for *RES* that is a finite, non-empty set. The animator requires an enumerated set, and the members of this set could be numbers or arbitrary names. Suppose you choose

```
{fork, spade, hoe, rake, trowel}
```

```
MACHINE

  RMan (RES)

VARIABLES

  rfree

INVARIANT

  rfree <: RES

INITIALISATION

  rfree := {}

OPERATIONS

  alloc (rr) =
    PRE
      rr : rfree
    THEN
      rfree := rfree - {rr}
    END
  ;
  free (rr) =
    PRE
      rr : RES & rr /: rfree
    THEN
      rfree := rfree \/ {rr}
    END
  ;
  setfree (rrs) =
    PRE
      rrs <: RES
    THEN
      rfree := rrs
    END

END
```

Figure 2.5 ASCII version of the resource manager.

The animator reports that the initial state has *rfree* empty, and invites you to choose an operation. If you choose *free*, the animator displays the precondition

```
rr : {fork, spade, hoe, rake, trowel}
```

and solicits an input. You must ensure that you choose the input so that the precondition is true. If you choose *hoe*, the animator evaluates the precondition, reports its value (in this case it is true), and then displays the new state.

```
rfree  {hoe}
```

Before each operation, the animator displays the precondition, so that you can supply sensible input, and after the input has been entered, it displays the value of the precondition and the new state. If you choose an input that makes the precondition false, the animator advises you that the precondition is false, but performs the operation anyway. (The animator provides an operation of its own to undo the last operation performed.)

You can save the state at any stage in the animation, and later animations can begin in a saved state.

In a real development, you could use the animator to show a client the behaviour of your machine for approval.

2.4.3 Proof obligation generator

We have seen that a machine definition has to have certain desirable properties before it is of much value as a specification of something we might wish to develop, and these properties have been expressed as proof obligations for showing the consistency of the initialization and the operations. Once you have analysed your machine, you can use the **proof obligation generator** to build the proof obligations described above. The generated proof obligations are then stored in the configuration control system.

2.4.4 Theorem provers

Once you have generated the proof obligations, you can use the B-Toolkit's **autoprover** to generate proofs. The autoprover is supplied with a large number of rules that express the properties of the mathematical notation in the proof obligations. The proof process attempts to rewrite the proof obligations in various ways by using the rules until it is reduced to a single true predicate. The completed proofs are also stored in the configuration control system. You can use the **proof printer** to print the obligations and the proofs.

Sometimes the autoprover fails to prove an obligation. This happens for one of the following reasons.

- The proof obligation is not a theorem because the machine definition contains mistakes, or insufficient information to prove the obligation.

- The obligation cannot be proved because the rules used by the autoprover are not powerful or subtle enough.

In the first case, you must rethink what the machine was trying to express, correct the error with the specification editor, and remake the machine. To cope with the second case, the B-Toolkit provides an **interprover** (interactive prover). The interprover allows you to investigate how the autoprover failed, and to add new rules to the machine's configuration. You can try out the effect of the new rules in the interprover, and if the interprover now succeeds in proving the obligation, you can return to the autoprover, which uses the new rules to generate the proof.

In this book we shall continue to present proof obligations, and to illustrate them with simple examples. However, the proofs even of simple examples can become tedious without the sort of mechanical help provided by the B-Toolkit.

2.4.5 Remaking after editing

Changes made to a machine might invalidate the proof obligations and proofs stored in the configuration control system. The commit mechanism that accepts edited machines distinguishes a **maths change**, something that affects the mathematical meaning of the machine, from an **annotation change**, which changes only comments, or rearranges the mathematical text in a purely visual way. If you edit a machine and the commit mechanism detects a maths change, the B-Toolkit remembers the analysis, proof obligation generation and proving that you had previously done on the machine, but discards the results. The toolkit has a **remake** operation, which attempts to re-establish the same information that was there before the change. If the machine has been through proof obligation generation, new proof obligations are generated. If the machine has been through the autoprover, the autoprover is invoked to attempt to prove the new proof obligations.

2.4.6 The markup generator

To help produce readable documentation, the B-Toolkit provides a **markup generator**. Once a machine has been analysed, it can be processed by the markup generator to produce a LaTeX source file. This file can be formatted and printed. Producing the marked-up version of the machine can be made part of the remake process, so the file is refreshed when a maths change makes it necessary to analyse the machine again.

2.4.7 Using the diskette with the B-Toolkit

If you have a full-function copy of the B-Toolkti, you can add the directories on the diskette to your system, and use them with the B-Toolkit. You should look at the README file on the diskette, and at the instructions on the World Wide Web, as described in the Preface to this book on page vii.

2.5 Summary and outlook

In this chapter we have learnt:

- how set theory and predicate calculus can be used to formalize ideas about the function of a simple software system;

- how to organize a machine to specify a software system;

- that machines have associated proof obligations that test their consistency;

- that programs can be regarded as generalized substitutions that act on predicates;

- that the B-Toolkit supports editing, analysis, animation, proof obligation generation, and proving of machines.

We are left with several problems in the domain of specifications. The repertoire of substitutions is very limited, and there are many intuitive ideas of specification that we cannot express. The burden that a machine with parameters places on the engineer who has to implement it is insupportable. In the next few chapters we learn more substitutions, and we learn how to exercise control over parameters, and eventually how to do without parameters altogether.

2.6 Exercises

(2.1) State and prove the theorem that guarantees that the operation *free* on page 21 preserves the invariant of *RMan*.

(2.2) State and prove the theorem that guarantees that the operation *setfree* on page 21 preserves the invariant of *RMan*.

(2.3) Make the indicated substitutions in the following predicates.

   (a) $[xx := 1] \, xx \neq yy$

   (b) $[xx := yy] \, xx = yy$

   (c) $[xx := 1] \, (\forall xx \bullet (xx \in \mathbb{N} \Rightarrow xx \geq yy) \lor xx \geq 0)$

   (d) $[xx := 0] \, yy > 0$

   (e) $[xx := xx + 1] \, xx > 0$

(2.4) Make the indicated substitutions in the following predicates.

   (a) $[\text{PRE } xx > 0 \text{ THEN } xx := xx - 1 \text{ END}] \, xx > yy$

   (b) $[\text{PRE } xx > yy \text{ THEN } xx := yy \text{ END}] \, xx > 0$

   (c) $[\text{PRE } xx \in \mathbb{N} \text{ THEN } xs := xs \cup \{xx\} \text{ END}] \, xs \subseteq \mathbb{N}$

   (d) $[\text{PRE } xx \in \mathbb{N} \text{ THEN } yy := xx \text{ END}]$
        $\forall xx \bullet (xx \in \mathbb{N} \Rightarrow yy > zz)$

Chapter 3
The class manager's assistant

Summary: Introducing the class manager's assistant (CMA) — the CONSTRAINTS clause — the SEES clause — the ASSERTIONS clause — multiple substitution — operations with outputs — IF-THEN-ELSE-END substitution — IF-THEN-ELSE-END rule — parallel substitution — BEGIN-END.

In this chapter we construct a component-layer machine, one that presents its users with a complete interface. The primary operations — those that change the state of the machine — have pre-conditions that must be true before the user of the machine can use the operations. In a component-layer machine there are auxiliary operations without preconditions that can be used to decide whether the preconditions of the primary operations are true.

3.1 The class manager's assistant: informal model

The class manager's assistant is an example that has been used in several books on formal methods of software development. The reader with a general interest in formal methods might look at the treatment of this example in Jones (1980), where it is formalized in VDM, and in Wordsworth (1992), where it is formalized in Z.

3.1.1 Informal requirements — a brief statement

The requirements can be described informally as follows. The class manager needs to keep track of students enrolled in the class, up to a certain number, and whether a student has done the exercises set for the class. Students may leave the class at any time, but only those who have done the exercises are entitled to a leaving certificate. The class manager needs to check from time to time whether a student has done the exercises.

3.1.2 A set-theoretic model

We propose to model these requirements by first introducing the set *STUDENT* of all students, and then considering two subsets of it. The first subset, called *enrolled*, is the set of students currently enrolled in the class. The second subset, called *tested*, is a subset of *enrolled*, and is the students who have done the exercises. We also introduce the maximum size *class_size* for the class.

The Venn diagram in Figure 3.1 shows a typical configuration of the model. The rectangle represents *STUDENT*, and the ellipses represent the sets *enrolled* and *tested*. Individual members of the set *STUDENT* are represented by small circles. In the class illustrated in the figure there are five students enrolled, of whom two have done the exercises. Of the many members of the set *STUDENT* who are not in *enrolled*, only three are shown on the diagram.

The operation to enrol a student is illustrated in Figure 3.2. The user of the operation is expected to identify the student to be enrolled. The diagram shows the successful case of the operation, in which the student to be enrolled is in the set *STUDENT*, but not in the set *enrolled*. There is room in *enrolled* for another student. The precondition is captured by the following predicate:

$st \in STUDENT \land$
$st \notin enrolled \land$
card (*enrolled*) < *class_size*

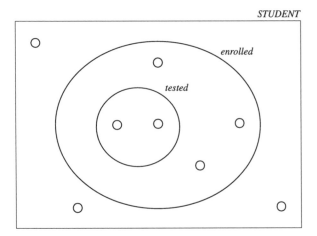

Figure 3.1 State of the class manager's assistant.

The value of the enrolled set after the operation is given by the following expression:

enrolled ∪ {*st*}

A number of other cases have to be considered:

• The student is already enrolled.

• The class is already full.

• Both of these.

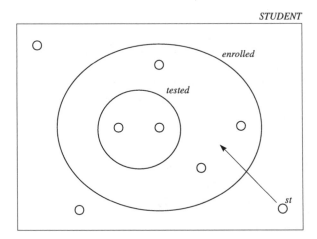

Figure 3.2 Enrolling a student.

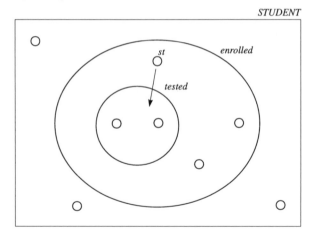

Figure 3.3 Recording that a student has done the exercises.

These possibilities must be discussed with the class manager, and satisfactory treatments of them decided on.

The operation to record that a student has done the exercises is illustrated in Figure 3.3. The student must be in *enrolled*, but not in *tested*. The precondition is captured by the following predicate:

> *st* ∈ *enrolled* ∧
> *st* ∉ *tested*

The value of the set *tested* after the operation is given by the following expression:

> *tested* ∪ {*st*}

The enrolled set is not changed.

If the student is not enrolled, or has already done the exercises, some indication of this must be given.

The operation to let a student leave the class has two main cases, illustrated in Figure 3.4. The precondition is captured by the following predicate:

> *st* ∈ *enrolled*

If the student is in *tested*, the operation should give some indication that a certificate is appropriate. The values of the enrolled and tested sets after the operation are given by

> *enrolled* − {*st*}

and

> *tested* − {*st*}

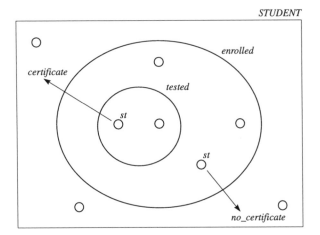

Figure 3.4 Discharging a student.

If the student is in *enrolled* but not in *tested*, a certificate is not appropriate. The value of the enrolled set after the operation is the same as it was in the previous case, but the tested set is unchanged.

If the student is *not* enrolled, some other behaviour is required.

The specification of the operations that the class manager requires is expressed informally in Table 3.1 on page 38. For each operation we list the inputs, the processing and the outputs. We make this description as complete as its informality will allow.

3.2 The class manager's assistant: formal model

3.2.1 Formalizing the class manager's assistant

The fragments of set theory given above are far from capturing the whole of the requirement expressed in the table. There are two ways of formalizing the function of the class manager's assistant:

- In the **component machine method**, we construct a machine that formalizes the successful cases of the operations, and we add enquiry operations that can be used to test whether the preconditions of the successful cases are true. The enquiry operations have outputs that the operator of the machine can use to decide whether it is safe to use the other operations. A component machine has to be put in an operating environment that can use the operations provided to meet the class manager's requirements.

- In the **full-function machine method**, we construct a machine that has just the operations described in the table. In this method the operations are robust, with relatively simple preconditions, but

Table 3.1 Informal state machine for the class manager's assistant.

Inputs	Processing	Outputs
Enrolling a student		
student	If the class is full, the response is 'No room'. If the class is not full, but the student is already enrolled, the response is 'Already enrolled'. If the class is not full and the student is not already enrolled, the response is 'Student enrolled', and the student is added to the enrolled set, but not to the tested set.	response
When a student does the exercises		
student	If the student is not enrolled, the response is 'Not enrolled'. If the student has already been tested, the response is 'Already tested'. If the student is enrolled, but not tested, the response is 'Test noted', and the student is added to the tested set.	response
When a student leaves the class		
student	If the student is not enrolled, the response is 'Not enrolled'. If the student has already been tested, the response is 'Certificate', and the student is removed from both the enrolled and tested sets. If the student is enrolled, but not tested, the response is 'No certificate', and the student is removed from the enrolled set.	response
Enquiries		
student	If the student is not enrolled, the response is 'Not enrolled'. If the student has already been tested, the response is 'Student tested'. If the student is enrolled, but not tested, the response is 'Enrolled but not tested'.	response

with quite elaborate operation definitions that enumerate the cases and specify the outputs that report whether an operation succeeded, and if not, why not.

We explore the component machine method first, deferring consideration of full-function machines to Chapter 6.

3.2.2 The MACHINE clause

The machine is called *CMA* (class manager's assistant), and it has two parameters.

MACHINE

CMA (*class_size*, *STUDENT*)

3.2.3 The CONSTRAINTS clause

The **CONSTRAINTS clause** is a predicate about the parameters, and it allows us to place any restrictions we like on the parameters. In this case we want *class_size* to be greater than zero, and we want the set *STUDENT* to be finite.

CONSTRAINTS

class_size $> 0 \land$ card $(STUDENT) \in \mathbb{N}$

The function card can be applied only to finite sets, and the function application denotes the number of members in the set. When a machine is instantiated, there is a proof obligation to show that the parameters satisfy the predicate in the CONSTRAINTS clause. You will be able to prove card $(STUDENT) \in \mathbb{N}$ if and only if you supply a finite set for *STUDENT*.

The effect of the CONSTRAINTS clause is to control the kinds of things the user of the machine can supply as parameters. One of the reasons for exercising this control is to make it more likely that we can find an implementation of the machine.

3.2.4 The SEES clause

The **SEES clause** introduces the names of machines that supply information that we need later in the machine definition. The machine *Bool_TYPE* supplies values *TRUE* and *FALSE* that are the outputs of some of the operations. This machine is a **library machine** provided with the B-Toolkit. The *Bool_TYPE* machine is one of a number of machines that specify the properties of simple data types that are used in most machine definitions. Appendix C contains the definitions of all the library machines that are used in this book.

SEES

Bool_TYPE

The form of the SEES clause is a list of machine names separated by commas. We shall see in Chapter 5 that the SEES clause is only one of several ways of using information in other machines in the machine we are defining.

3.2.5 The VARIABLES and INVARIANT clauses

The notion that two sets *enrolled* and *tested* are the model for the class is recorded in the VARIABLES clause, but the fact that these are sets of students is recorded in the predicate in the INVARIANT clause. The latter also records the fact that *tested* is a subset of *enrolled*, and that the size of *enrolled* cannot be greater than *class_size*.

VARIABLES

enrolled, tested

INVARIANT

$enrolled \subseteq (STUDENT) \wedge$
$tested \subseteq (STUDENT) \wedge$
$tested \subseteq enrolled \wedge$
$card\ (enrolled) \leq class\_size$

The INVARIANT clause of this machine is a conjunction of four conjuncts:

- The first conjunct fixes the type of *enrolled*.

- The second conjunct fixes the type of *tested*.

- The third conjunct expresses the constraint that *tested* is a subset of *enrolled*. We could have used this predicate to fix the type of *tested*, but it is good practice to make the type-fixing predicates as direct as possible.

- The fourth conjunct constrains the size of *enrolled* so that it cannot be greater than *class_size*.

3.2.6 Adding assertions to a machine

There are other predicates that describe properties of the variables that we could add to the invariant if we wish. For instance card *(tested)* $\leq$ *class_size* is such a predicate. We can derive this from the invariant by the laws of set theory, so it is not an essential part of the definition of the machine. Additional information of this sort serves to increase our confidence that we understand the mathematical properties of the machine, and we can put it in an **ASSERTIONS clause**:

ASSERTIONS

    card $(tested) \leq class\_size$

Having an ASSERTIONS clause in a machine introduces a new proof obligation. If $\mathbf{I_I}$ is the predicate in the INVARIANT clause, and $\mathbf{I_A}$ is the predicate in the ASSERTIONS clause, we have to prove that

$$\mathbf{I_I} \Rightarrow \mathbf{I_A}$$

With an ASSERTIONS clause the correctness of the initialization **G** is

$$[\mathbf{G}]\, \mathbf{I_I}$$

The correctness of an operation **G** with stated precondition **P** is

$$\mathbf{I_I} \wedge \mathbf{I_A} \wedge \mathbf{P} \Rightarrow [\mathbf{G}]\, \mathbf{I_I}$$

This is a bit easier to prove than the form introduced on page 26, as we now have the assertions in the antecedent.

3.2.7 Initialization and its correctness

The initialization promises an empty class, with no students enrolled or tested. It has the form of a **multiple assignment** substitution.

INITIALISATION

    enrolled, tested $:= \emptyset, \emptyset$

We should prove the correctness of this initialization, but this time we have a **multiple substitution** to make. We need to establish that

    $[enrolled, tested := \emptyset, \emptyset]$
    $(enrolled \subseteq (STUDENT) \wedge$
    $tested \subseteq (STUDENT) \wedge$
    $tested \subseteq enrolled \wedge$
    card $(enrolled) \leq class\_size)$

Making the substitution gives the following predicate:

$\emptyset \subseteq (STUDENT) \wedge$
$\emptyset \subseteq (STUDENT) \wedge$
$\emptyset \subseteq \emptyset \wedge$
card $(\emptyset) \leq class\_size$

Each of the first three conjuncts is a theorem of set theory. The last is, by a theorem of set theory, equivalent to $0 \leq class\_size$, and since *class_size* is a natural number, this is a theorem of arithmetic.

3.2.8 Specifying an operation with a precondition

The *enrol* operation is used to enrol a student. The input is to be a student, there must be room for another student, and the input student must not be already enrolled. In this operation the student is added to the set of enrolled students, provided that the precondition is true. Silence about the tested set means that the tested set does not change.

OPERATIONS

> *enrol* (*st*) =
>   PRE
>   *st* $\in$ *STUDENT* $\wedge$
>   card (*enrolled*) < *class_size* $\wedge$
>   *st* $\notin$ *enrolled*
>   THEN
>   *enrolled* := *enrolled* $\cup$ {*st*}
>   END

3.2.9 Preserving the invariant

For the *enrol* operation, we have to prove the following:

> *enrolled* $\subseteq$ (*STUDENT*) $\wedge$
> *tested* $\subseteq$ (*STUDENT*) $\wedge$
> *tested* $\subseteq$ *enrolled* $\wedge$
> card (*enrolled*) $\leq$ *class_size* $\wedge$
> *st* $\in$ *STUDENT* $\wedge$
> card (*enrolled*) < *class_size* $\wedge$
> *st* $\notin$ *enrolled*
> $\Rightarrow$
> [*enrolled* := *enrolled* $\cup$ {*st*}]
> (*enrolled* $\subseteq$ (*STUDENT*) $\wedge$
> *tested* $\subseteq$ (*STUDENT*) $\wedge$
> *tested* $\subseteq$ *enrolled* $\wedge$
> card (*enrolled*) $\leq$ *class_size*)

We simplify the consequent by making the substitution:

$enrolled \subseteq (STUDENT) \wedge$
$tested \subseteq (STUDENT) \wedge$
$tested \subseteq enrolled \wedge$
card $(enrolled) \leq class\_size \wedge$
$st \in STUDENT \wedge$
card $(enrolled) < class\_size) \wedge$
$st \notin enrolled$
$\Rightarrow$
$enrolled \cup \{st\} \subseteq (STUDENT) \wedge$
$tested \subseteq (STUDENT) \wedge$
$tested \subseteq enrolled \cup \{st\} \wedge$
card $(enrolled \cup \{st\}) \leq class\_size$

The consequent follows from the antecedent by the laws of set theory.

3.2.10 Specifying an operation to test a precondition

The *isenrolled* operation discloses whether a student is presently enrolled in the class. Here we see the method of specifying outputs of operations. A list of names of outputs (in this case only one) separated by commas followed by the **output sign** '⟵ ' precedes the name of the operation. This operation has a single output, referred to in the operation definition as *ans*, and a single input. The precondition is that the input is to be a student. The action is to set the output as follows. If the student is presently enrolled in the class, the output is *TRUE*, but if not the output is *FALSE*. As none of the machine's variables are changed, the proof obligation is trivially true.

```
ans ⟵  isenrolled (st) =
  PRE
    st ∈ STUDENT
  THEN
    IF
      st ∈ enrolled
    THEN
      ans := TRUE
    ELSE
      ans := FALSE
    END
  END
```

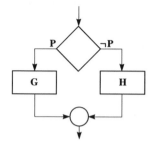

Figure 3.5 IF-THEN-ELSE-END illustrated.

3.2.11 The IF-THEN-ELSE-END substitution

The then-part of this PRE-THEN-END substitution is a new kind of substitution, the **IF-THEN-ELSE-END substitution**. To capture its meaning exactly we need to know how we can tell that the substitution establishes a predicate, so here is the **IF-THEN-ELSE-END rule**.

$$[\text{IF } \mathbf{P} \text{ THEN } \mathbf{G} \text{ ELSE } \mathbf{H}] \; \mathbf{Q}$$
$$\Leftrightarrow$$
$$(\mathbf{P} \Rightarrow [\mathbf{G}] \; \mathbf{Q}) \wedge (\neg \mathbf{P} \Rightarrow [\mathbf{H}] \; \mathbf{Q})$$

The predicate **P** is the **if-test**, the substitution **G** is the **then-part**, and the substitution **H** is the **else-part**. The rule says that if the if-test is true, the then-part must establish the predicate, and if the if-test is false, the else-part must establish the predicate.

The action of this substitution is illustrated in Figure 3.5 by a **flow chart**. It is intended to show that when the if-test **P** is true, the substitution **G** is made, and when the if-test is false, the substitution **H** is made. In this chart the diamond is a **decision box**, and we annotate the exits from the box with appropriate predicates. The rectangles are **substitution boxes**, and the circle is a **collection node**.

3.2.12 More operations

The *test* operation is used to record the fact that a student has done the exercises. It has a single input. Its precondition is that the input must be in the enrolled set (we can deduce that it must be a student), but not in the tested set. The action, specified with a simple substitution, is to add the input to the tested set without changing the enrolled set.

```
test (st) =
  PRE
    st ∈ enrolled ∧ st ∉ tested
  THEN
    tested := tested ∪ {st}
  END
```

The *istested* operation discloses whether an enrolled student has done the exercises.

```
ans ⟵ istested (st) =
  PRE
    st ∈ enrolled
  THEN
    IF
      st ∈ tested
    THEN
      ans := TRUE
    ELSE
      ans := FALSE
    END
  END
```

3.2.13 An operation to change two variables

The *leave* operation is used to record that a student has left the class. It has a single input, and its precondition is that the input must be in the enrolled set, so it must be a student. If the input student is in the tested set, the action is to remove it from the enrolled and tested sets. If the input student is not in the tested set, the action is to remove it from the enrolled set only.

```
leave (st) =
  PRE
    st ∈ enrolled
  THEN
    IF
      st ∈ tested
    THEN
      tested := tested − {st} ||
      enrolled := enrolled − {st}
    ELSE
      enrolled := enrolled − {st}
    END
  END
```

The then-part of the IF-THEN-ELSE-END substitution is a **parallel substitution**, and as the two substitutions are simple substitutions to different variables, it is equivalent to the following multiple substitution:

$$tested, enrolled := tested - \{st\}, enrolled - \{st\}$$

One last operation is proposed, and this reports the maximum class size and the number of students enrolled. There are therefore two outputs, but no inputs. The action has no precondition, and is expressed as a multiple substitution, with the maximum class size for *clmax* and the current class size for *sofar*.

3.2.14 The BEGIN-END substitution

The **BEGIN-END substitution** allows the keywords BEGIN and END to be used in operation definitions to enclose simple and multiple substitutions.

```
clmax, sofar ⟵ howmany =
  BEGIN
    clmax, sofar := class_size, card (enrolled)
  END
```

The **BEGIN-END rule** is very simple:

$$[\text{BEGIN } \mathbf{G} \text{ END }] \: \mathbf{P} \Leftrightarrow [\mathbf{G}] \: \mathbf{P}$$

3.3 Using a component-layer machine

This machine offers the class manager enough operations to solve the problems of class management described informally above. We might provide operating instructions for enrolling a student as follows.

First use the *isenrolled* operation to decide if the student is already enrolled. If the output is *FALSE*, then use the *howmany* operation to see if there is room for another enrolment. If the output *sofar* is less than the output *clmax*, then it is safe to use the *enrol* operation to enrol this student. (The *isenrolled* and *howmany* operations could be used in the opposite order.)

An easy way to play user of the class manager's assistant component machine is to animate it using the B-Toolkit animator.

3.3.1 Further development of the class manager's assistant

In later chapters we shall develop the machine described above in two directions. We shall see how it can be used to provide a more friendly interface for the class manager, and we shall see how it can be implemented using more primitive machines, which, in the end, will be the statements of a programming language like C or Pascal.

3.4 Summary and outlook

In this chapter we have learnt:

- the use of parameters that are not sets;
- the use of the CONSTRAINTS clause to control the instantiation of parameters;
- the use of multiple substitution;
- the characteristics of machines in the component layer of the layered software model;
- new substitutions for machines.

There are still several things left over from the previous chapter, especially how to define useful machines without parameters, and how to express non-determinism in specifications.

3.5 Exercises

(3.1)   Provide operating instructions for recording that a student has done the exercises.

(3.2)   Provide operating instructions for recording that a student has left the class.

(3.3)   Define a machine *Positive* to represent a natural number. The largest value to be stored should be a parameter of the machine. The initialization should set the number to zero. There should be operations to set the value, read the value, increase it by 1, decrease it by 1, add an input value, subtract an input value, and multiply by an input value.

(3.4)   Define a machine to represent an array. The machine should have two parameters, a natural number to fix the upper limit of the indexes (the lower limit is 1) and a set for the type of values to be stored in the array. Use a partial function from indexes to values for the model. There should be operations to read the value at a given index, to store a value at a given index, and to exchange the values at two indexes. The initialization and the operations to read values from the array and to exchange values in the array should warn the user of the array not to look at the values at an index that has not previously had a value stored.

(3.5)   Specify a machine *Nat_SET* whose model is a finite set of natural numbers in a limited range. There are two parameters: the size of the largest set to be modelled, and the largest natural number to be saved in the set. There are to be four operations as shown in Table 3.2.

Table 3.2 Informal requirements for a set of natural numbers.

Inputs	Processing	Outputs
Find size of set		
none	Return the current size of the set.	number
Add a number		
number	Add the number to the set if the number is in the appropriate range and the set is not full.	none
Remove a number		
number	If the number is in the appropriate range, remove it from the set.	none
Find number in set		
number	If the number is in the appropriate range, return 1 if it is in the set, and 0 if it is not.	number

Initially the set is empty.

(3.6)   Make the indicated substitutions in the following predicates.

(a) $[xx, yy := 1, 2]\ xx + yy \geq zz$

(b) $[xx, yy := 0, 1]\ \forall xx \bullet (xx \in \mathbb{N} \Rightarrow xx \geq yy)$

(c) $[xx, yy := yy, xx]\ xx > yy$

(3.7)   Make the indicated substitutions in the following predicates.

(a) $[\text{IF } x > 0 \text{ THEN } x := 1 \text{ ELSE } x := x + 1 \text{ END}]\ x = 1$

(b) [IF $x < 5$ THEN $x := x + 4$ ELSE $x := x - 1$ END]
$x \geq 4$

(c) [IF $x \in S$ THEN $T := T \cup \{x\}$ ELSE $S := S \cup \{x\}$ END]
$x \in S \cap T$

(3.8)   State and prove the proof obligation for the operation *leave* of the machine CMA.

Chapter 4
Deferred sets and non-determinism

Summary: Deferred sets — enumerated sets — constants — PROPERTIES clause — DEFINITIONS clause — CHOICE-OR-END — functional overriding — ANY-WHERE-THEN-END — choice from a set.

In this chapter we see how to introduce sets that are not parameters, sets whose contents can be specified by the implementer of a machine rather than by its user. We also see how to express non-determinism in operations.

4.1 Deferred and enumerated sets

4.1.1 What is a deferred set?

In the machines we have studied so far, we have used sets that were either parameters or the set of natural numbers. The value of a set parameter is decided when the machine is instantiated. Sometimes it is more convenient to define a set within the machine, and to leave decisions about the contents of the set to the implementer. Such a set is called a **deferred set** of the machine. Notice that the decision about what the set contains has moved from the instantiater to the implementer. The user of a machine needs to know what the deferred set is, because the user usually has to provide inputs or accept outputs whose values are taken from the set, but fixing the exact contents of the set is deferred until the machine is implemented.

If we think of the software interfaces we use, we see that deferred sets are very common. For instance, in a file manager we are expected to make the file names we use conform to a type defined by the provider of the interface, not by the user. The file names must be character strings, not floating point numbers or other more complex structures, and they have a certain maximum length. The format of bank account numbers is defined by a bank, not by its customers.

4.1.2 Specifying deferred sets

Consider a machine that might be a component machine in the development of a banking system. It has two sets, one for account numbers and one for customer numbers. It keeps track of the relationship between accounts (represented by account numbers) and customers (represented by customer numbers).

MACHINE

   Owners

SETS

   ACCTNO; CUSTNO

The **SETS clause** introduces the deferred sets. The names of the deferred sets in the SETS clause are separated by semicolons. The use of names in uppercase is not required by the abstract machine notation, nor by the B-Toolkit, but is a convention used in this book.

4.1.3 Specifying enumerated sets

The SETS clause is also the place to define small finite sets of values such as responses to operations. These are deferred sets of a kind, because the decision about what values they actually contain is left to the implementer of the machine. For the *Owners* machine we define such a set to contain two values, *success* and *noroom*, so the complete SETS clause is as follows:

> *ACCTNO; CUSTNO;*
> *O_RESP = {success, noroom}*

The set *O_RESP* is called an **enumerated set**. It is a convention of the abstract machine notation that where enumerated sets are introduced in a SETS clause, the different names denote distinct values, and the set contains no other values.

4.2 The CONSTANTS and PROPERTIES clauses

4.2.1 Specifying constants

For administrative purposes in the bank, we need to have a special account number and a special customer number, and these are introduced in the **CONSTANTS clause**.

> CONSTANTS

> *specacct, speccust*

The form of the CONSTANTS clause is a list of names separated by commas. The use of lowercase names for constants is a convention used in this book.

4.2.2 The PROPERTIES clause

We must say what the types of these constants are, and the **PROPERTIES clause** allows us to do this.

> PROPERTIES

> *specacct $\in$ ACCTNO $\wedge$*
> *speccust $\in$ CUSTNO*

The form of the PROPERTIES clause is a predicate. It can be used to express any desired relationship between the constants and the deferred sets. You can also refer to the parameters of the machine in the predicate that fixes the properties of the deferred sets and constants.

4.3 Making additional definitions

4.3.1 Variables and invariant

Now we come to the VARIABLES and INVARIANT clauses. We have a function to record for each account number which customer owns it.

VARIABLES

owner

INVARIANT

$owner \in ACCTNO \rightarrowtail CUSTNO \wedge$
$specacct \mapsto speccust \in owner$

The invariant clause gives the type of the *owner* variable, and says that the special account is owned by the special customer.

The initialization of the machine must establish this invariant.

INITIALISATION

$owner := \{specacct \mapsto speccust\}$

4.3.2 The DEFINITIONS clause

It helps the expression of preconditions and other aspects of the operations if we give names to the set of account numbers in use and the set of customers who own accounts. We do this in a **DEFINITIONS clause** as follows:

DEFINITIONS

$accounts == \text{dom}\,(owner);$
$customers == \text{ran}\,(owner)$

In this machine, the names *accounts* and *customers* mean the domain and range of the *owner* function.

The form of the DEFINITIONS clause is a list of definitions separated by semicolons. Each definition consists of:

- the name being defined

- the **definition sign** '=='

- the expression that is to replace the name being defined.

4.4 Non-determinism

4.4.1 An operation of the banking system

Consider an operation to add a new account for an existing customer. The customer number must be an input to the operation, and it is the user's responsibility to supply a customer number that is in *customers*. As for the account number, there are two possibilities.

- The new account number might be an input to the operation. In this case, it is the user's responsibility to make sure that the account number is not already in use. This allows the user to control how account numbers are used, but makes the user keep a record of the account numbers in use.

- The machine decides what account number to use for the new account. In this case the new account number is an output from the operation.

Consideration of these two possibilities leads us to some new substitutions. We also consider how to specify that the operation cannot be completed because of a lack of resources in the implementation. This leads us to study how non-determinism can be expressed in machines.

We first document the case in which the new account number is an input, but the operation might fail for lack of implementation resources. Here is the operation definition:

$$resp \longleftarrow new\_acct\_old\_cust\ (cust, acct) =$$
```
    PRE
      cust ∈ customers ∧
      acct ∈ ACCTNO ∧
      acct ∉ accounts
    THEN
      CHOICE
        resp := success ||
        owner (acct) := cust
      OR
        resp := noroom
      END
    END
```

The output *resp* reports whether the operation succeeded (*success*) or failed (*noroom*).

This operation definition contains new notations, which we now examine.

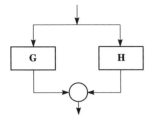

Figure 4.1 CHOICE-OR-END illustrated.

4.4.2 The CHOICE-OR-END substitution

The then-part of the PRE-THEN-END substitution is a **CHOICE-OR-END substitution**. The idea of this substitution is that either of the two substitutions specified can happen, and the choice as to which happens is made inside the machine, that is, by the implementation. In this case the informal intention is that the new account is established if possible, but if not, then nothing happens except the output *noroom*.

The **CHOICE-OR-END rule** is

[CHOICE **G** OR **H** END] **P** $\Leftrightarrow$ [**G**] **P** $\wedge$ [**H**] **P**

The rule can be paraphrased by saying that since either substitution might happen, each of them must be able to establish the predicate. The CHOICE-OR-END substitution can be extended by adding more ORs to it, and the CHOICE-OR-END rule is extended in an obvious way. The substitution can be illustrated by a flow chart like the one used for IF-THEN-ELSE-END, but in this case we do not put in a decision box. Figure 4.1 illustrates the substitution.

4.4.3 The functional overriding substitution

The substitution that is used to update the *owner* function is the **functional overriding substitution**. It has the form of a simple substitution

f (**x**) := **E**

but its meaning is more elaborate:

f := **f** $\rhd$ {**x** $\mapsto$ **E**}

Here **f** must be a variable of function type, **x** a variable of the type of the arguments of **f**, and **E** an expression of the type of the values of **f**. The function **f** is unchanged except that **x** is now associated with **E** in it.

4.4.4 Non-deterministic outputs

The second way of defining the operation to add a new account for an existing customer allows the implementation to choose the account number. It is specified as follows:

$$resp, acct \longleftarrow alt\_new\_acct\_old\_cust (cust) =$$
    PRE
        $cust \in customers \wedge$
        $accounts \neq ACCTNO$
    THEN
        CHOICE
            ANY
                ac
            WHERE
                $ac \in ACCTNO \wedge$
                $ac \notin accounts$
            THEN
                $resp := success \mid \mid$
                $owner (ac) := cust \mid \mid$
                $acct := ac$
            END
        OR
            $resp := noroom \mid \mid$
            $acct :\in ACCTNO$
        END
    END

4.4.5 The ANY-WHERE-THEN-END substitution

The first part of the CHOICE-OR-END substitution is a new substitution, the **ANY-WHERE-THEN-END substitution**. This substitution is used here to say that any member of $ACCTNO$ that is not already in use as an account number can be the new account number. It is another way of introducing non-determinism into a specification. The substitution has three parts:

- The ANY keyword introduces **local variables** that are used only in this substitution.

- The WHERE keyword introduces a predicate that must fix the types of the local variables, and may constrain them in other ways. In this case it constrains ac to be a member of $ACCTNO$, but not of $accounts$.

- The THEN keyword introduces the then-part of the substitution, which is a substitution that uses the local variables.

The **ANY-WHERE-THEN-END rule** is as follows:

$$[\text{ANY x WHERE } \mathbf{P} \text{ THEN } \mathbf{G} \text{ END}]\ \mathbf{Q} \Leftrightarrow \forall x \bullet (\mathbf{P} \Rightarrow [\mathbf{G}]\ \mathbf{Q})$$

Here **x** is a list of variables, **P** a predicate that constrains their values, and **G** a substitution. The rule can be paraphrased by saying that whatever values are chosen for the local variables, if they satisfy the predicate after the WHERE keyword, then the substitution from the then-part must establish the predicate. The local nature of the variables introduced after the ANY keyword is reflected by their being bound variables in the rule.

4.4.6 Choice-from-a-set substitution

The second part of the CHOICE-OR-END substitution deals with the case in which the operation cannot be completed satisfactorily. The value to be used for *resp* is determined by the requirements, but the value for *acct* is not. We need a substitution to say that any member of the set *ACCTNO* will do, and it is convenient to use the **choice-from-a-set substitution**. This substitution is another way of expressing non-determinism.

The **choice-from-a-set rule** is as follows:

$$[\mathbf{x} :\in \mathbf{S}]\ \mathbf{P} \Leftrightarrow \forall \mathbf{y} \bullet (\mathbf{y} \in \mathbf{S} \Rightarrow [\mathbf{x} := \mathbf{y}]\ \mathbf{P})$$

Here **x** is a variable, and **S** is a set expression. The rule expresses the idea that whichever member of **S** is chosen, replacement of **x** by it establishes **P**. The rule supposes that the bound variable **y** is not free in **P**.

4.5 More about animation

4.5.1 Animating machines with deferred sets and constants

If you animate a machine with deferred sets or constants, the B-Toolkit gives you the opportunity to choose the values of the deferred sets and the constants. This is really quite wrong, because the user of the machine can *never* fix the values of deferred sets and constants, but it is convenient for animation to allow the user to do so.

4.5.2 Animation and non-determinism

Animating a machine with non-deterministic substitutions involves the user in making the choices that would be made by the implementation. If you animate *Owners*, and select the operation *new_acct_old_cust*, you will be asked first to supply the inputs *cust* and *acct*. Then you will be asked to make the choice offered by the CHOICE-OR-END substitution. When an operation has non-deterministic outputs, you will be asked to choose the output value.

4.6 Summary and outlook

In this chapter we have learnt:

- how to specify machines with deferred and enumerated sets;

- how to specify constants in a machine;

- more substitutions, especially substitutions that specify non-determinism;

- the use of the DEFINITIONS clause to simplify writing machines.

Our next need is for constructing larger machines from smaller ones in order to promote reuse of specifications.

4.7 Exercises

(4.1)   Write more operations for *Owners* as follows:

- Add a new account for a new customer. The customer number is an input, and it is the user's responsibility to supply a customer number that is not in *customers*. The user must also ensure that there is an unused account number. The account number is selected by the machine, and is an output from the operation. If the response is *success*, the input customer number and output account number will be paired in *owner*. Sometimes, however, the response is *no_room*, and *owner* will not be changed.

- Inquire about a customer number. The response is *TRUE* if the input customer number is in *customers*, and *FALSE* if it is not.

- Output any customer number not in *customers*, with a response of *TRUE* if there are any, and *FALSE* if there are not.

(4.2)   The following machine is a number server. It provides as output to its single operation a number in the range 1 to 100, without repeating itself.

MACHINE

   Server

SEES

   Bool_TYPE

VARIABLES

   gone

INVARIANT

   $gone \subseteq 1 .. 100$

INITIALISATION

   $gone := \varnothing$

OPERATIONS

```
resp, num ⟵ go =
  IF
    gone = 1 .. 100
  THEN
    resp := FALSE ||
    num := 1
  ELSE
    resp := TRUE ||
    ANY
      nn
    WHERE
      nn ∈ 1 .. 100 ∧
      nn ∉ gone
    THEN
      num := nn ||
      gone := gone ∪ {nn}
    END
  END
```

END

List the proof obligations associated with this machine.

(4.3)   The informal requirements of Table 4.1 describe a storage manager for an operating system. An extended version of this example is to be found in Woodcock and Loomes (1988), where it is specified in Z. The storage manager has a certain number *maxblocks* of blocks to manage on behalf of users of the operating system. A block can only be allocated to one user at once, and a user must free a block before it can be allocated to another user. The blocks are identified by natural numbers in the range 1 .. *maxblocks*. There are user identifiers, but what these are has not yet been decided. In Table 4.1, 'user' is used for user identifier, and 'block' for block number.

Table 4.1 Informal requirements for a storage manager.

Inputs	Processing	Outputs
Acquire a free block		
user	There must be at least one free block. The output is the number of any free block, and that block is allocated to the input user.	block
Release a block of storage		
user block	The input block number must be the number of a block allocated to the input user. The block is freed.	none
Find the number of free blocks		
none	The output is the number of free blocks.	number
Release all the storage for a user		
user	All the blocks allocated to the input user identifier are freed.	none

Initially all the blocks are free.

The operation to get a block has a precondition that there is at least one block free, and you can test this precondition with the third operation. The operation to free a block has a very demanding precondition: the user can only free blocks previously allocated to this user. However, there is no operation to test this precondition. It is the user's responsibility to keep track of the blocks allocated to the user, and to attempt to free only those blocks.

MACHINE

   Storman

SETS

   USER

CONSTANTS

   maxblocks

PROPERTIES

   $maxblocks \in \mathbb{N} \ \wedge$
   $maxblocks > 0$

VARIABLES

   alloc

INVARIANT

   $alloc \in 1 \mathbin{..} maxblocks \nrightarrow USER$

INITIALISATION

   $alloc := \emptyset$

Figure 4.2 Storage manager machine begun.

     Figure 4.2 shows how the machine definition begins, and you must write the rest of it.

(4.4)   Show that

        [ANY xx WHERE $xx \in \mathbb{N} \wedge xx > 5$ THEN $yy := xx$ END]
        $yy > 5$

(4.5)   Show that

        [ANY xx WHERE $xx \in \mathbb{N} \wedge xx > 0$
        THEN $yy := xx + 1$ END] $yy > 1$

(4.6)   Show that

        [ANY xx WHERE $xx \in \mathbb{N} \wedge xx > yy$ THEN $zz := xx$ END]
        $zz > yy$

(4.7)   Show that

$$[\text{CHOICE } xx := 1 \text{ OR } xx := 2 \text{ END}] \ xx > 0$$

(4.8)   Show that

$$[\text{CHOICE } xx := yy - 1 \text{ OR } xx := yy + 1 \text{ END}] \ xx \neq yy$$

(4.9)   Show that if xx is a natural number, then

$$[\text{CHOICE } xx := 1 \text{ OR } xx := 2 \text{ END}] \ xx = 1$$

and

$$[\text{CHOICE } xx := 1 \text{ OR } xx := 2 \text{ END}] \ xx \neq 1$$

are both false.

(4.10)   Show that

$$[xx :\in \mathbb{N}] \ xx \in \mathbb{N}$$

(4.11)   Show that

$$[xx :\in \{yy\}] \ xx = yy$$

(4.12)   Show that

$$[xx :\in \{0, 1, 2\}] \ xx \neq 3$$

(4.13)   Show that

$$[xx :\in yy \cap zz] \ xx \in yy$$

(4.14)   Show that

$$[xx :\in yy \cap zz] \ xx \in yy \cup zz$$

(4.15)   Show that $\mathbf{x} :\in \mathbf{S}$ is equivalent to

$$\text{ANY } \mathbf{y} \text{ WHERE } \mathbf{y} \in \mathbf{S} \text{ THEN } \mathbf{x} := \mathbf{y} \text{ END}$$

Chapter 5
Constructing large machines

Summary: INCLUDES clause — PROMOTES and EXTENDS clauses — USES and SEES clauses — machine characteristics — dependency and subordination.

In this chapter we see how to reuse small machines in larger machines. We see how relations of dependency between machines cause changes in one machine to invalidate the analysis of others.

5.1 Constructing large machines

5.1.1 The recoverable resource manager

We now consider how *RMan*, manager of a single set of resources, can be adapted to construct a more usable resource manager, which we first describe informally in Table 5.1.

Table 5.1 Informal requirements for a resource manager.

Inputs	Processing	Outputs
Allocate a resource		
none	If there are any free resources, one is chosen, and the resource and a response of 'Resource allocated' are output. Otherwise the response is 'No more free resources'.	resource response
Deallocate a resource		
resource	If the resource is allocated, it is made free, and the response is 'Resource freed'. Otherwise the response is 'Already free'.	response
Back up the resource manager's state		
none	The current state of resources is saved.	none
Restore the resource manager's state		
none	The mostly recently saved state of resources is restored.	none

5.1.2 Machine inclusion

The machine *RRMan* (recoverable resource manager) develops the simple machine *RMan* in two ways. It includes two versions of *RMan*, one to represent the current state of the resources and one to represent the most recently saved state, and it provides enquiry operations to test the precondition of the operations that allocate and free resources.

The parameters are the set *RESOURCE*, from which resources are drawn, and the natural number *max_res*, which is the largest number of free resources our machine will have to cope with.

MACHINE

RRMan (RESOURCE, max_res)

The CONSTRAINTS clause says that there are at least *max_res* resources in *RESOURCE*.

CONSTRAINTS

card (*RESOURCE*) $\geq$ *max_res*

A user of this machine must make sure that the values supplied for the parameters satisfy this predicate.

The SEES clause introduces *Bool_TYPE* so that we can use the values *TRUE* and *FALSE* as output indicators on the enquiry operations.

SEES

Bool_TYPE

The **INCLUDES clause** introduces previously defined machines whose variables are to be variables of the new machine. It is much more powerful than the SEES clause, which allows limited reference to the variables of a machine, but does not allow us to change them. It has the form of a list of machine names separated by commas. If the same machine is to be included several times, it is necessary to distinguish the several instances by **renaming** them. The distinguishing names are prefixed to the machine names, and separated from them by a dot. In *RRMan* we include two copies of *RMan*, one of them plain and the other renamed with *bkup* to *bkup.RMan*. This latter copy is where the saved state will be put by the *rec_backup* operation ready to be brought out again by *rec_restore*. The parameters of the included machines are instantiated with the set *RESOURCE*, which is a parameter of *RRMan*. The state of *RRMan* is illustrated in Figure 5.1 on page 66. In this case there are 12 resources to be managed.

Renaming affects the names of the variables, so the variable *rfree* of *RMan* becomes *bkup.rfree* in *bkup.RMan*. The operations are also renamed, so *alloc* becomes *bkup.alloc*. However, the operations of the included machines are not necessarily operations of the machine that includes them, as we shall see later. Renaming does not affect the deferred sets or constants of a machine. The B-Toolkit analyser does not allow the same machine to be included more than once if it contains deferred sets or constants.

The variables of the included machines are variables of the new machine, so their names can be used in predicates like the invariant of the new machine, or the preconditions of its operations. There is however one important restriction: the values of the variables of the included machines can only be changed by using the operations of the included machines in the definitions of the operations of the new

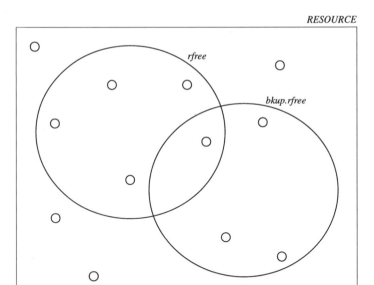

Figure 5.1 State of the recoverable resource manager.

machine. This restriction simplifies the proofs of correctness of the operations, since the operations of a previously proved included machine are known to respect the invariants of the included machine.

INCLUDES

> RMan (RESOURCE),
> bkup.RMan (RESOURCE)

RRMan has no variables other than rfree and bkup.rfree, but we need to put constraints on the values of those variables in their new environment. Neither rfree nor bkup.rfree can have more than max_res resources in them, so we supply the following INVARIANT clause:

INVARIANT

> card (rfree) ≤ max_res ∧
> card (bkup.rfree) ≤ max_res

There is no new initialization: the initialization is that of the included machines:

> rfree, bkup.rfree := Ø, Ø

5.1.3 Operations of the recoverable resource manager

The operation to allocate a resource is *rec_alloc*. It produces an output, the resource to be allocated. The operation definition is a PRE-THEN-END substitution. Note that the precondition refers directly to a variable of an included machine. There must be a free resource in the current version. In the then-part, any free resource is chosen and presented as output and is allocated in *RMan* (so it is removed from *rfree*).

$$res \longleftarrow rec\_alloc =$$
  PRE
    $rfree \neq \emptyset$
  THEN
    ANY
      rr
    WHERE
      $rr \in rfree$
    THEN
      $res := rr \;||$
      $alloc\,(rr)$
    END
  END

We can apply the ANY-WHERE-THEN-END rule to check that *rec_alloc* preserves the invariant of *RRMan*. Since *bkup.rfree* is not part of the operation, we omit it from the theorem, so we have to prove

  card $(rfree) \leq max\_res \wedge rfree \neq \emptyset \Rightarrow$
  [ANY rr WHERE $rr \in rfree$ THEN $alloc\,(rr)$ END]
  card $(rfree) \leq max\_res$

Applying the ANY-WHERE-THEN-END rule to the consequent gives

  $\forall rr \bullet (rr \in rfree \Rightarrow [alloc\,(rr)]$ card $(rfree) \leq max\_res)$

Replacing *alloc* by its definition from *RMan* gives the following consequent:

  $\forall rr \bullet (rr \in rfree \Rightarrow$
  [PRE $rr \in rfree$ THEN $rfree := rfree - \{rr\}$ END]
  card $(rfree) \leq max\_res)$

Applying the PRE-THEN-END rule and doing the simple substitution gives the following consequent:

$$\forall rr \bullet (rr \in rfree \Rightarrow rr \in rfree \wedge \text{card} (rfree - \{rr\}) \leq max\_res)$$

This will be true if and only if the quantified predicate is true for arbitrary rr:

$$rr \in rfree \Rightarrow rr \in rfree \wedge \text{card} (rfree - \{rr\}) \leq max\_res$$

Now we bring back the antecedent of the proof obligation, and consolidate the antecedents:

$$\text{card} (rfree) \leq max\_res \wedge rfree \neq \emptyset \wedge rr \in rfree \Rightarrow$$
$$rr \in rfree \wedge \text{card} (rfree - \{rr\}) \leq max\_res$$

The consequent follows from the antecedent by the laws of set theory.

5.1.4 The Boolean substitution

To help the user of *RRMan* make use of *rec_alloc*, we provide an enquiry operation to see if there are any free resources. This operation, *is_any_free*, has a single output that is *TRUE* when there are free resources and *FALSE* when there are not.

A useful shorthand for associating predicates with the values *TRUE* and *FALSE* is the **Boolean substitution**. The form of the substitution is

$$\mathbf{x} := \text{bool} (\mathbf{P})$$

and its meaning is as follows.

$$\text{IF } \mathbf{P} \text{ THEN } \mathbf{x} := TRUE \text{ ELSE } \mathbf{x} := FALSE \text{ END}$$

If **P** is true, then **x** is replaced by *TRUE*, otherwise it is replaced by *FALSE*.

Here is the substitution in use:

$$ans \longleftarrow is\_any\_free =$$
$$ans := \text{bool} (rfree \neq \emptyset)$$

In this operation, since none of the variables are changed, there is no proof obligation.

5.1.5 More operations of the recoverable resource manager

The operation to free a resource is *rec_free*. This has a single input *rr*, and the precondition says that *rr* must be an allocated resource. The then-part adds *rr* to *rfree*, leaving *bkup.rfree* unchanged.

```
rec_free (rr) =
  PRE
    rr ∈ RESOURCE − rfree ∧
    card (rfree) < max_res
  THEN
    free (rr)
  END
```

The definition of *rec_free* as a PRE-THEN-END substitution is supported by *is_free*, which takes a resource as input and returns a Boolean value to indicate whether the input is in *rfree*.

```
ans ⟵ is_free (rr) =
  PRE
    rr ∈ RESOURCE
  THEN
    ans := bool (rr ∈ rfree)
  END
```

The *rec_backup* operation modifies *bkup.rfree* using the *bkup.setfree* operation. Its input is *rfree*, so it saves the current value of *rfree* in *bkup.rfree*.

```
rec_backup =
  BEGIN
    bkup.setfree (rfree)
  END
```

The *rec_restore* operation modifies *rfree* using the *setfree* operation. Its input is *bkup.rfree*, so it replaces the current value of *rfree* by the saved value of *bkup.rfree*.

```
rec_restore =
  BEGIN
    setfree (bkup.rfree)
  END
```

5.1.6 The PROMOTES and EXTENDS clauses

When a machine **M** includes other machines M_1, M_2, ... M_n, the operations of the included machines are not themselves operations of **M**. In *RRMan*, the only operations are those defined in the OPER-ATIONS clause, namely *rec_alloc*, *is_any_free*, *rec_free*, *is_free*, *rec_backup* and *rec_restore*. The operations of *RMan* and *bkup.RMan* are not operations of *RRMan*. The **EXTENDS clause** allows a machine to be included in another, and at the same time makes all its operations into operations of the larger machine. The

EXTENDS clause has the same form as the INCLUDES clause, that is, a list of machines, with renaming if desired, separated by commas.

The **PROMOTES clause** allows some of the operations of a machine named in the INCLUDES clause to become operations of the larger machine. The PROMOTES clause has the form of a list of names of operations of included machines separated by commas.

The INCLUDES, PROMOTES and EXTENDS clauses can be used in any desired combination, subject to the following rules:

(1) The same name cannot appear in both the INCLUDES and EXTENDS clauses.

(2) If an operation name appears in the PROMOTES clause, the name of the machine to which the operation belongs must appear in the INCLUDES clause.

5.1.7 Notes on the recoverable resource manager machine

RRMan is a component-layer machine in the layered model of software structure. It supplies functions from which a recoverable resource manager can easily be constructed. The model contains enough information to meet the needs described informally in Table 5.1 on page 64, and the operations are supported by enquiry operations that can be used to determine the preconditions.

RRMan will be implemented from library components. The machine *RMan* merely supplies some of the ingredients for *RRMan*, and is not itself implemented in the development of *RRMan*.

RRMan is not robust because its operations have non-trivial preconditions, and its behaviour is unpredictable if an operation is attempted when its precondition is not true.

5.1.8 Animating the recoverable resource manager

When *RRMan* has been analysed, it can be animated. The constraint is displayed so that the user can enter appropriate values for *RESOURCE* and *max_res*. In *rec_alloc*, the user is required to resolve the non-determinism of the ANY-WHERE-THEN-END substitution for choosing the resource to be allocated. The animator displays a list of alternatives, and the user has to choose one of them.

5.2 Structuring large machines

In this section we look at how the INCLUDES, USES and SEES clauses can be used to structure a large machine.

5.2.1 The USES clause

The purpose of the **USES clause** is to let one machine have access to information in another before both machines are included in a larger machine. It often happens that we wish to construct a single machine to be the specification of a software object, but it is convenient to present two smaller machines first. For an example of this approach we consider a specification of the oil terminal control system described informally in Chapter 1.

We propose to write first two specifications as follows:

- *TankerM* is a machine to manage the queue of tankers. It contains a deferred set *TANKER* for the set of all possible tankers. Its state is an injective sequence of tankers, that is, a sequence without repetitions.

- *BerthM* is a machine to manage the berths. It contains a deferred set *BERTH* for the set of berths to be managed. Its state is a function relating berths to tankers, so it needs to use the set *TANKER*. This machine is also a convenient place to record the invariant that no tanker can be both queued and berthed.

The outline of the machine *TankerM* is as follows:

MACHINE

   TankerM

SETS

   TANKER

VARIABLES

   waiting

INVARIANT

   waiting ∈ iseq (*TANKER*)

OPERATIONS

   ...

END

The outline of the machine *BerthM* is as follows:

MACHINE

  BerthM

SETS

  BERTH

USES

  TankerM

VARIABLES

  docked

INVARIANT

  docked $\in$ *BERTH* $\nrightarrow$ *TANKER* $\wedge$
  ran (*docked*) $\cap$ ran (*waiting*) $= \varnothing$

OPERATIONS

  ...

END

The USES clause allows *BerthM* to use the set *TANKER* and the variable *waiting* in its invariant.

After these two specifications have been separately presented in the specification document for the oil terminal control system, the specification of *OTCS* can be constructed by including both machines.

MACHINE

  OTCS

INCLUDES

  BerthM, TankerM

OPERATIONS

  ...

END

5.2.2 The SEES clause

The purpose of the SEES clause, which we have met in several examples already, is to let one machine have access to information in another that is to be separately implemented. Three kinds of machine usually appear in SEES clauses.

(1) Stateless machines that define widely used types. The library machines *Bool_TYPE* and *Scalar_TYPE* are examples.

(2) Machines that define deferred and enumerated sets used in common by many machines in a development. Enumerated sets of responses to operations are often treated in this way.

(3) Mathematical context machines that define mathematical functions.

Here is an example of the last kind of use.

MACHINE

  Mathfac

CONSTANTS

  mathfac

PROPERTIES

$mathfac \in \mathbb{N} \rightarrow \mathbb{N} \wedge$
$mathfac\ (0) = 1 \wedge$
$\forall nn \bullet (nn \in \mathbb{N}_1 \Rightarrow$
$mathfac\ (nn) = nn \times mathfac\ (nn - 1))$

END

This machine simply provides a definition of the mathematical factorial function.

A machine that uses the *mathfac* function might be constructed as follows:

MACHINE

  Myfac

SEES

  Mathfac

OPERATIONS

$nn \longleftarrow fac\ (mm) =$
   PRE
     $mm \in \mathbb{N}$
   THEN
     $nn := mathfac\ (mm)$
   END

END

This machine relies on the function *mathfac* defined in the machine *Mathfac*.

5.3 Defining characteristics of a machine

The examples in this and the preceding chapters illustrate the principal features of machines and the substitutions that can be used in them. In this section we explore the nature of the machine further, consolidating and extending what we have already learnt.

5.3.1 Variables

We have seen that a machine can have variables, invariant and operations, and these can be established by the corresponding clauses of the machine definition. Other clauses of the machine can also contribute to a machine's variables as follows.

We shall call the variables named in the VARIABLES clause of the machine the **native variables** of the machine. The native variables of the machine can be used in the INVARIANT clause, and can be modified in the substitutions that define the operations.

Almost as good as the native variables are the variables acquired from machines named in the INCLUDES and EXTENDS clauses. The native variables of these machines become **included variables** of the machines that include them. The included variables of a machine can be used in the INVARIANT clause, and can be referred to in the substitutions that define the operations, but in the operations they can be modified only by the operations of their own machines. Machine inclusion is transitive in the sense that if $\mathbf{M}_1$ includes or extends $\mathbf{M}_2$, the included variables of $\mathbf{M}_2$ become included variables of $\mathbf{M}_1$.

A machine can make limited use of variables of machines named in a USES clause, which is a list of names of machines separated by commas. The native and included variables of such a machine become **used variables** of the machine that uses them. The used variables can appear in the INVARIANT clause, and can be referred to in the operations, but cannot be modified by them. The renaming mechanism described above (page 65) is available in the USES clause.

A machine can also make limited use of variables of machines in the SEES clause, and we shall call the native and included variables of these machine **seen variables** of the machine that sees them. The seen variables cannot be used in the INVARIANT clause of the machine that sees them, but they can be referred to, but not changed, in the operations. The renaming mechanism described above (page 65) is available in the SEES clause.

5.3.2 Sets

Many machines have sets associated with them. A machine might have one or more parameters that are sets, and these will be called the **parametric sets** of the machine. The machine *RMan* has one parametric set, *RES*. Sets can be introduced explicitly in the SETS clause, and as we saw earlier in this chapter, these sets can be deferred or enumerated. Sets introduced explicitly in the SETS clause, whether deferred or enumerated, will be called the **native sets** of the machine. A machine can acquire sets from the machines named in the INCLUDES and EXTENDS clauses. The deferred and enumerated sets of these machines become **included sets** of the machine that includes them. A machine can acquire sets from the machines named in the USES clause. The native and included sets of such a machine become **used sets** of the machine. A machine can acquire sets from the machines named in the SEES clause. The native and included sets of such a machine become **seen sets** of the machine.

5.3.3 Constants

A machine may have constants of various types. The parameters that are not sets are the **parametric constants** of the machine. If they are not typed in the CONSTRAINTS clause, they are assumed to be natural numbers. Constants can also be introduced to the machine in the CONSTANTS clause. These names are the names of the **native constants** of the machine. Native constants also arise from the use of enumerated sets in the SETS clause of a machine. Each of the members of an enumerated set is a native constant of the machine. Constants are also inherited from other machines. The native constants of machines named in the INCLUDES and EXTENDS clauses become the **included constants** of the machine. The native constants of machines named in the USES clause become **used constants** of the machine. The native constants of machines named in the SEES clause become **seen constants** of the machine.

5.3.4 Constraints

The **constraints** of a machine are predicates about the parameters, and they are introduced explicitly in the CONSTRAINTS clause. Some constraints are implicit – these are the constraints that say that a parametric set is non-empty.

5.3.5 Context

The **context** of a machine is a collection of predicates about the machine's sets and constants. It must contain a constraining predicate for each native constant that was not in an enumerated set, and these constraining predicates must be introduced explicitly in the machine's PROPERTIES clause. The PROPERTIES clause may fix other relationships among the machine's sets and constants. It must not, however, attempt to type the deferred and enumerated sets, nor can it give a value to the deferred or enumerated sets. An important part of the context of a machine is the implicit predicates about enumerated sets. These implicit predicates and the contents of the PROPERTIES clause make up the **native context** of the machine. The machine *Bool_TYPE* has the following predicates in its context.

$$BOOL \neq \emptyset$$
$$BOOL = \{FALSE, TRUE\}$$
$$\text{card}\,(BOOL) = 2$$
$$FALSE \neq TRUE$$

Parts of a machine's context are inherited from elsewhere, so we can speak of **included context** from the native context of machines named in the INCLUDES and EXTENDS clauses, **used context** from the native context of machines named in the USES clause, and **seen context** from the native context of machines named in the SEES clause.

5.3.6 Invariant

The machine's invariant is a predicate, usually a conjunction, about the machine's variables. The INVARIANT clause provides the **native invariant**, and it must contain constraining predicates to fix the types of the machine's native variables, and can also specify relationships between the native variables and the included and used variables, but cannot refer to the seen variables. The invariants of machines mentioned in the INCLUDES and EXTENDS clauses are the **included invariant**. The included invariant contains constraining predicates for the included variables. The invariants of machines mentioned in the USES clause are the **used invariant**. The invariants of machines mentioned in the SEES clause are the **seen invariant**.

The operations of the machine must preserve the native invariant. They cannot violate the included invariant because they can only modify the included variables by using the operations of the included machines. They cannot violate the used or seen invariants because they are not allowed to change used or seen variables.

5.3.7 Initialization

The initialization of a machine is a substitution that establishes the invariant. If there are several variables, it will usually be a parallel substitution. The **native initialization** is to be found in the INITIAL-ISATION clause of the machine, and this substitution must establish the native invariant. The initialization of the machines in the INCLUDES and EXTENDS clauses is the **included initialization**, which establishes the included invariant. The **used initialization** is the initialization of the machines in the USES clause. The native, included and used initializations must together (in parallel) establish the native invariant.

5.3.8 Operations

The operations of a machine are all of the following:

- Operations of machines named in the EXTENDS clause

- Operations named in the PROMOTES clause

- Operations defined in the OPERATIONS clause.

In an operation definition, the precondition must establish the types of the inputs, and may specify any other requirements on the state and inputs. An operation definition can refer to the native, included, used and seen variables, and may refer to any of the machine's sets and constants. The operation definition can change the native variables in any way you please; it can change included variables only through the operations of the machines in which they are native variables; it cannot change used or seen variables. It can, however, use any of the operations of used or seen machines that do not change the variables.

5.4 Dependency and subordination

When a machine is analysed by the B-Toolkit analyser, a relation of **dependency** is established between the machine being analysed and the machines named in the SEES, USES, INCLUDES and EXTENDS clauses. For instance, if machine M_1 includes machine M_2, we shall say that M_1 is dependent on M_2. The **subordination**

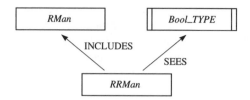

Figure 5.2 Dependencies of the recoverable resource manager.

relation between machines is the converse of the dependency relation, and in this example we would say that M_2 is subordinate to M_1.

The dependency relation can be illustrated in a **dependency diagram** like Figure 5.2, in which the dependencies of *RRMan* are illustrated.

The boxes represent machines; the machine *Bool_TYPE*, being a library machine and so not able to be changed by the user, is represented by a box with double ends. The dependency relation is represented by the arrows, and each arrow is annotated with the name of the clause that introduced it. Although *RMan* is included twice in *RRMan*, once as *RMan* and once as *bkup.RMan*, we need record the dependency only once in the diagram.

The dependency diagram shows that a maths change to *RMan* would invalidate the analysis of *RRMan*, and both would need to be re-analysed. We shall use the dependency diagram elsewhere in the book to illustrate the progress of developments.

5.5 Summary and outlook

In this chapter we have learnt:

- how to include machines in larger machines;
- how to use the operations of included machines in operations of the including machine;
- the visibility and usability rules for the elements of machines in combination;
- the complementary ideas of subordination and dependency.

Now we are almost ready to think about how a machine can be developed into a software object, but first we have a few more substitutions.

5.6 Exercises

(5.1) Define a machine *Student_array* with two parameters *max_size* and *STUDENT* by extending the machine *Array* defined in a previous exercise. Add a new operation to find a particular value in an initial segment of the array. The operation will have two inputs: the highest array index to be considered, and the value to be searched for. The output will be the index of an occurrence of the input value in the segment of the array that ends at the input limit, or zero if there is no such occurrence.

(5.2) The following machine is supplied.

MACHINE

Students (*max_students*, *STUDENT*)

CONSTRAINTS

max_students > *0*

VARIABLES

studentset

INVARIANT

studentset $\subseteq$ *STUDENT* $\wedge$
card (*studentset*) $\leq$ *max_students*

INITIALISATION

studentset := $\emptyset$

OPERATIONS

enter (*st*) =
  PRE
    st $\in$ *STUDENT* $\wedge$
    st $\notin$ *studentset* $\wedge$
    card (*studentset*) < *max_students*
  THEN
    studentset := *studentset* $\cup$ {*st*}
  END
  ;

$$remove\ (st) =$$
PRE

$st \in studentset$

THEN

$studentset := studentset - \{st\}$

END

END

Construct a machine *CMA_built* that has the same operations as *CMA* by including two versions of *Students*, one for the enrolled set and one for the tested set.

(5.3) Draw dependency diagrams for the examples in Section 5.2 on structuring large machines.

Chapter 6
More substitutions for machines

Summary: Skip substitution — IF-THEN-END — IF-THEN-ELSIF — choice-by-predicate — SELECT — CASE — LET-BE-IN-END — full-function machines — parallel substitution rules.

In this chapter we complete the repertoire of substitutions that can be used in machines, and exploit some of them in full-function machines. The rules for giving meanings to parallel substitutions are made precise.

6.1 More substitutions for machines

In this section we review some substitutions that have not appeared in examples, but that will be useful in machine construction. (Some of these substitutions will be needed for some of the exercises.)

6.1.1 The substitution that does nothing

The first new substitution is *skip*, a substitution that does nothing. The **skip rule** is very simple:

$$[skip] \textbf{ P} \Leftrightarrow \textbf{P}$$

which is to say *skip* establishes **P** if and only if **P**.

6.1.2 Variations on IF-THEN-ELSE-END

There are a couple of variations on IF-THEN-ELSE-END that are often useful. The first of these is the **IF-THEN-END substitution**, which takes some action when the if-test is true, but does nothing when the if-test is false. We define

IF **P** THEN **G** END

to mean

IF **P** THEN **G** ELSE *skip* END

and illustrate its action with a flow chart in Figure 6.1.

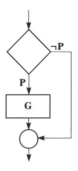

Figure 6.1 IF-THEN-END illustrated.

Using the IF-THEN-ELSE-END rule and the skip rule we can derive the **IF-THEN-END rule** as follows. We begin with the following predicate:

[IF **P** THEN **G** END] **Q**

Replacing the IF-THEN-END substitution with its definition gives

[IF **P** THEN **G** ELSE *skip* END] **Q**

Applying the IF-THEN-ELSE-END rule gives

$(\mathbf{P} \Rightarrow [\mathbf{G}]\, \mathbf{Q}) \wedge (\neg \mathbf{P} \Rightarrow [skip]\, \mathbf{Q})$

Applying the skip rule gives us the result:

$(\mathbf{P} \Rightarrow [\mathbf{G}]\, \mathbf{Q}) \wedge (\neg \mathbf{P} \Rightarrow \mathbf{Q})$

The other variation on IF-THEN-ELSE-END is an extension to cover more cases. We give a simple example of the **IF-THEN-ELSIF substitution**.

IF **P** THEN **G** ELSIF **Q** THEN **H** ELSE **I** END

is defined to mean

IF **P** THEN **G** ELSE (IF **Q** THEN **H** ELSE **I** END) END

and this is illustrated in Figure 6.2.

We derive a rule for the IF-THEN-ELSIF substitution as follows.

[IF **P** THEN **G** ELSIF **Q** THEN **H** ELSE **I** END] **R**

Expanding the ELSIF part gives

[IF **P** THEN **G** ELSE (IF **Q** THEN **H** ELSE **I** END) END] **R**

Applying the IF-THEN-ELSE-END rule gives

$(\mathbf{P} \Rightarrow [\mathbf{G}]\, \mathbf{R}) \wedge (\neg \mathbf{P} \Rightarrow [\text{IF } \mathbf{Q} \text{ THEN } \mathbf{H} \text{ ELSE } \mathbf{I} \text{ END}]\, \mathbf{R})$

Applying the same rule again gives

$(\mathbf{P} \Rightarrow [\mathbf{G}]\, \mathbf{R}) \wedge (\neg \mathbf{P} \Rightarrow (\mathbf{Q} \Rightarrow [\mathbf{H}]\, \mathbf{R}) \wedge (\neg \mathbf{Q} \Rightarrow [\mathbf{I}]\, \mathbf{R}))$

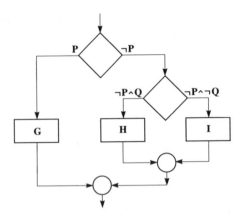

Figure 6.2 IF-THEN-ELSIF-ELSE-END illustrated.

Simplifying this with some properties of propositional functions gives the following result:

$$(P \Rightarrow [G] \: R) \wedge (\neg P \wedge Q \Rightarrow [H] \: R) \wedge (\neg P \wedge \neg Q \Rightarrow [I] \: R)$$

The ELSIF ... THEN ... can be repeated as often as you like. The ELSE ... can be omitted, and ELSE *skip* is assumed.

6.1.3 Non-deterministic substitutions

The substitutions discussed so far in this section, *skip* and the variations of IF-THEN-ELSE-END, are all deterministic substitutions. We now look at some more ways of expressing non-determinism.

First we have the **choice-by-predicate substitution**. The notation is

$$x : P$$

and the rule expresses that fact that **x** is to be replaced by any value that satisfies **P**. **x** must occur free in **P** and must be constrained there. Here is the **choice-by-predicate rule**:

$$[x : P] \: Q \Leftrightarrow \forall y \bullet ([x := y] \: P \Rightarrow [x := y] \: Q)$$

The bound variable **y** must not occur free in **P** or **Q**.

We now examine a method of using predicates to influence which part of a non-deterministic choice is selected. The modified form of choice is appropriately called a **SELECT substitution**. Here is a simple example:

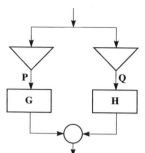

Figure 6.3 SELECT illustrated.

```
SELECT
    x ≥ 0 THEN x := x + 1
WHEN
    x > 0 THEN skip
WHEN
    x > 1 THEN x := x − 1
END
```

The predicates $x \geq 0$, $x > 0$, and $x > 1$ are called the **guards** of the simple substitutions $x := x + 1$, *skip*, and $x := x - 1$. The substitution in a then-part can be selected only if its guard is true. When x is greater than 1, there is a non-deterministic choice between the three simple substitutions. When x is equal to 1, there is a non-deterministic choice between two of them. When x is zero, the substitution $x := x + 1$ is selected. The SELECT substitution cannot be represented using conventional flow charts, so Figure 6.3 uses a large arrowhead annotated with a guard to emphasize that passage to the following substitution is permitted only if the guard is true. This figure illustrates the substitution SELECT **P** THEN **G** WHEN **Q** THEN **H** END.

We give the **SELECT rule** for two guards, and the extension to more guards is obvious.

[SELECT **P** THEN **G** WHEN **Q** THEN **H** END] **R**
⇔
$(\mathbf{P} \Rightarrow [\mathbf{G}] \, \mathbf{R}) \wedge (\mathbf{Q} \Rightarrow [\mathbf{H}] \, \mathbf{R})$

The guards do not need to be mutually exclusive, but they should cover every case.

The SELECT substitution can have an ELSE keyword and an else-part to catch the cases not selected by the guards. Figure 6.4 on page 86 illustrates the substitution.

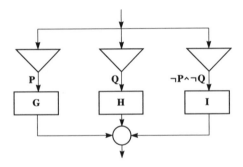

Figure 6.4 SELECT-with-ELSE illustrated.

For a two-guard SELECT substitution, the **SELECT-with-ELSE rule** is as follows.

[SELECT **P** THEN **G** WHEN **Q** THEN **H** ELSE **I** END] **R**
$\Leftrightarrow$
$(\mathbf{P} \Rightarrow [\mathbf{G}]\,\mathbf{R}) \wedge (\mathbf{Q} \Rightarrow [\mathbf{H}]\,\mathbf{R}) \wedge (\neg(\mathbf{P} \vee \mathbf{Q}) \Rightarrow [\mathbf{I}]\,\mathbf{R})$

The next substitution that we shall study is a variation on SELECT where the guards are membership predicates. This is the **CASE substitution**, of which a typical instance follows.

```
CASE E OF
  EITHER S THEN G
  OR T THEN H
  END
END
```

which is equivalent to

```
SELECT
  E ∈ S THEN G
WHEN
  E ∈ T THEN H
END
```

The **CASE rule** for this example is

[CASE **E** OF EITHER **S** THEN **G** OR **T** THEN **H** END END] **P**
$\Leftrightarrow$
$(\mathbf{E} \in \mathbf{S} \Rightarrow [\mathbf{G}]\,\mathbf{P}) \wedge (\mathbf{E} \in \mathbf{T} \Rightarrow [\mathbf{H}]\,\mathbf{P})$

The CASE substitution can also have an ELSE keyword and an else-part to catch the defaults.

The last substitution we need for machine construction allows us to introduce locally defined names for expressions that might be complex. It is explained as a variation of ANY-WHERE-THEN-END, but is not really a non-deterministic substitution, since the value to be used is fixed uniquely. The substitution is the **LET-BE-IN-END substitution**, and its form is as follows.

LET x BE x $=$ **E** IN **G** END

The meaning of this substitution is the following.

ANY x WHERE x $=$ **E** THEN **G** END

The **LET-BE-IN-END rule** is therefore

[LET x BE x $=$ **E** IN **G** END] **P**
$\Leftrightarrow$
$\forall x \bullet (x = E \Rightarrow [G] \, P)$

provided that x is not free in **P**.

6.2 Full-function machines

The idea of a full-function machine was introduced briefly in Chapter 3. Here we study an example based on the class manager's assistant.

The main characteristics of a full-function machine are these:

- The operations are all robust, with relatively simple preconditions. The preconditions are usually just enough to fix the types of the inputs.

- The operation definitions enumerate the cases, and produce outputs that explain the success or failure of the operation. The SELECT or IF-THEN-ELSIF substitutions are common.

- The inquiry operations are just those demanded by the requirements. Extra operations to test preconditions are not provided.

These principles are illustrated by the machine *FFCMA*. In this example we present only one operation, and leave the others as an exercise.

MACHINE

FFCMA (class_size, STUDENT)

CONSTRAINTS

$class\_size > 0 \wedge$
card $(STUDENT) \in \mathbb{N}$

SETS

$Response = \{no\_room, already\_enrolled,$
$student\_enrolled, not\_enrolled, already\_tested,$
$test\_noted, certificate, no\_certificate,$
$student\_tested, enrolled\_but\_not\_tested\}$

VARIABLES

enrolled, tested

INVARIANT

$enrolled \subseteq STUDENT \wedge$
$tested \subseteq enrolled \wedge$
card $(enrolled) \leq class\_size$

INITIALISATION

$enrolled, tested := \varnothing, \varnothing$

OPERATIONS

```
resp ⟵ enrol (st) =
  PRE
    st ∈ STUDENT
  THEN
    SELECT
      st ∈ enrolled
    THEN
      resp := already_enrolled
    WHEN
      card (enrolled) = class_size
    THEN
      resp := no_room
    WHEN
      st ∉ enrolled ∧
      card (enrolled) < class_size
    THEN
      enrolled := enrolled ∪ {st} ||
      resp := student_enrolled
    END
  END
```

The use of the SELECT substitution in the definition of *enrol* means that when the class is full and the input is already enrolled, the implementer can choose whether to respond *no_room* or *already_enrolled*. Specifying the other operations is left as an exercise.

In the layered model of software, full-function machines are part of the API layer.

6.3 Rules for parallel substitutions

The idea of substitutions that operate in parallel was introduced in the machine *CMA* on page 45 to express the idea that two variables in the state were to be changed by an operation. The two substitutions in parallel were both simple substitutions, so the parallel composition of the substitutions was equivalent to a multiple substitution. This interpretation of parallelism applied also to the operation *new_acct_old_cust* in the machine *Owners* on page 54, since the functional overriding substitution used there is just an abbreviation for a simple substitution.

We expect the notation for parallelism to obey some simple rules. For instance we expect the order of substitutions in a parallel substitution not to matter, as follows:

$$G \mid\mid H = H \mid\mid G$$

The equals sign denotes equivalence of substitutions. Two substitutions are equivalent if and only if they establish the same predicates.

We should also expect an associative law:

$$(G \mid\mid H) \mid\mid I = G \mid\mid (H \mid\mid I)$$

Another simple rule concerns the substitution *skip*:

$$G \mid\mid skip = G$$

In the operation *go* of the machine *Server* on page 59 however, we have a simple substitution in parallel with ANY-WHERE-THEN-END. The operation definition could just as well have been written as follows:

```
ANY
    nn
WHERE
    nn ∈ 1 .. 100 ∧
    nn ∉ gone
THEN
```

```
        num := nn | |
        gone := gone ∪ {nn} | |
        resp := TRUE
    END
END
```

This leads us to formulate the following general rule for parallelism with ANY-WHERE-THEN-END.

```
ANY x WHERE P THEN G END | | H
=
ANY x WHERE P THEN G | | H END
```

provided that **x** is not free in **H**. (If **x** is free in **H**, rewrite the ANY-WHERE-THEN-END substitution with a different name for the local variable.)

A more exciting situation occurs in the operation *rec_alloc* in the machine *RRMan* on page 67. Here we have a simple substitution in parallel with an operation of an included machine. If we look at the definition of the operation *alloc* in the machine *RMan* in Chapter 2, we find that it is a PRE-THEN-END substitution. Applying the same technique to this example as we did to the ANY-WHERE-THEN-END example, we see that

$$res := rr \mid\mid alloc\ (rr)$$

is equivalent to

```
PRE rr ∈ rfree THEN rfree := rfree − {rr} | | res := rr END
```

We therefore formulate the general rule:

```
PRE P THEN G END | | H
=
PRE P THEN G | | H END
```

We can formulate similar rules for other substitutions, and there are more given in Appendix B.

6.4 Summary and outlook

In this chapter we have learnt:

- several new substitutions that can be used in machines;
- how to write full-function machines;
- the rules for parallel substitutions.

Now we look forward to developing machines into programs.

6.5 Exercises

(6.1)   Show that if xx is a natural number, then

$$[\text{IF } xx = 0 \text{ THEN } xx := xx + 1 \text{ END}] \, xx > 0$$

(6.2)   Show that if xx is a natural number, then

```
[IF xx = 0
THEN xx := xx + 1
ELSIF xx > 1
THEN  xx := 1
END]
xx = 1
```

(6.3)   Show that

$$[\text{LET } xx \text{ BE } xx = 5 \text{ IN } yy := xx \text{ END}] \, yy = 5$$

(6.4)   Show that

$$[\text{LET } xx \text{ BE } xx = yy + zz \text{ IN } yy := xx - yy \text{ END}] \, yy = zz$$

(6.5)   Show that

$$[\text{LET } xx \text{ BE } xx = yy \cap zz \text{ IN } ww := xx \text{ END}] \, ww \subseteq yy$$

(6.6)   Show that

$$[xx : xx \in \mathbb{N} \wedge xx > 0] \, xx > 0$$

(6.7)   Show that

$$[xx : xx \in \mathbb{N} \wedge xx = 0] \, xx \neq 1$$

(6.8)   Show that

$$[xx : xx \in \mathbb{N} \wedge xx > 5] \, xx \neq 0$$

(6.9)   Show that

$$[xx : xx \in \mathbb{N} \wedge xx < 1] \, xx = 0$$

(6.10)   Show that

SELECT **P** THEN **G** WHEN $\neg$**P** THEN **H** END

is equivalent to

IF **P** THEN **G** ELSE **H** END

(6.11)   Show that

x : P

is equivalent to

ANY **y** WHERE [**x** := **y**] **P** THEN **x** := **y** END

(6.12)   Complete the full-function machine *FFCMA* by providing the operations *test*, *leave* and *inquire*.

(6.13)   Write a full-function machine for the oil terminal control system. Use the informal state machine of Chapter 1 as the basis of your machine.

(6.14)   Define a full-function machine *Birthday_book* to keep track of the relationship between people's names and their birthdays. The idea of a birthday book is taken from Spivey (1992), where a specification of it is presented in Z. Make *NAME* and *DATE* the deferred sets of the machine, and define an enumerated set *REPORT* for the responses to the operations. Use the informal requirements in Table 6.1.

Table 6.1 Informal requirements for a birthday book.

Inputs	Processing	Outputs
Add a birthday		
name date	If the name is already registered with a birthday, report 'Already known'. Otherwise report 'Birthday added', and associate the name with the date, unless there is no more room, in which case report 'No room'.	report
Find a birthday		
name	If the name is associated with a date, report 'Name found', and output the date. Otherwise report 'Not known'.	report date
Start reminder list		
date	If there are no birthdays for this date, report 'No birthdays'. If there are some, report 'Birthdays found', output one of them, and remember the rest for later.	report name

Inputs	Processing	Outputs
Show next birthday in reminder list		
none	If there are any names left for the date provided on 'Start reminder list', report 'Another birthday', and output another name, remembering the rest. If there are no more, report 'No more birthdays'.	report name

Initially the birthday book is empty.

Chapter 7
Software design

7.1 Software design	**7.4 Algorithm design: local vari-**
7.2 Data design	**ables**
7.3 Algorithm design:	**7.5 Algorithm design: loops**
sequences	

Summary: Software design — concrete and abstract states — retrieve relation — data design — correctness of initialization — non-deterministic abstract initializations — correctness of operations — algorithm design — sequence — local variables — loop — loop variant — loop invariant — the five rules — principles of loop construction.

In this chapter we explore ideas of software design, and categorize design decisions as data design or algorithm design. We see that design decisions can be recorded in a precise way, and that proofs can be used to show that a design is correct. We meet two new substitutions that can be used to express algorithm designs, the sequence and the loop.

7.1 Software design

The specification of a software object is represented in the B-Method by a machine. The development process that begins with the machine must produce programs and data that are the software object. We shall call the process of producing the software object from its specification **software design**. Software design has two aspects:

- **Data design**, in which data structures that can be easily programmed are chosen to represent the variables of the machine;

- **Algorithm design**, in which the program instructions that manipulate the data structures are organized into the operations promised in the machine.

To do software design well, you need to understand the specification, and know about the capabilities of the available data structures and the operations on them. If you are a newcomer to software engineering, I should like to be able to tell you that the producers of programming languages and other programming interfaces document them well enough to make software design easy, or at least possible, but experienced software engineers will know that this is not the case. Sometimes (perhaps I should say 'usually'), it is necessary to experiment with an interface to find out its properties and assess its suitability for design purposes. Ideally any interface that is to be used in design should have a precise specification − a machine definition in AMN would be ideal, and the B-Toolkit supplies a number of such interfaces in its library.

A good design must have certain properties. Efficiency of use of computing resources is one useful property, and speed of operation is another. In this book we are concentrating on the property of being correct, that is, of refining the behaviour of the machine so that the promises made in it are fulfilled.

In the B-Method, the results of software design for a machine are recorded in an implementation.

In discussing the relationship between a machine and its implementation, we shall call the variables of the machine **abstract variables**. The implementation also has variables, and we shall call these **concrete variables**. The concrete variables are chosen so that the implementation is easily translated into program code by the B-Toolkit, and so that they represent the abstract variables. The idea is that given any **concrete state** (that is, a set of values for the concrete variables), we can discover which **abstract state** (that is, a set of values for the abstract variables) it represents. Recording the relationship between the abstract and the concrete is an important part of constructing an implementation of a machine. This relation is called the **retrieve relation**. It is often a function, so that one or more concrete states represent each abstract state. Very rarely it is an injection, so that each abstract state is represented by exactly one concrete state. Occasionally it is a more general relation.

Before studying the details of implementations, we study the idea of correctness of design, and the proof obligations that guarantee it. In this study we make some assumptions about the kinds of data structures that can be used in design, and the operations on them.

7.2 Data design

In this section we consider how choices of data representation are related to the initialization and operations of a machine. The general process of data representation is to represent abstract data by data that is more concrete. Sets, which are abstract, might be represented by sequences, which are more concrete. If you think sequences are abstract, you might choose to represent a sequence by an array. A relation, which is abstract, might be represented by two arrays, with corresponding members of pairs in the relation in corresponding cells in the arrays.

7.2.1 Data design and correctness of initialization

The simplest kind of data design makes no change between the abstract and concrete representations of the data. Suppose for instance that the abstract state has a natural number variable xx in the range 0 .. 100. We can represent this in the concrete state by a natural number variable yy in the same range. The retrieve relation in this case is just $xx = yy$, which has one concrete state to represent each abstract state, and is therefore an injection. It is often useful in data design to make a tabular representation of the abstract and concrete states and the invariants as follows.

	Abstract	Concrete
VARIABLES	xx	yy
INVARIANT	$xx \in 0 .. 100$	$yy \in 0 .. 100 \wedge$ $xx = yy$

It is convenient for what follows to put the retrieve relation in the concrete invariant, as we do in this example.

The initialization of the concrete state must agree with the initialization of the abstract state when seen through the retrieve relation. If the abstract initialization sets xx to zero, the concrete initialization must do the same, so we can extend the table as follows:

	Abstract	Concrete
INITIALISATION	$xx := 0$	$yy := 0$

Sometimes a design removes non-determinism in a specification. For instance consider the following initializations:

	Abstract	Concrete
INITIALISATION	$xx :\in 0 .. 100$	$yy := 0$

In this case the abstract initialization does not fix the value of xx; any number in the range will do. The concrete initialization chooses a particular value in the range, namely 0.

The question remains: how shall we formalize the idea of correctness of initialization when we are given the two states and the retrieve relation? We first state a condition derived from the set-theoretic model of abstract machines developed in Abrial (1993), and then apply it to the two examples given. If $\mathbf{P_C}$ is the invariant of the concrete state, which includes the retrieve relation, and if $\mathbf{G_A}$ is the initialization of the abstract state, and $\mathbf{G_C}$ is the initialization of the concrete state, the correctness condition is

$$[\mathbf{G_C}] \, \neg [\mathbf{G_A}] \, \neg \mathbf{P_C}$$

The condition can be paraphrased as follows: the concrete initialization makes it impossible for the abstract initialization to fail to establish the concrete invariant. The appearance of two negations in this condition prompts the question as to whether they can be dispensed with. We might ask in what circumstances could this condition be simplified to

$$[\mathbf{G_C}] \, [\mathbf{G_A}] \, \mathbf{P_C}$$

and the answer depends on the nature of the substitution $[\mathbf{G_A}]$.

If we apply the condition to the first initialization, we get the following proof obligation:

$$[yy := 0] \, \neg [xx := 0] \, \neg (yy \in 0 .. 100 \wedge yy = xx)$$

Making the second substitution in the concrete invariant gives the following:

$$[yy := 0] \, \neg \neg (yy \in 0 .. 100 \wedge yy = 0)$$

Using the law of double negation gives:

$$[yy := 0]\ (yy \in 0 \mathinner{.\,.} 100 \wedge yy = 0)$$

Now making the remaining substitution gives us the following theorem:

$$0 \in 0 \mathinner{.\,.} 100 \wedge 0 = 0$$

We see that when the abstract initialization is a simple substitution, the two negations cancel each other out in a simple way.

If we apply the condition to the second initialization, we get the following proof obligation:

$$[yy := 0]\ \neg[xx :\in 0 \mathinner{.\,.} 100]\ \neg(yy \in 0 \mathinner{.\,.} 100 \wedge yy = xx)$$

We make the second substitution by using the choice-from-a-set rule.

$$[yy := 0]$$
$$\neg\forall zz \bullet (zz \in 0 \mathinner{.\,.} 100 \Rightarrow [xx := zz]\ \neg(yy \in 0 \mathinner{.\,.} 100 \wedge yy = xx))$$

The law of double negation cannot be used yet, so we make the substitution of zz for xx.

$$[yy := 0]\ \neg\forall zz \bullet (zz \in 0 \mathinner{.\,.} 100 \Rightarrow \neg(yy \in 0 \mathinner{.\,.} 100 \wedge yy = zz))$$

Now we make the remaining substitution of 0 for yy.

$$\neg\forall zz \bullet (zz \in 0 \mathinner{.\,.} 100 \Rightarrow \neg(0 \in 0 \mathinner{.\,.} 100 \wedge 0 = zz))$$

Using the rule for negating a universal quantification and the rule for negating an implication gives the following:

$$\exists zz \bullet (zz \in 0 \mathinner{.\,.} 100 \wedge \neg\neg(0 \in 0 \mathinner{.\,.} 100 \wedge 0 = zz))$$

Using the law of double negation and dropping the theorem $0 \in 0 \mathinner{.\,.} 100$ gives the following:

$$\exists zz \bullet (zz \in 0 \mathinner{.\,.} 100 \wedge 0 = zz)$$

To this we can apply the one-point rule to leave the following theorem:

$$0 \in 0 \mathinner{.\,.} 100$$

In this case we see that the two negations can only be disposed of after the universal quantifier has been turned into an existential quantifier. Had we attempted to apply the version of the correctness condition without the negations, we should have been unable to prove the correctness of the initialization, even though the initialization is intuitively correct. The form with two negations is essential if we are to cope with abstract initializations that are non-deterministic.

sequences

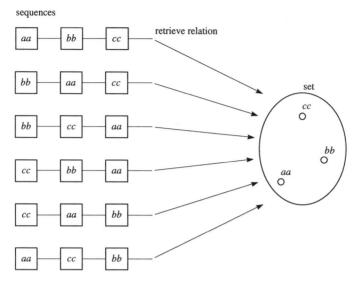

Figure 7.1 Many sequences representing a single set.

Now we look at a more elaborate relation between abstract and concrete. This example uses part of the state of the machine *RRMan*.

	Abstract	**Concrete**
VARI-ABLES	*rfree*	*rseq*
INVAR-IANT	*rfree* $\subseteq$ *RESOURCE* $\wedge$ card (*rfree*) $\leq$ *max_res*	*rseq* $\in$ iseq (*RESOURCE*) $\wedge$ *rfree* = ran (*rseq*)
INITIAL-ISATION	*rfree* := $\varnothing$	*rseq* := []

The abstract state is a set of resources of a given maximum size. The concrete state is a sequence, without repetitions, of resources, and the abstract set is just the range of the concrete sequence. Figure 7.1 shows how a set of three resources can be represented by any one of six different concrete states, each being a sequence of three resources. In this design the retrieve relation (concrete to abstract) is many – one.

The abstract initialization sets *rfree* empty. The concrete initialization sets *rseq* to the empty sequence. The proof obligation for correctness of the initialization is as follows:

$$[rseq := []]$$
$$\neg [rfree := \varnothing]$$
$$\neg (rseq \in \text{i}\,\text{seq}\,(RESOURCE) \land rfree = \text{ran}\,(rseq))$$

Making the second substitution and using the law of double negation gives the following:

$$[rseq := []]\,(rseq \in \text{i}\,\text{seq}\,(RESOURCE) \land \varnothing = \text{ran}\,(rseq))$$

Making the remaining substitution gives the following:

$$[] \in \text{i}\,\text{seq}\,(RESOURCE) \land \varnothing = \text{ran}\,([])$$

This is a theorem of set theory.

7.2.2 Data design and correctness of operation

The two data designs discussed in the previous section will now be used to investigate correctness of operation. We consider first operations that have no outputs.

Suppose that the machine whose abstract state consists of xx in the range 1 .. 100 has an operation to increase xx by 1.

	Abstract	**Concrete**
VARIABLES	xx	yy
INVARIANT	$xx \in 0 .. 100$	$yy \in 0 .. 100 \land$ $xx = yy$
up	PRE $\quad xx < 100$ THEN $\quad xx := xx + 1$ END	$yy := yy + 1$

The abstract operation has a precondition that xx is less than 100. The concrete operation does not need a precondition, because the concrete variable yy always has the same value as xx, and the responsibility for making sure that the precondition is true lies with the user of the abstract operation. The correctness condition for an operation without outputs can be stated as follows. Suppose that P_A is the abstract invariant, P_C is the concrete invariant, Q_A is the precondition of the abstract operation, H_A is the substitution that is the then-part of the abstract operation, and H_C is the substitution that is the concrete operation. The proof obligation for correctness of the operation is as follows:

$$P_A \land P_C \land Q_A \Rightarrow [H_C]\,\neg[H_A]\,\neg P_C$$

The condition may be paraphrased as follows: if the concrete and abstract invariants are true, and the precondition of the abstract operation is true, then the concrete operation makes it impossible for the then-part of the abstract operation to fail to establish the concrete invariant. Again the two negations are necessary to cope with the situation where the abstract operation is non-deterministic. (We shall have an example in a moment.)

First we apply this to the operation *up*. In this case the proof obligation is as follows:

$$xx \in 0 .. 100 \wedge yy \in 0 .. 100 \wedge yy = xx \wedge xx < 100 \Rightarrow$$
$$[yy := yy + 1] \neg [xx := xx + 1] \neg (yy \in 0 .. 100 \wedge yy = xx)$$

Making the second substitution and using the law of double negation gives the following:

$$xx \in 0 .. 100 \wedge yy \in 0 .. 100 \wedge yy = xx \wedge xx < 100 \Rightarrow$$
$$[yy := yy + 1] (yy \in 0 .. 100 \wedge yy = xx + 1)$$

Making the remaining substitution gives the following:

$$xx \in 0 .. 100 \wedge yy \in 0 .. 100 \wedge yy = xx \wedge xx < 100 \Rightarrow$$
$$yy + 1 \in 0 .. 100 \wedge yy + 1 = xx + 1$$

This result is a simple theorem of set theory and arithmetic.

Now for a non-deterministic example. Suppose that we have an operation *bigger* as follows:

	Abstract	Concrete

bigger	PRE
	  $xx < 100$
	THEN
	  ANY
	  zz
	  WHERE
	    $zz \in 1 .. 100 \wedge$
	    $zz > xx$
	  THEN
	    $xx := zz$
	  END
	END
		$yy := yy + 1$

The abstract operation has a precondition that xx is less than 100, and it increases xx to any value not exceeding 100. The concrete operation increases yy by 1. The following proof obligation is the result of this design:

$xx \in 0 .. 100 \wedge yy \in 0 .. 100 \wedge yy = xx \wedge xx < 100 \Rightarrow$
$[yy := yy + 1]$
$\neg[\text{ANY } zz \text{ WHERE } zz \in 0 .. 100 \wedge zz > xx \text{ THEN } xx := zz \text{ END}]$
$\neg(yy \in 0 .. 100 \wedge yy = xx)$

For the moment we ignore the antecedent, and concentrate on simplifying the consequent. First we use the ANY-WHERE-THEN-END rule:

$[yy := yy + 1]$
$\neg\forall zz \bullet (zz \in 0 .. 100 \wedge zz > xx \Rightarrow$
$[xx := zz]$
$\neg(yy \in 0 .. 100 \wedge yy = xx))$

Next we make the second substitution:

$[yy := yy + 1]$
$\neg\forall zz \bullet (zz \in 0 .. 100 \wedge zz > xx \Rightarrow$
$\neg(yy \in 0 .. 100 \wedge yy = zz))$

Next we make the remaining substitution:

$\neg\forall zz \bullet (zz \in 0 .. 100 \wedge zz > xx \Rightarrow$
$\neg(yy + 1 \in 0 .. 100 \wedge yy + 1 = zz))$

Next we use the rule for the negation of a universal quantification and the rule for negating an implication:

$\exists zz \bullet$
$(zz \in 0 .. 100 \wedge zz > xx \wedge yy + 1 \in 0 .. 100 \wedge yy + 1 = zz)$

Next we use the one-point rule, replacing zz by $yy + 1$:

$yy + 1 \in 0 .. 100 \wedge yy + 1 > xx \wedge yy + 1 \in 0 .. 100$

This result follows from the antecedent by the laws of set theory and arithmetic.

For our last example we consider the following design of the operation *rec_free* from the machine *RRMan* discussed in Chapter 5.

	Abstract	**Concrete**
VARI-ABLES	*rfree*	*rseq*
INVAR-IANT	*rfree* $\subseteq$ *RESOURCE* $\wedge$ card (*rfree*) $\leq$ *max_res*	*rseq* $\in$ iseq (*RESOURCE*) $\wedge$ *rfree* = ran (*rseq*)

	Abstract	**Concrete**
rec_free	PRE $rr \in RESOURCE - rfree \wedge$ card $(rfree) < max\_res$ THEN $rfree := rfree \cup \{rr\}$ END	$rseq := rseq \,\widehat{}\, [rr]$

Here we propose to represent the adding of a resource to *rfree* by adding the resource to the end of the sequence. The proof obligation for the correctness of this operation is as follows:

$rfree \subseteq RESOURCE \wedge$
card $(rfree) \leq max\_res \wedge$
$rseq \in \mathsf{i\,seq}\,(RESOURCE) \wedge$
$rfree = \mathsf{ran}\,(rseq) \wedge$
$rr \in RESOURCE - rfree \wedge$
card $(rfree) < max\_res$
$\Rightarrow$
$[rseq := rseq \,\widehat{}\, [rr]]$
$\neg [rfree := rfree \cup \{rr\}]$
$\neg (rseq \in \mathsf{i\,seq}\,(RESOURCE) \wedge rfree = \mathsf{ran}\,(rseq))$

For the moment we ignore the antecedent, and concentrate on simplifying the consequent. Making the second substitution and using the law of double negation gives the following:

$[rseq := rseq \,\widehat{}\, [rr]]$
$(rseq \in \mathsf{i\,seq}\,(RESOURCE) \wedge rfree \cup \{rr\} = \mathsf{ran}\,(rseq))$

Making the remaining substitution gives the following:

$rseq \,\widehat{}\, [rr] \in \mathsf{i\,seq}\,(RESOURCE) \wedge$
$rfree \cup \{rr\} = \mathsf{ran}\,(rseq \,\widehat{}\, [rr])$

This can be derived from the antecedent by the laws of set theory.

7.2.3 Correctness of operations with outputs

All the operations so far studied have had no outputs. If an abstract operation has an output, we should expect the concrete operation to have an output as well, and we should expect that the output of the concrete operation would be one allowed by the abstract operation. (We do not say 'the one specified by the abstract operation' because the abstract operation might be non-deterministic about its outputs.) We modify the correctness rule given earlier to allow for the presence of outputs as follows. Suppose that $\mathbf{P}_A$ is the abstract invariant, $\mathbf{P}_C$ is the concrete invariant, Q_A is the precondition of the abstract operation, H_A is the substitution that is the then-part of the abstract operation, H_C is the substitution that is the concrete operation, and y is the output of the operation. The proof obligation for correctness of the operation is as follows:

$$P_A \wedge P_C \wedge Q_A \Rightarrow [H_C] \neg [H'_A] \neg (P_C \wedge y' = y)$$

where H'_A is the same as H_A but with the output renamed y'.

The condition may be paraphrased as follows: if the concrete and abstract invariants are true, and the precondition of the abstract operation is true, then the concrete operation makes it impossible for the then-part of the abstract operation to fail to establish the concrete invariant and equality of outputs. Again the two negations are necessary to cope with the situation where the abstract operation is non-deterministic.

First we look at a deterministic example.

	Abstract	**Concrete**
VARIABLES	xx	yy
INVARIANT	$xx \in 0 .. 100$	$yy \in 0 .. 100 \wedge$ $xx = yy$
$op \longleftarrow tell$	$op := xx$	$op := yy$

The proof obligation is as follows:

$$xx \in 0 .. 100 \wedge yy \in 0 .. 100 \wedge yy = xx \wedge xx > 0 \Rightarrow$$
$$[op' := yy]$$
$$\neg [op := xx]$$
$$\neg (yy \in 0 .. 100 \wedge yy = xx \wedge op' = op)$$

For the moment we ignore the antecedent, and concentrate on simplifying the consequent. Making the second substitution and using the law of double negation gives the following:

$$[op' := yy]$$
$$(yy \in 0 .. 100 \wedge yy = xx \wedge op' = xx)$$

Finally we make the remaining substitution:

$$yy \in 0 .. 100 \wedge yy = xx \wedge yy = xx$$

All these conjuncts are in the antecedent.

For a non-deterministic example, consider the following.

	Abstract	**Concrete**
VARIABLES	xx	yy
INVARIANT	$xx \in 0 .. 100$	$yy \in 0 .. 100 \wedge$ $xx = yy$
$op \longleftarrow anyless$	PRE $\quad xx > 0$ THEN $\quad$ ANY $\quad\quad zz$ $\quad$ WHERE $\quad\quad zz \in \mathbb{N} \wedge$ $\quad\quad zz < xx$ $\quad$ THEN $\quad\quad op := zz$ $\quad$ END END	$op := 0$

The abstract operation *anyless* has a precondition that xx is greater than zero. Its output is some natural number less than xx. The concrete operation always outputs zero.

The proof obligation is as follows:

$xx \in 0 .. 100 \wedge yy \in 0 .. 100 \wedge yy = xx \wedge xx > 0 \Rightarrow$
$[op' := 0]$
$\neg [$ANY zz WHERE $zz \in \mathbb{N} \wedge zz < xx$ THEN $op := zz$ END$]$
$\neg (yy \in 0 .. 100 \wedge yy = xx \wedge op' = op)$

For the moment we ignore the antecedent, and concentrate on simplifying the consequent. Making the second substitution gives the following:

$[op' := 0]$
$\neg \forall zz \bullet (zz \in \mathbb{N} \wedge zz < xx \Rightarrow$
$[op := zz] \neg (yy \in 0 .. 100 \wedge yy = xx \wedge op' = op))$

Now we make the inner substitution:

$[op' := 0]$
$\neg \forall zz \bullet (zz \in \mathbb{N} \wedge zz < xx \Rightarrow$
$\neg (yy \in 0 .. 100 \wedge yy = xx \wedge op' = zz))$

Next we use the rule for negating a universal quantifier and the rule for negating an implication:

$[op' := 0]$
$\exists zz \bullet (zz \in \mathbb{N} \wedge zz < xx \wedge yy \in 0 \mathinner{..} 100 \wedge yy = xx \wedge op' = zz)$

Next we apply the one-point rule, using op' for zz:

$[op' := 0]$
$(op' \in \mathbb{N} \wedge op' < xx \wedge yy \in 0 \mathinner{..} 100 \wedge yy = xx)$

Finally we make the remaining substitution:

$0 \in \mathbb{N} \wedge 0 < xx \wedge yy \in 0 \mathinner{..} 100 \wedge yy = xx$

All these conjuncts are in the antecedent, or are theorems of arithmetic.

7.3 Algorithm design: sequences

In a machine, the operations are expressed in an abstract way by the substitutions described earlier in this book. In an algorithm design we choose to ban certain substitutions that have unprogramlike qualities, and to introduce three others without which programming would be impossible: the sequence, local variables, and the loop.

7.3.1 Sequences

A **sequence** in algorithm design is a substitution built from two others. The intention is that the changes of state represented by the two substitutions should take place one after the other. If **G** and **H** are substitutions, the sequence of **G** followed by **H** is represented by the following notation:

G ; H

The semicolon is the sequence sign for substitutions.

Figure 7.2 on page 107 illustrates the sequence substitution with a flow chart.

Whenever we have introduced a new substitution, it has always been accompanied by a rule that explains what it means for the substitution to establish a predicate. Here is the **sequence rule**:

[G ; H] P ⇔ [G] [H] P

The rule can be paraphrased as follows: a sequence of two substitutions establishes a predicate if and only if the first substitution establishes that the second substitution establishes the predicate.

A left association rule is used to interpret an extended sequence, so

G$_1$; G$_2$; G$_3$; G$_4$

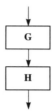

Figure 7.2 Sequence substitution illustrated.

means

$$((G_1 \; ; \; G_2) \; ; \; G_3) \; ; \; G_4$$

We now look at a few examples of how the sequence substitution can be used in simple algorithm designs.

7.3.2 Abstract state with a single variable

For our first example we consider an abstract state consisting of a single numeric variable. The abstract operation increases the value by 2. We are designing for an environment in which increasing a number variable by 1 is easy, but increasing it by a larger amount requires repeated applications of increase by 1, so we use a sequence.

	Abstract	**Concrete**
VARIABLES	xx	yy
INVARIANT	$xx \in \mathbb{N}$	$yy \in \mathbb{N} \wedge yy = xx$
$up2$	$xx := xx + 2$	$yy := yy + 1 \; ;$ $yy := yy + 1$

The correctness condition for this design is as follows:

$$xx \in \mathbb{N} \wedge yy \in \mathbb{N} \wedge yy = xx \Rightarrow$$
$$[yy := yy + 1 \; ; yy := yy + 1]$$
$$\neg [xx := xx + 2]$$
$$\neg (yy \in \mathbb{N} \wedge yy = xx)$$

For the moment we ignore the antecedent, and concentrate on simplifying the consequent. Making the second substitution and using the law of double negation gives the following:

$$[yy := yy + 1 \; ; yy := yy + 1]$$
$$(yy \in \mathbb{N} \wedge yy = xx + 2)$$

Now we apply the sequence rule:

$$[yy := yy + 1]$$
$$[yy := yy + 1]$$
$$(yy \in \mathbb{N} \wedge yy = xx + 2)$$

Making the second substitution gives the following:

$$[yy := yy + 1]$$
$$(yy + 1 \in \mathbb{N} \wedge yy + 1 = xx + 2)$$

Making the remaining substitution gives the following:

$$yy + 1 + 1 \in \mathbb{N} \wedge yy + 1 + 1 = xx + 2$$

This follows from the antecedent by the laws of arithmetic.

7.3.3 Abstract state with two variables

In our second example, the state has two variables that have to be changed independently.

	Abstract	Concrete
VARIABLES	xx, yy	vv, ww
INVARIANT	$xx \in \mathbb{N} \wedge yy \in \mathbb{N}$	$vv \in \mathbb{N} \wedge ww \in \mathbb{N} \wedge$ $vv = xx \wedge ww = yy$
up_both	$xx, yy := xx + 1,$ $yy + 1$	$vv := vv + 1 ;$ $ww := ww + 1$

The correctness condition for this design is as follows:

$$xx \in \mathbb{N} \wedge yy \in \mathbb{N} \wedge vv \in \mathbb{N} \wedge ww \in \mathbb{N} \wedge vv = xx \wedge ww = yy \Rightarrow$$
$$[vv := vv + 1 ; ww := ww + 1]$$
$$\neg [xx, yy := xx + 1, yy := yy + 1]$$
$$\neg (vv \in \mathbb{N} \wedge ww \in \mathbb{N} \wedge vv = xx \wedge ww = yy)$$

For the moment we ignore the antecedent, and concentrate on simplifying the consequent. Making the second substitution and using the law of double negation gives the following:

$$[vv := vv + 1 ; ww := ww + 1]$$
$$(vv \in \mathbb{N} \wedge ww \in \mathbb{N} \wedge vv = xx + 1 \wedge ww = yy + 1)$$

Now we apply the sequence rule:

$$[vv := vv + 1]$$
$$[ww := ww + 1]$$
$$(vv \in \mathbb{N} \wedge ww \in \mathbb{N} \wedge vv = xx + 1 \wedge ww = yy + 1)$$

Making the second substitution gives the following:

$$[vv := vv + 1]$$
$$(vv \in \mathbb{N} \land ww + 1 \in \mathbb{N} \land vv = xx + 1 \land ww + 1 = yy + 1)$$

Making the remaining substitution gives the following:

$$vv + 1 \in \mathbb{N} \land ww + 1 \in \mathbb{N} \land$$
$$vv + 1 = xx + 1 \land ww + 1 = yy + 1$$

This follows from the antecedent by the laws of arithmetic.

7.3.4 Representing a set by an array and a counter

For our third example we use an array and a counter as concrete variables to represent an abstract set.

	Abstract	**Concrete**
VARI-ABLES	*nset*	*narr, ctr*
INVAR-IANT	$nset \subseteq 0 .. 100 \land$ card $(nset) \leq mm$	$ctr \in 0 .. 100 \land$ $narr \in 1 .. mm \twoheadrightarrow 0 .. 100 \land$ $1 .. ctr \lhd narr \in$ $1 .. ctr \rightarrowtail 0 .. 100 \land$ $nset = \text{ran} \, (1 .. ctr \lhd narr)$
INITIAL-ISATION	$nset = \emptyset$	$ctr := 0 \, ; \, narr := \emptyset$ ／

enter (num)	PRE
	  $num \in 0 .. 100 \land$
	  card $(nset) < mm \land$
	  $num \notin nset$
	THEN
	  $nset := nset \cup \{num\}$
	END
		$ctr := ctr + 1 \, ;$
		$narr := narr \cup \{ctr \mapsto num\}$

Figure 7.3 illustrates the concrete invariant.

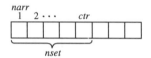

Figure 7.3 Representing a set by an array and a counter.

The correctness condition for the initialization is as follows:

$[ctr := 0 \; ; narr := \varnothing]$
$\neg [nset := \varnothing]$
$\neg (ctr \in 0 .. 100 \wedge narr \in 1 .. mm \twoheadrightarrow 1 .. 100 \wedge$
$1 .. ctr \vartriangleleft narr \in 1 .. ctr \rightarrowtail 1 .. 100 \wedge nset = \mathrm{ran}\,(1 .. ctr \vartriangleleft narr))$

Making the second substitution and using the law of double negation gives the following:

$[ctr := 0 \; ; narr := \varnothing]$
$(ctr \in 0 .. 100 \wedge narr \in 1 .. mm \twoheadrightarrow 1 .. 100 \wedge$
$1 .. ctr \vartriangleleft narr \in 1 .. ctr \rightarrowtail 1 .. 100 \wedge \varnothing = \mathrm{ran}\,(1 .. ctr \vartriangleleft narr))$

Using the sequence rule and making the remaining substitutions gives the following:

$0 \in 0 .. 100 \wedge \varnothing \in 1 .. mm \twoheadrightarrow 1 .. 100 \wedge$
$1 .. 0 \vartriangleleft \varnothing \in 1 .. 0 \rightarrowtail 1 .. 100 \wedge \varnothing = \mathrm{ran}\,(1 .. 0 \vartriangleleft \varnothing)$

The conjuncts are theorems of arithmetic and set theory.

The correctness condition for the operation *enter* (*num*) is as follows:

$nset \subseteq 0 .. 100 \wedge$
$\mathrm{card}\,(nset) \leq mm \wedge$
$ctr \in 0 .. 100 \wedge$
$narr \in 1 .. mm \twoheadrightarrow 1 .. 100 \wedge$
$1 .. ctr \vartriangleleft narr \in 1..ctr \rightarrowtail 1 .. 100 \wedge$
$nset = \mathrm{ran}\,(1 .. ctr \vartriangleleft narr) \wedge$
$num \in 1 .. 100 \wedge$
$\mathrm{card}\,(nset) < mm \wedge$
$num \notin nset$
$\Rightarrow$
$[ctr := ctr + 1 \; ; narr := narr \cup \{ctr \mapsto num\}]$
$\neg [nset := nset \cup \{num\}]$
$\neg (ctr \in 0 .. 100 \wedge$
$narr \in 1 .. mm \twoheadrightarrow 1 .. 100 \wedge$
$1 .. ctr \vartriangleleft narr \in 1 .. ctr \rightarrowtail 1 .. 100 \wedge$
$nset = \mathrm{ran}\,(1 .. ctr \vartriangleleft narr))$

For the moment we ignore the antecedent, and concentrate on simplifying the consequent. Making the second substitution and using the law of double negation gives the following:

$[ctr := ctr + 1 \; ; narr := narr \cup \{ctr \mapsto num\}]$
$(ctr \in 0 .. 100 \wedge$
$narr \in 1 .. mm \twoheadrightarrow 1 .. 100 \wedge$

$1 \mathbin{..} ctr \lhd narr \in 1 \mathbin{..} ctr \rightarrowtail 1 \mathbin{..} 100 \wedge$
$nset \cup \{num\} = \operatorname{ran}(1 \mathbin{..} ctr \lhd narr))$

Using the sequence rule and making the remaining substitutions gives the following:

$ctr + 1 \in 0 \mathbin{..} 100 \wedge$
$narr \cup \{ctr \mapsto num\} \in 1 \mathbin{..} mm \nrightarrow 1 \mathbin{..} 100 \wedge$
$1 \mathbin{..} (ctr + 1) \lhd narr \cup \{ctr \mapsto num\} \in 1 \mathbin{..} (ctr + 1) \rightarrowtail 1 \mathbin{..} 100 \wedge$
$nset \cup \{num\} = \operatorname{ran}(1 \mathbin{..} (ctr + 1) \lhd narr \cup \{ctr \mapsto num\})$

The derivation of the conjuncts of the consequent from the antecedent is long, but straightforward.

7.4 Algorithm design: local variables

It is often convenient to introduce local variables into a program to hold the results of calculations. The following example illustrates the technique, and how the proof obligations cope with local variables.

	Abstract	**Concrete**
VARIABLES	xx, yy	vv, ww
INVARIANT	$xx \in \mathbb{N} \wedge yy \in \mathbb{N}$	$vv \in \mathbb{N} \wedge ww \in \mathbb{N} \wedge$ $vv = xx \wedge ww = yy$
swap	$xx, yy := yy, xx$	$tt := vv \,;$ $vv := ww \,;$ $ww := tt$

Here tt is used as a local variable to hold the value of vv for later assignment to ww.

The correctness condition for this refinement is as follows:

$xx \in \mathbb{N} \wedge yy \in \mathbb{N} \wedge vv \in \mathbb{N} \wedge ww \in \mathbb{N} \wedge vv = xx \wedge ww = yy \Rightarrow$
$[tt := vv \,; vv := ww \,; ww := tt]$
$\neg [xx, yy := yy, xx]$
$\neg (vv \in \mathbb{N} \wedge ww \in \mathbb{N} \wedge vv = xx \wedge ww = yy)$

For the moment we ignore the antecedent, and concentrate on simplifying the consequent. Making the second substitution and using the law of double negation gives the following:

$[tt := vv \,; vv := ww \,; ww := tt]$
$(vv \in \mathbb{N} \wedge ww \in \mathbb{N} \wedge vv = yy \wedge ww = xx)$

Now we apply the sequence rule:

$$[tt := vv] \; [vv := ww \;] \; [ww := tt]$$
$$(vv \in \mathbb{N} \wedge ww \in \mathbb{N} \wedge vv = yy \wedge ww = xx)$$

Making the third substitution gives the following:

$$[tt := vv] \; [vv := ww \;]$$
$$(vv \in \mathbb{N} \wedge tt \in \mathbb{N} \wedge vv = yy \wedge tt = xx)$$

Making the second substitution gives the following:

$$[tt := vv]$$
$$(ww \in \mathbb{N} \wedge tt \in \mathbb{N} \wedge ww = yy \wedge tt = xx)$$

Making the remaining substitution gives the following:

$$ww \in \mathbb{N} \wedge vv \in \mathbb{N} \wedge ww = yy \wedge vv = xx$$

The conjuncts in this predicate are all in the antecedent.

7.5 Algorithm design: loops

7.5.1 The loop as a programming construct

The **loop** is a means in programming of executing a sequence of instructions (the **loop body**) several times. Most programming languages have various different styles of loop, but in this book we are concerned only with what is usually called a while-loop. The operation of the loop is controlled by a predicate (the **while-test**). The body of the loop is executed repeatedly as long as the predicate is true. As soon as the predicate becomes false, the loop terminates. A loop is usually preceded by a sequence of instructions (the **loop initialization**) that prepares the values in variables that will be used in the loop. Figure 7.4 on page 113 illustrates some of the parts of a loop and their intended significance as a program structure.

In ordinary programs the loop is a powerful but dangerous tool. Even experienced programmers find that their loops sometimes do not do what they want. Either they end too soon, and fail to process something that should have been processed, or they go on too long, and attempt to process something that is not there, often with unfortunate results. Occasionally they fail to end at all, and go on for ever processing the same thing over and over again. As conscientious software engineers, we seek an approach to the design of loops that guarantees that they do exactly what we want, and stop at exactly the right time.

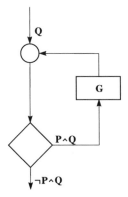

Figure 7.4 Elements of a loop.

7.5.2 Format of the loop substitution

The format that we shall use for recording loops is as follows:

WHILE **P** DO **G** VARIANT **E** INVARIANT **Q** END

This is the **loop substitution.** The parts of the substitution are those used in the flow chart, but there are a couple of extra things that could not be shown in the flow chart.

- The **loop variant** is an expression that denotes a natural number. Informally it is the maximum number of iterations of the loop body that are required to get the while-test to become false. It is the key to making sure that the loop terminates.

- The **loop invariant** is a predicate that makes a statement about the values of the variables in the loop body. The invariant must be true each time the while-test is made. It is the key to making sure that when the loop terminates, it produces the desired result.

7.5.3 Rules for the correctness of a loop

Instead of a single proof obligation for the loop substitution, it is convenient to consider five separate proof rules. Each rule establishes a different aspect of the correctness of the assertion that the loop establishes a predicate.

Suppose we want to be sure that a loop establishes a predicate **R** as follows:

[WHILE **P** DO **G** VARIANT **E** INVARIANT **Q** END] **R**

The first rule says that the loop invariant must be true before the while-test is made for the first time.

Q

We call this the **I-rule**.

The loop is usually used as part of a sequence, and is preceded by substitutions that serve to establish the invariant. If the loop is part of a sequence like this:

[H ; WHILE P DO G VARIANT E INVARIANT Q END] R

then the I-rule is

[H] **Q**

The second rule says that when the loop ends, the predicate **R** is true. When the loop ends we know that

- the invariant is true (because the invariant is true every time the while-test is made);
- the while-test is false (because if it were true we should go through the body once more).

The rule is therefore as follows:

$\neg P \wedge Q \Rightarrow R$

We call this the **F-rule**. This is the only rule that says anything about the predicate that the loop is supposed to establish.

The third and fourth rules go together: they are both concerned with termination. The third says that if the invariant is true, the variant expression denotes a natural number.

$Q \Rightarrow E \in \mathbb{N}$

We call this the **T1-rule**.

The fourth says that the body of the loop decreases the variant.

$P \wedge Q \Rightarrow [y := E] [G] E < y$

We call this the **T2-rule**.

The form of this rule is unusual because it introduces a new variable, **y**, which should not be one of the variables being used in the loop. The rule says that if you store the variant in **y**, then run the loop body, the new value of the variant will be less than the stored value.

These two rules together guarantee that the loop will terminate.

The last rule limits the action of the body. It says that if the while-test is true, the body must preserve the invariant.

$$\mathbf{P} \wedge \mathbf{Q} \Rightarrow [\mathbf{G}] \, \mathbf{Q}$$

We call this the **P-rule**.

7.5.4 Example of a simple loop

The five rules will now be illustrated by applying them to a simple loop.

The loop in the following example is supposed to increase xx by 5. We save the original value of xx in yy. We write a predicate that says that the initialized loop establishes $xx = yy + 5$, and then check the rules for the loop.

```
[yy := xx ; ctr := 1 ;
WHILE
  ctr ≤ 5
DO
  xx := xx + 1 ;
  ctr := ctr + 1
VARIANT
  6 − ctr
INVARIANT
  ctr ∈ 1 .. 6 ∧ xx = yy + ctr − 1
END] xx = yy + 5
```

First we check the I-rule – the initialization establishes the invariant:

$$[yy := xx \; ; \; ctr := 1] \, (ctr \in 1 \, .. \, 6 \wedge xx = yy + ctr - 1)$$

Applying the sequence rule and making the substitutions gives the following:

$$1 \in 1 \, .. \, 6 \wedge xx = xx + 1 - 1$$

The conjuncts are theorems of arithmetic.

Next we check the F-rule – the invariant and the negation of the while-test establish the predicate to be established:

$$ctr \in 1 \, .. \, 6 \wedge xx = yy + ctr - 1 \wedge ctr > 5 \Rightarrow xx = yy + 5$$

The conjuncts $ctr \in 1 \, .. \, 6$ and $ctr > 5$ imply that ctr must be 6, so the second conjunct of the antecedent is the same as the consequent.

Next we check the T1-rule – the invariant implies that the variant is a natural number:

$$ctr \in 1 \mathinner{.\,.} 6 \wedge xx = yy + ctr - 1 \Rightarrow 6 - ctr \in \mathbb{N}$$

This is a theorem of arithmetic.

Next we check the T2-rule – the body of the loop decreases the variant.

$$ctr \in 1 \mathinner{.\,.} 6 \wedge xx = yy + ctr - 1 \wedge ctr \leq 5 \Rightarrow$$
$$[ww := 6 - ctr]$$
$$[xx := xx + 1 \; ; ctr := ctr + 1]$$
$$6 - ctr < ww$$

For the moment we ignore the antecedent, and concentrate on simplifying the consequent. Applying the substitution rule gives the following:

$$[ww := 6 - ctr]$$
$$[xx := xx + 1] [ctr := ctr + 1]$$
$$6 - ctr < ww$$

Making the third substitution gives the following:

$$[ww := 6 - ctr]$$
$$[xx := xx + 1]$$
$$6 - (ctr + 1) < ww$$

Making the second substitution gives the following:

$$[ww := 6 - ctr]$$
$$6 - (ctr + 1) < ww$$

Making the remaining substitution gives the following:

$$6 - (ctr + 1) < 6 - ctr$$

This result can be deduced from the antecedent by the laws of arithmetic.

Lastly we check the P-rule – the body preserves the invariant.

$$ctr \in 1 \mathinner{.\,.} 6 \wedge xx = yy + ctr - 1 \wedge ctr \leq 5 \Rightarrow$$
$$[xx := xx + 1 \; ; ctr := ctr + 1]$$
$$ctr \in 1 \mathinner{.\,.} 6 \wedge xx = yy + ctr - 1$$

For the moment we ignore the antecedent, and concentrate on simplifying the consequent. Applying the sequence rule and making the substitutions gives the following:

$$ctr + 1 \in 1 \mathinner{.\,.} 6 \wedge xx + 1 = yy + ctr + 1 - 1$$

This follows from the antecedent.

7.5.5 Principles of loop construction

The rules described above give us a method of loop construction that will guarantee that the loop is correct. The hardest part of loop construction is choosing the loop invariant. The invariant is based on our informal intentions about how the loop is to achieve the desired result. It records the types of the variables in the loop, and expresses essential relationships between their values. The invariant must be a predicate that is true each time the while-test is made, but it need not be true during the execution of the loop body. Once the invariant has been recorded, loop construction proceeds as follows:

(1) Choose the initialization to satisfy the I-rule. The initialization is something that is easy to program that establishes the invariant.

(2) Choose the while-test to satisfy the F-rule. The while-test must be a predicate that is easily evaluated in the programming language for which the loop is written.

(3) Choose a variant expression to satisfy the T1-rule. The variant expression must be an upper limit for the number of iterations through the body still to do.

(4) To satisfy the T2-rule, put something in the body to decrease the variant.

(5) To satisfy the P-rule, put something in the loop body to preserve the invariant.

7.5.6 Application of the principles

We apply these principles to the loop just described. For the invariant, the informal intention is to use a counter to track the number of times we have been round the loop, and to add 1 to yy each time. Our invariant is therefore as follows:

$$ctr \in 1 \mathinner{\ldotp\ldotp} 6 \wedge xx = yy + ctr - 1$$

To satisfy the I-rule, we choose to set yy to xx, and so we must set ctr to 0.

Now we deal with the while test. We are trying to find a value of **P** to satisfy the F-rule:

$$ctr \in 1 \mathinner{\ldotp\ldotp} 6 \wedge xx = yy + ctr - 1 \wedge \neg \mathbf{P} \Rightarrow xx = yy + 5$$

There are many predicates that will do for **P**, but we choose a simple one that involves the loop counter:

$$ctr \leq 5$$

Since, according to the invariant, the counter ranges from 0 to 6, an appropriate expression for the variant must be $6 - ctr$.

To satisfy the T2-rule, we choose the following substitution:

$ctr := ctr - 1$

The invariant was true at the start of the body, but decreasing ctr by 1 upsets the invariant. To redress the balance, and satisfy the P-rule, we must increase yy by the same amount.

$yy := yy + 1$

7.5.7 Using a loop in algorithm design

Now we must study the loop in the context of an algorithm design. Consider the following algorithm design of an operation without outputs:

	Abstract	**Concrete**
INVARIANT	P_A	P_C
op	PRE	H ;
	Q_A	WHILE
	THEN	P
	H_A	DO
	END	G
		VARIANT
		E
		INVARIANT
		Q
		END

Here the concrete operation consists of some substitutions denoted by **H** followed by a loop. The proof obligation for correctness of this design is as follows:

$P_A \wedge P_C \wedge Q_A \Rightarrow$
[H ; WHILE P DO G VARIANT E INVARIANT Q END]
$\neg [H_A] \neg P_C$

If we use **R** as a name for the predicate $\neg [H_A] \neg P_C$, this becomes

$P_A \wedge P_C \wedge Q_A \Rightarrow$
[H ; WHILE P DO G VARIANT E INVARIANT Q END] **R**

We can apply the sequence rule to give the following:

$$\mathbf{P_A} \wedge \mathbf{P_C} \wedge \mathbf{Q_A} \Rightarrow$$
$$[\mathbf{H}]\ [\text{WHILE } \mathbf{P} \text{ DO } \mathbf{G} \text{ VARIANT } \mathbf{E} \text{ INVARIANT } \mathbf{Q} \text{ END}]\ \mathbf{R}$$

Now the I-rule for the loop can be written as

$$\mathbf{P_A} \wedge \mathbf{P_C} \wedge \mathbf{Q_A} \Rightarrow [\mathbf{H}]\ \mathbf{Q}$$

and the rest of the rules are the same as before.
The F-rule:

$$\mathbf{Q} \wedge \neg \mathbf{P} \Rightarrow \mathbf{R}$$

Since **R** includes all the type information from the concrete invariant, the type information must also be part of the loop invariant.
The T1-rule:

$$\mathbf{Q} \Rightarrow \mathbf{E} \in \mathbb{N}$$

The T2-rule:

$$\mathbf{Q} \wedge \mathbf{P} \Rightarrow [\mathbf{y} := \mathbf{E}]\ [\mathbf{G}]\ \mathbf{E} < \mathbf{y}$$

The P-rule:

$$\mathbf{Q} \wedge \mathbf{P} \Rightarrow [\mathbf{G}]\ \mathbf{Q}$$

Figure 7.5 shows the loop with its initialization in the context of an algorithm design. The diagram is annotated with the predicates that are true at each stage in the execution of the loop.

7.5.8 Example of a loop in algorithm design

We now apply the rules to a simple example of the use of a loop in algorithm design. The abstract operation is to find the product of two natural number variables, one of which is greater than zero. We suppose that the programming language for the design allows addition, but not multiplication. The details of the loop are not yet filled in.

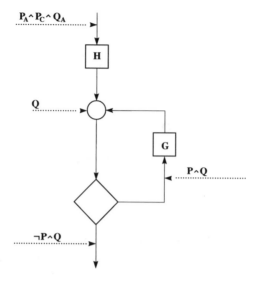

Figure 7.5 The initialized loop in algorithm design.

	Abstract	**Concrete**
VARIABLES	xx, yy	vv, ww
INVARIANT	$xx \in \mathbb{N} \wedge$ $yy \in \mathbb{N} \wedge$ $yy > 0$	$vv \in \mathbb{N} \wedge ww \in \mathbb{N} \wedge$ $vv = xx \wedge ww = yy \wedge$ $ww > 0$
mult	$xx := xx \times yy$	**H** ; WHILE **P** DO **G** VARIANT **E** INVARIANT **Q** END

The predicate to be established by the loop is

$\neg [xx := xx \times yy]$
$\neg (vv \in \mathbb{N} \wedge ww \in \mathbb{N} \wedge ww > 0 \wedge vv = xx \wedge ww = yy)$

By making the substitution and using the law of double negation we get the following:

$$vv \in \mathbb{N} \wedge ww \in \mathbb{N} \wedge ww > 0 \wedge vv = xx \times yy \wedge ww = yy$$

The informal intention is to save the value of vv in a local variable (tt), and then accumulate the product in vv by repeated addition of the saved value, using another local variable (zz) as a counter. At each stage the value in vv is $zz \times tt$, so the invariant must be the following:

$$tt = xx \wedge vv = zz \times tt \wedge$$
$$zz \in 1 .. ww \wedge vv \in \mathbb{N} \wedge$$
$$ww \in \mathbb{N} \wedge ww > 0 \wedge ww = yy$$

We can analyse the invariant as follows, conjunct by conjunct:

(1) $tt = xx$ — confirms our intention to save the initial value of vv. It is essential to refer to the abstract value xx here, since vv will change in the course of the loop.

(2) $vv = zz \times tt$ — confirms our intention of using zz to count how many tts we have accumulated in vv.

(3) $zz \in 1 .. ww$ — constrains zz tightly enough to make sure that we do not get too many tts into vv.

(4) $vv \in \mathbb{N}$ — type information in the concrete invariant that the operation of the loop must maintain.

(5) $ww \in \mathbb{N}$ — type information in the concrete invariant that the operation of the loop must maintain.

(6) $ww > 0$ — part of the concrete invariant that the operation of the loop must maintain.

(7) $ww = yy$ — more of the concrete invariant that the operation of the loop must maintain.

In practice, constructing the invariant might be a more tentative process than what has been illustrated here. Usually we get the part that concerns the rôles of the local variables, but forget parts of the concrete invariant. It is only when we begin the proofs that we discover what is missing.

For the initialization, we can establish the first conjunct in the invariant by assigning vv to tt. The second conjunct can then be satisfied by assigning 1 to zz, and this satisfies the third conjunct also, since $1 .. ww$ is not empty. The full form of the I-rule is an implication whose antecedent is the concrete invariant, the abstract invariant, and the abstract precondition:

$$xx \in \mathbb{N} \wedge yy \in \mathbb{N} \wedge yy > 0 \wedge vv \in \mathbb{N} \wedge$$
$$ww \in \mathbb{N} \wedge vv = xx \wedge ww = yy \wedge ww > 0$$

$\Rightarrow$

$[tt := vv \; ; \; zz := 1]$

$(tt = xx \wedge vv = zz \times tt \wedge zz \in 1 \; .. \; ww \wedge vv \in \mathbb{N} \wedge ww \in \mathbb{N} \wedge ww > 0 \wedge ww = yy)$

Using the sequence rule and making the substitutions gives the following:

$xx \in \mathbb{N} \wedge yy \in \mathbb{N} \wedge yy > 0 \wedge vv \in \mathbb{N} \wedge$
$ww \in \mathbb{N} \wedge vv = xx \wedge ww = yy \wedge ww > 0$

$\Rightarrow$

$vv = xx \wedge vv = 1 \times vv \wedge 1 \in 1 \; .. \; ww \wedge vv \in \mathbb{N} \wedge ww \in \mathbb{N} \wedge$
$ww > 0 \wedge ww = yy$

The deduction of the consequent from the antecedent is straightforward.

For the F-rule, we have to choose **P** so that

$\neg \mathbf{P} \wedge$
$tt = xx \wedge$
$vv = zz \times tt \wedge$
$zz \in 1 \; .. \; ww \wedge$
$vv \in \mathbb{N} \wedge ww \in \mathbb{N} \wedge$
$ww > 0 \wedge ww = yy$

$\Rightarrow$

$vv \in \mathbb{N} \wedge ww \in \mathbb{N} \wedge ww > 0 \wedge vv = xx \times yy \wedge ww = yy$

The obvious choice for **P** is

$zz < ww$

For the variant, since we intend to count through the loop with zz, we choose $ww - zz$.

The body is to decrease the variant, so we choose to increase zz by 1. If the value of zz goes up, the value of vv must go up by tt to preserve the invariant. Thus the body of the loop can be

$zz := zz + 1 \; ; \; vv := vv + tt$

(Of course the sequence could be the other way round in this case, as neither assignment changes a value in the other.)

This completes the development of the loop.

7.6 Summary and outlook

In this chapter we have learnt:

- a plausible meaning for the vague term 'software design';
- the principles of data design:
  - representation of abstract variables by concrete variables
  - the importance of recording retrieve relations
  - correctness conditions for a concrete initialization
  - correctness conditions for concrete operations
  - reduction of non-determinism;
- the principles of algorithm design:
  - the use of the sequence substitution
  - the use of local variables
  - how to design and record loops.

The examples we have studied in this chapter have raised some questions that have so far been unanswered.

In talking about concrete states we have made some assumptions about the kinds of variables that can be used there. We have used natural number variables, sequences and arrays. We need to know more exactly what kinds of concrete variables will be in the programming language we shall be using.

We have also made assumptions about the kinds of substitutions that can be used in the design of concrete operations. We have used simple assignment, concatenation of sequences and assignment to elements of arrays. We need to know what operations are available on the permitted concrete variables.

In the proof of correctness, there has been nothing to check that the types of expressions being assigned matched the types of variables into which they were being assigned. In a proof involving arrays, there seemed to be no formal obligation to check that the index was within the valid range. In what has been presented as a simple assignment there has often been concealed a preconditioned operation. In real programming languages, $xx := xx + yy$ is a preconditioned operation; it is the programmer's responsibility to make sure that the mathematical value of $xx + yy$ is not greater than the maximum value that can be stored in xx. These are signs that certain simplifications have been made, simplifications that we shall dispense with when we study the implementation abstract machine.

7.7 Exercises

(7.1)   Show that

$$[xx := 0 ; xx := xx + 1] \, xx = 1$$

(7.2)   Show that

$$[xx := 5 ; yy := 3 ; zz := xx \times yy] \, zz = 15$$

(7.3)   Show that, if xx and yy are natural numbers,

$$[xx := yy ; yy := yy + 1] \, yy > xx$$

(7.4)   Show that, if xx, yy and zz are natural numbers,

$$[xx := yy ; yy := yy + zz] \, yy \geq xx$$

(7.5)   Show that

$$[xx := 0] \, [\text{CHOICE } yy := 0 \text{ OR } yy := 1 \text{ END}]$$
$$(xx \in \mathbb{N} \wedge xx = yy)$$

is false, but

$$[xx := 0] \, \neg[\text{CHOICE } yy := 0 \text{ OR } yy := 1 \text{ END}]$$
$$\neg(xx \in \mathbb{N} \wedge xx = yy)$$

is true.

(7.6)   Show that the following initialization is correct.

	Abstract	Concrete
VARIABLES	xx	yy
INVARIANT	$xx \in \mathbb{N}$	$yy \in \mathbb{N} \wedge$ $yy = xx$
INITIALISATION	$xx :\in 0 \,..\, 5$	$yy := 3$

(7.7)   Show that the following initialization is correct.

	Abstract	Concrete
VARIABLES	xx	yy
INVARIANT	$xx \in 0 \,..\, 10$	$yy \in 0 \,..\, 10 \wedge$ $yy = xx$
INITIALISATION	$xx :\in 0 \,..\, 10$	$yy :\in 0 \,..\, 5$

In this example, non-determinism is reduced but not removed.

(7.8)   Show that the following operation is correct.

	Abstract	Concrete
VARIABLES	xx	yy
INVARIANT	$xx \in \mathbb{N}$	$yy \in \mathbb{N} \wedge$ $yy = xx$
Operation	$xx :\in 0 .. 5$	IF $yy > 5$ THEN $yy := 5$ END

(7.9)   Show that

$$xx \in \mathbb{N} \wedge yy \in \mathbb{N} \Rightarrow$$

```
[ww := xx ;
 zz := yy ;
 WHILE
   zz ≠ 0
 DO
   ww := ww + 1 ; zz := zz − 1
 VARIANT
   zz
 INVARIANT
   ww + zz = xx + yy  ∧
   ww ∈ ℕ ∧
   xx ∈ ℕ ∧
   yy ∈ ℕ ∧
   zz ∈ ℕ
 END] ww = xx + yy
```

(7.10)   Verify the following loop.

```
[xx := 0 ;
 WHILE
   xx < 10
 DO
   xx := xx + 1
 VARIANT
   10 − xx
 INVARIANT
   xx ∈ ℕ ∧ xx ≤ 10
 END]
 xx = 10
```

(7.11)   For each of the following loops, determine which of the five
          rules is not satisfied, and suggest how the loop might be
          amended to make it satisfy all five. In each case you should
          make all five tests even if one of them fails.

(a)

$$[xx := 100 \; ; \; \text{WHILE } xx < 10 \text{ DO } xx := xx + 1$$
$$\text{VARIANT } 10 - xx \text{ INVARIANT } xx \in 0 \,..\, 10 \text{ END}]$$
$$xx = 10$$

(b)

$$[xx := 0 \; ; \; \text{WHILE } xx < 10 \text{ DO } skip$$
$$\text{VARIANT } 10 - xx \text{ INVARIANT } xx \in \mathbb{N} \wedge xx \leq 10 \text{ END}]$$
$$xx = 10$$

(c)

$$[xx := 0 \; ; \; \text{WHILE } xx \neq 10 \text{ DO } xx := xx + 1$$
$$\text{VARIANT } 10 - xx \text{ INVARIANT } xx \in \mathbb{N} \text{ END}] \; xx = 10$$

(d)

$$[xx := 10 \; ; \; \text{WHILE } xx = xx \text{ DO } xx := xx + 1$$
$$\text{VARIANT } 10 - xx \text{ INVARIANT } xx = 10 \text{ END}] \; xx = 10$$

(e)

$$[xx := 0 \; ; \; \text{WHILE } xx < 10 \text{ DO } xx := xx + 2$$
$$\text{VARIANT } 10 - xx \text{ INVARIANT } xx \in \mathbb{N} \wedge xx \leq 10 \text{ END}]$$
$$xx = 10$$

(7.12)   This exercise illustrates the use of a loop to find a value in
          an array when the value is known to be present. In this
          example, *narr* is an array of natural numbers between 1
          and 100, *mm* is the largest index in the array, *num* is the
          number to be found, and *ctr* is a local variable for counting
          through the array.

$$mm \in \mathbb{N} \wedge$$
$$mm > 0 \wedge$$
$$num \in 1 \,..\, 100 \wedge$$
$$narr \in 1 \,..\, mm \to 1 \,..\, 100 \wedge$$
$$num \in \text{ran}\,(narr) \wedge$$
$$ctr \in \mathbb{N} \Rightarrow$$
$$[ctr := 1 \; ;$$
$$\text{WHILE}$$
$$\quad narr\,(ctr) \neq num$$
$$\text{DO}$$
$$\quad ctr := ctr + 1$$
$$\text{VARIANT}$$

$$mm - ctr$$
INVARIANT
$$num \notin ran (1 .. (ctr - 1) \lhd narr) \land ctr \in 1 .. mm$$
END] $narr (ctr) = num$

Verify this initialized loop.

(7.13)   Given *narr*, an array of natural numbers with indexes 1 .. *nn*, where *nn* is greater than zero, and *where* is a natural number variable, write a loop to store an index of the largest number in the array in the variable *where*. Prove your loop correct.

(7.14)   Given *numseq*, a sequence of length *nn* of natural numbers, write a loop to store the sum of the numbers in the sequence in the natural number variable *sum*. Prove your loop correct.

(7.15)   Show that the following initialization is correct:

	Abstract	Concrete
VARIABLES	xx	yy
INVARIANT	$xx \subseteq 1 .. 10$	$yy : 1 .. 10 \rightarrow BOOL \land$ $xx = dom (yy \rhd$ $\{TRUE\})$

INITIAL-ISATION	$xx := \emptyset$	$ctr := 0 ;$
		WHILE
		   $ctr < 10$
		DO
		   $ctr := ctr + 1 ;$
		   $yy (ctr) := FALSE$
		VARIANT
		   $10 - ctr$
		INVARIANT
		   $ctr \in 0 .. 10 \land$
		   $dom (1 .. ctr \lhd yy \rhd$
		   $\{TRUE\}) = \emptyset$
		END

(7.16)   Show that the following operation is correct:

	Abstract	Concrete
VARIABLES	xx	yy
INVARIANT	$xx \in \mathbb{N}$	$yy \in \mathbb{N} \wedge$ $xx = yy$

Operation	$xx :\in 0 .. 5$	WHILE
		   $yy > 5$
		 DO
		   $yy := yy - 1$
		 VARIANT
		   yy
		 INVARIANT
		   $yy \in \mathbb{N}$
		 END

Chapter 8
Implementations

Summary: The implementation in software development — library machines — importing library machines — dependencies — invariant of an implementation — initialization and its verification — VAR-IN-END — operations of an implementation — verifying the operations — parameterized implementations — code generation — sample application.

In this chapter we see how to record design decisions in an implementation, how to generate code for an implementation, and how to generate a sample application to test an implementation.

8.1 What is an implementation?

In the B-Method an **implementation** is an abstract machine from which program code (data declarations and executable statements) can be generated. For this generation to be possible, some restrictions have to be placed on the kinds of variables that can be used, and on the substitutions that can appear in the definitions of the operations. To be of any practical value in software development, an implementation must also be a correct design of some machine that promises useful function.

Before we can write an implementation in the abstract machine notation, we must understand the programming language that is provided for an implementation. In an ordinary programming language like COBOL or C, the language rules prescribe the kinds of data that can be used, the kinds of operations allowed on the data, the control structures into which the operation can be organized, and the kinds of expressions that can appear in operations and control structures. In this chapter we shall study the programming language for implementations in the B-Method.

8.1.1 The variables of an implementation

All the data used in an implementation (apart from local variables used in algorithm design, which we discuss later) must be encapsulated in machines. The implementation therefore has no VARIABLES clause. Instead it has an **IMPORTS clause** that names the machines from which its concrete state is constructed. You can use any machines you like to build up the concrete state. The B-Toolkit provides a library of machines that provide the kinds of concrete data types found in many programming languages.

When you import a machine, you must supply parameters that respect any constraints of the imported machine. The values you supply for the parameters can be:

- parameters of the machine being implemented
- sets or constants of the machine being implemented
- sets or constants of imported machines.

8.1.2 The invariant of an implementation

Implementations have an INVARIANT clause which serves two purposes:

- To specify constraints among the permissible values of the variables of the imported machines.

- To specify how the variables of the imported machines represent the variables of the machine being refined. This part of the invariant is the retrieve relation described in Chapter 7.

The predicate in the INVARIANT clause is the **native invariant** of the implementation. The types of the variables are specified in the invariants of the imported machines. The invariants of the imported machines are the **imported invariant** of the implementation.

You can supplement the native invariant with an ASSERTIONS clause. The predicate in the ASSERTIONS clause of an implementation must be provable from the invariant of the machine being refined and the native and imported invariants of the implementation. There is a proof obligation to prove it. The assertions appear in the antecedent of the other proof obligations.

8.1.3 The initialization of an implementation

The implementation has an initialization substitution, just like a machine, though the implementation's initialization establishes the initial values of the concrete state. There is a correctness condition for initialization, because any concrete state that results from the initialization substitution must correspond under the retrieve relation to an abstract state resulting from the machine's initialization. The proof obligations for correctness of an initialization were discussed in Chapter 7.

8.1.4 The operations of an implementation

The implementation has operations (the **concrete operations**) that correspond to the operations of the machine (the **abstract operations**). In the B-Method, corresponding operations must have identical names, and they must have the same number of inputs and outputs, and the types of corresponding inputs and outputs must be the same. The B-Toolkit provides a facility for generating a template for an implementation of an analysed machine.

You implement the operations by using the operations of the imported machines. This ensures that the imported invariant is always preserved.

In constructing an operation definition, only certain substitutions are allowed:

(1) A substitution to introduce local variables. This is the VAR-IN-END substitution described on page 141.

(2) BEGIN-END.

(3) IF-THEN-ELSE-END and its variations.

(4) CASE.

(5) Sequence.

(6) Loop.

(7) An assignment in which the receiver is a local variable or an output, and the source expression is an input, a local variable, or an arithmetic expression constructed from inputs and local variables.

(8) Operations of imported or seen machines. The outputs of these operations must be local variables, or outputs of the operation being implemented. The inputs must be local variables, or inputs of the operation being implemented.

The following substitutions are not allowed: assignments that are more elaborate than defined above, PRE-THEN-END, ANY-WHERE-THEN-END, LET-BE-IN-END, CHOICE-OR-END, Boolean, choice-by-predicate, choice-from-a-set, functional over-riding, multiple, parallel and SELECT (except when disguised as CASE).

In if-tests and while-tests, elementary predicates can be combined with $\neg$, $\wedge$, $\vee$ and $\Rightarrow$ in any desired level of complexity. The elementary predicates can only be the following:

(1) Arithmetic comparisons in which the expressions are constructed from:

  (a) numbers

  (b) local variables

  (c) inputs

  (d) constants of the machines mentioned in the REFINES, IMPORTS and SEES clauses of the implementation.

(2) Equality or inequality predicates. The terms being compared can be:

  (a) local variables

  (b) inputs

  (c) constants of the machines mentioned in the REFINES, IMPORTS and SEES clauses of the implementation.

8.1.5 What do we do about parameters?

We can do nothing about these, as the parameters will be supplied by the user of the machine. We will need to use the parameters by passing them as parameters to machines that the implementation imports.

8.1.6 What do we do about deferred and enumerated sets?

In the implementation, you must fix the values of the machine's native and included deferred and enumerated sets. You use the PROPERTIES clause of the implementation to do this. You can identify sets with sets of numbers, or with deferred or enumerated sets of imported machines. You can identify the members of an enumerated set with natural numbers, or with the constants of imported machines, including the members of the enumerated sets of imported machines.

8.2 Some useful library machines

8.2.1 A library machine for sequences

In the development that follows we shall be using sequences of resources to represent the sets of resources in *RRMan*, and the B-Toolkit library provides a machine *seq_obj* to help with this. We study here as much of the machine definition as we need for the implementation of *RRMan*. The general idea is that the *seq_obj* machine maintains a number of sequences, each sequence being identified by a token from the set *SEQOBJ*. The set of tokens currently in use is *seqtok*, and the relation between them and the sequences is *seqstruct*. All this is illustrated in Figure 8.1 on page 134. The rectangle representing *SEQOBJ* is shown as having five members, of which two are shown as being in *seqtok*. Four of the many sequences of *VALUE* are shown in the rectangle on the right of the figure. The first is an empty sequence, the second a sequence with three members, and the last two each have one member. The function *seqstruct* relating the tokens to the sequences is represented by the two arrows each connecting a token to a sequence.

The machine has three parameters:

- the set *VALUE* of things that are to go in the sequences

- the maximum number *maxobj* of sequences that are to be used

- the maximum number *maxmem* of elements in all the sequences combined.

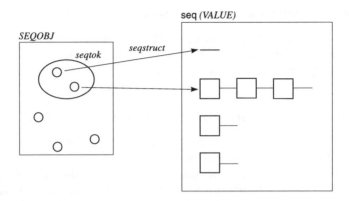

Figure 8.1 Sequences and their tokens.

The last two parameters are for the benefit of the implementation of *seq_obj*, which promises not to run out of storage. A CONSTRAINTS clause is used here to ensure that users of the machine supply a value for *maxobj* that is strictly positive.

MACHINE

seq_obj (*VALUE, maxobj, maxmem*)

CONSTRAINTS

maxobj > 0

SEES

Bool_TYPE

The SETS clause introduces the set *SEQOBJ*, the tokens that will be used to refer to the sequences. The PROPERTIES clause is used to express conditions on the sets defined in the SETS clause. In this case the set *SEQOBJ* from which tokens will be drawn is to have exactly *maxobj* members.

SETS

SEQOBJ

PROPERTIES

card (*SEQOBJ*) = *maxobj*

As usual the VARIABLES and INVARIANT clauses establish the state illustrated in Figure 8.1. The state has an additional component *seqmem*, whose function is to keep account of the amount of storage being used.

VARIABLES

seqtok, seqstruct, seqmem

INVARIANT

seqtok ⊆ *SEQOBJ* ∧
seqstruct ∈ *seqtok* → seq (*VALUE*) ∧
seqmem ∈ ℕ

The INITIALISATION clause promises that the relation and set will be empty, and that the count will be zero.

INITIALISATION

seqtok, seqstruct, seqmem := ∅, ∅, 0

We first study the operation *CRE_SEQ_OBJ*, whose main function is to create a new (empty) sequence, and to provide a token that can be used to refer to it. Provided that there are still unused tokens, a new token is selected and associated with an empty sequence, and *TRUE* and the new token are output. If there are no more tokens, *FALSE* is output.

```
bb, pp ⟵ CRE_SEQ_OBJ =
  IF
    seqtok ≠ SEQOBJ
  THEN
    ANY
      qq
    WHERE
      qq ∈ SEQOBJ − seqtok
    THEN
      seqstruct (qq) := [ ] ||
      seqtok := seqtok ∪ {qq} ||
      pp := qq ||
      bb := TRUE
    END
  ELSE
    bb := FALSE ||
    pp :∈ SEQOBJ
  END
```

The operation *LEN_SEQ_OBJ* reports the length of the sequence corresponding to the input token.

```
nn ⟵  LEN_SEQ_OBJ (pp) =
  PRE
    pp ∈ seqtok
  THEN
    nn := size (seqstruct (pp))
  END
```

The operation *VAL_SEQ_OBJ* has two inputs: the token of the sequence being referred to, and the position in the sequence of the value to be returned as output.

```
vv ⟵  VAL_SEQ_OBJ (pp, ii) =
  PRE
    pp ∈ seqtok ∧
    ii ∈ 1 .. size (seqstruct (pp))
  THEN
    vv := seqstruct (pp) (ii)
  END
```

The operation *POP_SEQ_OBJ* amends the sequence identified by the input token by dropping the last element.

```
POP_SEQ_OBJ (pp) =
  PRE
    pp ∈ seqtok ∧
    seqstruct (pp) ≠ [ ]
  THEN
    seqstruct (pp) := front (seqstruct (pp)) ||
    seqmem := seqmem − 1
  END
```

The operation *EMP_SEQ_OBJ* is an enquiry operation that returns *TRUE* if the sequence is empty, and *FALSE* if it is not.

```
bb ⟵  EMP_SEQ_OBJ (pp) =
  PRE
    pp ∈ seqtok
  THEN
    bb := bool (seqstruct (pp) = [ ])
  END
```

The operation *PSH_SEQ_OBJ* has two inputs: the token of the sequence being referred to, and the value to be added to the end of the sequence.

$bb \longleftarrow PSH\_SEQ\_OBJ (pp, vv) =$
  PRE
    $pp \in seqtok \land$
    $vv \in VALUE$
  THEN
    IF
      $seqmem < maxmem$
    THEN
      $seqstruct (pp) := seqstruct (pp) \leftarrow vv \; ||$
      $seqmem := seqmem + 1 \; ||$
      $bb := TRUE$
    ELSE
      $bb := FALSE$
    END
  END

The last operation that we shall need is *CPY_SEQ_OBJ*. It takes two input parameters: the token identifying the source sequence, and the token identifying the target sequence. The operation replaces the target with the source, leaving the source unchanged.

$bb \longleftarrow CPY\_SEQ\_OBJ (pp, qq) =$
  PRE
    $pp \in seqtok \land$
    $qq \in seqtok$
  THEN
    IF
      $seqmem -$
      $(\text{size} (seqstruct (qq)) + \text{size} (seqstruct (pp)))$
      > 0
    THEN
      $seqstruct (qq) := seqstruct (pp) \; ||$
      $seqmem :=$
      $seqmem - \text{size} (seqstruct (qq)) +$
      $\text{size} (seqstruct (pp)) \; ||$
      $bb := TRUE$
    ELSE
      $bb := FALSE$
    END
  END

8.2.2 A library machine for variables

In our implementation we need two variables to store the tokens that represent the sequences. The B-Toolkit library provides a machine *Vvar* for simple variables. The machine has a single parameter, the set of values eligible to be stored in the variable. The INITIAL-ISATION clause says only that the initial value is one of the eligible values. There are two operations: *VAL_VAR* delivers the value of the variable as an output, and *STO_VAR* accepts an eligible value as input, and stores it in the variable. Figure 8.2 is the complete specification of *Vvar*.

MACHINE

   Vvar (VALUE)

VARIABLES

   Vvar

INVARIANT

   Vvar ∈ *VALUE*

INITIALISATION

   Vvar :∈ *VALUE*

OPERATIONS

   vv ⟵ *VAL_VAR* =
    vv := *Vvar*
   ;
   STO_VAR (vv) =
    PRE
     vv ∈ *VALUE*
    THEN
     Vvar := *vv*
    END

END

Figure 8.2 The library machine for a variable.

8.3 Implementing the recoverable resource manager

We shall study an implementation of the machine *RRMan*. The **IMPLEMENTATION clause** names the implementation — we have called it *RRManI*, and the **REFINES clause** explains that it is an implementation of *RRMan*. This implementation needs *TRUE* and *FALSE*, so it has a SEES clause that names the *Bool_TYPE* machine.

IMPLEMENTATION

   RRManI

REFINES

   RRMan

SEES

   Bool_TYPE

8.3.1 Importing library machines into an implementation

When library machines are imported into an implementation, they have to be renamed. The method of renaming is to join a user-defined name to the beginning of the name of the library machine with an underscore. The user-defined name must not contain an underscore. This kind of renaming renames the native variables, native constants, native sets and operations of the machine being renamed. One of the machines we import into *RRManI* is called *Current_Vvar*. This is an instance of the library machine *Vvar* discussed above. Its variable is *Current_Vvar*, and its operations are *Current_VAL_VAR*, and *Current_STO_VAR*. Another machine we import is *Resource_seq_obj*, an instance of the library machine *seq_obj*. The variables of this machine are *Resource_seqtok*, *Resource_seqstruct* and *Resource_seqmem*. The deferred set of this machine is *Resource_SEQOBJ*, and its operations are *Resource_CRE_SEQ_OBJ*, and so on. We also import *Backup_Vvar*, another instance of *Vvar*.

The IMPORTS clause lists the machines that are to be used to provide the concrete variables of the implementation.

IMPORTS

   Resource_seq_obj (RESOURCE, 2, 2 × max_res),
   Current_Vvar (Resource_SEQOBJ),
   Backup_Vvar (Resource_SEQOBJ)

The form of the IMPORTS clause is a list of instantiated machine names separated by commas. *Resource_seq_obj* is instantiated with a set and two numbers. *Current_Vvar* and *Backup_Vvar* are instantiated with a set that is a deferred set of the imported machine *Resource_seq_obj*.

8.3.2 Dependencies of an implementation

The REFINES and IMPORTS clauses introduce new dependencies. An implementation must be analysed with the machine that it refines and the machines that it imports in mind, since the implementation makes reference to the contents of all these machines. The dependency diagram for *RRManI* is illustrated in Figure 8.3.

The machines are represented by boxes as before, and the implementation is represented by a round-ended box. A maths change to *RMan* would mean that *RMan*, *RRMan* and *RRManI* would all have to be re-analysed.

8.3.3 Invariant in an implementation

The INVARIANT clause of *RRManI* has four conjuncts. The first two conjuncts state constraints local to the implementation, namely that the two values *Current_Vvar* and *Backup_Vvar* will always be tokens that give access to sequences in *Resource_seq_obj*. The last two conjuncts are the retrieve relation. The machine variable *rfree* is the set of elements of the sequence identified by *Current_Vvar*, and the machine variable *bkup.rfree* is the set of elements of the sequence identified by *Backup_Vvar*.

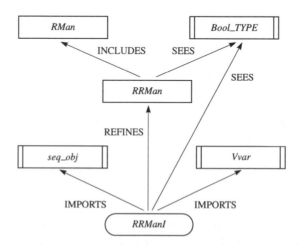

Figure 8.3 Dependencies of an implementation.

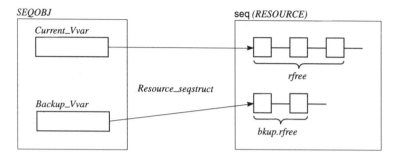

Figure 8.4 Invariant of an implementation.

INVARIANT

> $Current\_Vvar \in Resource\_seqtok \wedge$
> $Backup\_Vvar \in Resource\_seqtok \wedge$
> $rfree = \mathrm{ran}\,(Resource\_seqstruct\,(Current\_Vvar)) \wedge$
> $bkup.rfree = \mathrm{ran}\,(Resource\_seqstruct\,(Backup\_Vvar)) \wedge$
> $Current\_Vvar \neq Backup\_Vvar \wedge$
> $Resource\_seqmem = \mathrm{card}\,(rfree) + \mathrm{card}\,(bkup.rfree)$

The invariant is illustrated in Figure 8.4.

8.3.4 Initializing the implementation

The INITIALISATION clause contains a pseudo-program to establish the invariant.

> INITIALISATION
> ```
> VAR
>   bb, cc, bpp, cpp
> IN
>   bb, cpp ⟵ Resource_CRE_SEQ_OBJ ;
>   Current_STO_VAR (cpp) ;
>   cc, bpp ⟵ Resource_CRE_SEQ_OBJ ;
>   Backup_STO_VAR (bpp)
> END
> ```

The pseudo-program here is a **VAR-IN-END substitution**. This substitution, which can be used only in implementations, introduces local variables, in this case four of them. These variables are not variables of *RRManI*, but are used in the body of the substitution to hold outputs of *Resource_SEQ_OBJ*, and deliver some of them as inputs to operations of *Current_Vvar* and *Backup_Vvar*. The operation *Resource_CRE_SEQ_OBJ* is used twice to get tokens for the two sequences, and each token is stored in the appropriate variable with *Current_STO_VAR* and *Backup_STO_VAR.*

The body of a VAR-IN-END substitution is allowed to use only the operations of the imported machines, and assignments to local variables and to the outputs. The body of a VAR-IN-END substitution must establish the type of each of the local variables introduced. Each local variable must appear in the body as the output of an operation of an imported machine, so that its type can be determined from the definition of the operation of the imported machine. No local variable can appear as an input to an operation before it has been used as an output.

The meaning of the VAR-IN-END substitution is fixed by the **VAR-IN-END rule**.

$$[\text{VAR } x \text{ IN } \mathbf{G} \text{ END}] \ \mathbf{P} \Leftrightarrow \forall x \bullet (\mathbf{Q} \Rightarrow [\mathbf{G}] \ \mathbf{P})$$

provided that **x** is not free in **P**. The predicate **Q**, which appears on the right hand side of the rule, but is not in the pseudo-program, is constructed from the substitution **G**. It is a predicate that establishes the types of the local variables.

The local nature of the variables in the pseudo-program is reflected by the fact that the variables are bound on the right hand side of the rule.

8.3.5 Verifying the initialization

By the initialization of the implementation we mean a sequence substitution consisting of the initializations of the imported machines followed by the substitution in the INITIALISATION clause of the implementation. In this example the proof obligation is as follows.

[*Current_Vvar* :∈ *Resource_SEQOBJ* ;
Backup_Vvar :∈ *Resource_SEQOBJ* ;
Resource_seqtok := Ø ;
Resource_seqstruct := Ø ;
Resource_seqmem := 0 ;
bb, cpp ⟵ *Resource_CRE_SEQ_OBJ* ;
Current_STO_VAR (*cpp*) ;
cc, bpp ⟵ *Resource_CRE_SEQ_OBJ* ;
Backup_STO_VAR (*bpp*)]
¬[*rfree, bkup.rfree* := Ø, Ø]
¬(*Current_Vvar* ∈ *Resource_seqtok* ∧
Backup_Vvar ∈ *Resource_seqtok* ∧
rfree = ran (*Resource_seqstruct* (*Current_Vvar*)) ∧
bkup.rfree = ran (*Resource_seqstruct* (*Backup_Vvar*)))

If we make the first substitution and use the law of double negation we get the following:

[...]
(*Current_Vvar* ∈ *Resource_seqtok* ∧
Backup_Vvar ∈ *Resource_seqtok* ∧
∅ = ran (*Resource_seqstruct* (*Current_Vvar*)) ∧
∅ = ran (*Resource_seqstruct* (*Backup_Vvar*)))

From here we can argue informally as follows. The first conjunct follows from the substitutions that first assign a member of *Resource_seqtok* to a local variable, and then store the same variable in *Current_Vvar*. The second conjunct follows in the same way. The last two conjuncts follow from the allocation of empty sequences by *Resource_CRE_SEQ_OBJ*.

8.3.6 Implementing the operations

The implementations of the operations appear in the OPERATIONS clause.

The design chosen for *rec_alloc* is typical of the style of programming in implementations. Three local variables are introduced in a VAR-IN-END substitution whose body is a sequence of operations. The value of the token for the sequence representing the current state of the resources is obtained using *Current_VAL_VAR*. This value is used in *Resource_LEN_SEQ_OBJ* to get the size of the sequence, and this is used to find the last resource in the sequence. The resource is removed from the sequence by using *Resource_POP_SEQ_OBJ*, and the same resource is returned in the output.

```
res ⟵ rec_alloc =
  VAR
    pp, rr, ll
  IN
    pp ⟵ Current_VAL_VAR ;
    ll ⟵ Resource_LEN_SEQ_OBJ (pp) ;
    rr ⟵ Resource_VAL_SEQ_OBJ (pp, ll) ;
    Resource_POP_SEQ_OBJ (pp) ;
    res := rr
  END
```

The design of *is_any_free* is a VAR-IN-END substitution that introduces two local variables. The token that identifies the sequence representing the current state of the resources is retrieved and used to enquire if the sequence is empty. The output is the negation of the response to that enquiry. (*NEG_BOOL* is an operation of the library machine *Bool_TYPE*.)

```
ans ⟵ is_any_free =
  VAR
    pp, bb
  IN
    pp ⟵ Current_VAL_VAR ;
    bb ⟵ Resource_EMP_SEQ_OBJ (pp) ;
    ans ⟵ NEG_BOOL (bb)
  END
```

The design of *rec_free* retrieves the token for the current resources, and then pushes the input on to the end of the sequence with *Resource_PSH_SEQ_OBJ*.

```
rec_free (rr) =
  VAR
    pp, bb
  IN
    pp ⟵ Current_VAL_VAR ;
    bb ⟵ Resource_PSH_SEQ_OBJ (pp, rr)
  END
```

The design of *is_free* searches the sequence for an occurrence of the input resource, and returns *TRUE* if it is found there and *FALSE* if it is not.

```
ans ⟵ is_free (rr) =
  VAR
    pp, ll, ff, vv
  IN
    pp ⟵ Current_VAL_VAR ;
    ll ⟵ Resource_LEN_SEQ_OBJ (pp) ;
    ff := FALSE ;
    WHILE
      ff = FALSE ∧ ll ≠ 0
    DO
      vv ⟵ Resource_VAL_SEQ_OBJ (pp, ll) ;
      IF
        vv = rr
      THEN
        ff := TRUE
      END ;
      ll := ll − 1
```

```
VARIANT
    ll
INVARIANT
```

$ll \in \mathbb{N} \land$ (1)

$ff \in BOOL \land$ (2)

$pp = Current\_Vvar \land$ (3)

$(ll \neq 0 \Rightarrow$

$ll \in$ dom $(Resource\_seqstruct (Current\_Vvar)) \land$ (4)

$(ff = TRUE \Rightarrow$

$rr \in$ ran $(1 .. ll \triangleleft$

$Resource\_seqstruct (Current\_Vvar))) \land$ (5)

$(ff = FALSE \Rightarrow$

$(rr \notin$ ran $(1 .. ll \triangleleft$

$Resource\_seqstruct (Current\_Vvar)))) \land$ (6)

$Current\_Vvar \in Resource\_seqtok \land$ (7)

$Backup\_Vvar \in Resource\_seqtok \land$ (8)

$Current\_Vvar \neq Backup\_Vvar \land$ (9)

$rfree =$ ran $(Resource\_seqstruct (Current\_Vvar)) \land$ (10)

$bkup.rfree =$

ran $(Resource\_seqstruct (Backup\_Vvar))) \land$ (11)

$Resource\_seqmem =$ card $(rfree) +$ card $(bkup.rfree)$ (12)

```
END ;
    ans := ff
END
```

In this VAR-IN-END substitution, four local variables are introduced. In the loop, we start at the end of the sequence and work backwards, examining each resource in turn, until either we find an instance of *rr*, or we have examined all the resources.

As we saw in Chapter 7, construction of a loop is often a tentative process. The method described there began with the invariant, but often the best invariant depends on the chosen initialization, while-test, variant and loop body. The following analysis of the invariant of the loop in *is_free* illustrates this dependency.

A loop invariant usually contains predicates of five kinds:

- Predicates that fix the types of the local variables. In this example, (1), (2) and (3) are of this kind. We do not type *vv* because it is local to the loop body.

- Predicates that ensure that the preconditions of operations in the body are satisfied. In this example, (3) and (4) are of this kind.

- Predicates that protect the variant, ensuring that it is a natural number. In this example, (1) is of this kind.

- Predicates that approximate the predicate that the loop is to establish. These predicates figure prominently in the proof of the F-rule for the loop. In this example, (5) and (6) are of this kind.

- Predicates of the native invariant for variables that are not changed in the loop body. These will include the parts of the retrieve relation for the abstract variables that are not changed in the loop body. In this example (7), (8), (9), (10), (11) and (12) are of this kind. They are the whole of the retrieve relation, since this operation does not change any of the abstract variables.

The informal intention of predicates (5) and (6) is as follows:

- If $ff = TRUE$, we must have found an instance of rr in the part of the sequence searched so far. This is illustrated in the following diagram.

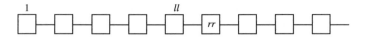

- If $ff = FALSE$, we know that there is no instance of rr in the part of the sequence searched so far. This is illustrated in the following diagram.

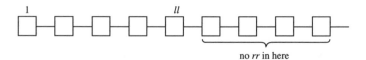

This example reminds us that the loop invariant is one of the places we are allowed to refer to the values of the variables of imported machines.

For the I-rule, we see that the initialization certainly establishes two of the conjuncts in the invariant: $ll \in \mathbb{N}$ and $ff \in BOOL$. Since ff has been assigned the value $FALSE$, we need only seek to establish the following:

$$rr \notin \text{ran} (1 \mathinner{\ldotp\ldotp} ll \lhd Resource\_seqstruct (Current\_Vvar))$$

Since $1 \mathinner{\ldotp\ldotp} ll$ is the whole of the domain of $Resource\_seqstruct$ $(Current\_Vvar)$, the predicate is

$$rr \notin \varnothing$$

which is a theorem of set theory.

For the F-rule, we first decide what predicate the loop is supposed to establish. In order for this implementation to be a proper implementation of the abstract operation, it must set *ans* to *TRUE* if *rr* ∈ *rfree*, and it must set *ans* to *FALSE* if *rr* ∉ *rfree*. The invariant of the implementation identifies *rfree* with ran (*Resource_seqstruct* (*Current_Vvar*)), so the loop must establish the following predicate:

[*ans* := *ff*]
((*rr* ∈ ran (*Resource_seqstruct* (*Current_Vvar*)) ⇒ *ans* = *TRUE*) ∧
(*rr* ∉ ran (*Resource_seqstruct* (*Current_Vvar*)) ⇒ *ans* = *FALSE*))

which is the same as

((*rr* ∈ ran (*Resource_seqstruct* (*Current_Vvar*)) ⇒ *ff* = *TRUE*) ∧
(*rr* ∉ ran (*Resource_seqstruct* (*Current_Vvar*)) ⇒ *ff* = *FALSE*))

From here we can argue informally by cases. There are three cases in which the while-test is false:

- *ff* = *TRUE* ∧ *ll* = 0

- *ff* = *TRUE* ∧ *ll* ≠ 0

- *ff* = *FALSE* ∧ *ll* = 0

In the first case, we need only consider the first conjunct of the loop invariant:

rr ∈ ran ((1 .. 0) ⩤ *Resource_seqstruct* (*Current_Vvar*))

Since the set on the left of the domain subtraction is empty, this is equivalent to the desired result in this case:

rr ∈ ran (*Resource_seqstruct* (*Current_Vvar*))

In the second case, the first conjunct of the invariant gives the following:

rr ∈ ran ((1 .. *ll*) ⩤ *Resource_seqstruct* (*Current_Vvar*))

If *ll* is less than the length of the sequence, then *rr* is a member of what is left after the domain subtraction, and so must be in the sequence. If *ll* is equal to the length of the sequence, then we have *rr* ∈ ∅, which is false; and so the implication ¬**P** ∧ **Q** ⇒ **R** is true. (Although we know that *ff* = *TRUE* means that we have been through the loop body once, so that *ll* must now be less than the length of the sequence, we have not recorded this fact in the invariant, so we have to consider it as a possibility. We could amend the invariant to include a predicate to assert this truth about *ll* in the consequent of the first conjunct.)

In the third case we must look at the second conjunct of the loop invariant:

$$rr \notin \text{ran} ((1 .. 0) \lhd Resource\_seqstruct \ (Current\_Vvar))$$

Since the set on the left of the domain subtraction is empty, this is equivalent to the desired result in this case:

$$rr \notin \text{ran} \ (Resource\_seqstruct \ (Current\_Vvar))$$

For the T1-rule, we have ll as the variant, and the invariant has a conjunct $ll \in \mathbb{N}$, which is just what we need to satisfy the rule.

For the T2-rule, we see that the only part of the loop body that affects the variant is the substitution $ll := ll - 1$. We have to show that

$$ll \in \mathbb{N} \wedge ll \neq 0 \Rightarrow [yy := ll] \ [ll := ll - 1] \ ll < yy$$

which is equivalent to

$$ll \in \mathbb{N} \wedge ll \neq 0 \Rightarrow [yy := ll] \ ll - 1 < yy$$

which is equivalent to

$$ll \in \mathbb{N} \wedge ll \neq 0 \Rightarrow ll - 1 < ll$$

which is a theorem of arithmetic.

For the P-rule, we first look at ll, and observe that what we have to prove is just the following theorem of arithmetic.

$$ll \in \mathbb{N} \wedge ll \neq 0 \Rightarrow ll - 1 \in \mathbb{N}$$

The conjunct $ll \in \mathbb{N}$ is in **Q**, the invariant of the loop. The conjunct $ll \neq 0$ is in **P**, the while-test. The consequent $ll - 1 \in \mathbb{N}$ is in **[G] Q**, since the loop body **G** always reduces ll by 1.

The fate of ff is as follows. If the loop body does not change ff, we can reduce the proof obligation to:

$$ff \in BOOL \Rightarrow [skip] \ ff \in BOOL$$

and this is equivalent, by the skip rule, to the following tautology:

$$ff \in BOOL \Rightarrow ff \in BOOL$$

If the loop body does change ff, we can reduce the proof obligation to the following:

$$ff \in BOOL \Rightarrow [ff := TRUE] \ ff \in BOOL$$

and this is equivalent to the theorem

$$ff \in BOOL \Rightarrow TRUE \in BOOL$$

and the consequent is part of the context of *Bool_TYPE*, which is in the SEES clause of the implementation.

Now we investigate the first two conjuncts of the invariant. If the body sets *ff* to *TRUE*, this means that

$$rr = Resource\_seqstruct\ (Current\_Vvar)\ (ll)$$

so

$$rr \in \mathrm{ran}\ (1\ ..\ (ll - 1) \lhd Resource\_seqstruct\ (Current\_Vvar))$$

and this is what we need to show in this case.
   If the body leaves *ff* equal to *FALSE*, then

$$rr \neq Resource\_seqstruct\ (Current\_Vvar)\ (ll)$$

and because

$$rr \notin \mathrm{ran}\ ((1\ ..\ ll) \lhd Resource\_seqstruct\ (Current\_Vvar))$$

we have

$$rr \notin \mathrm{ran}\ (1\ ..\ (ll - 1) \lhd Resource\_seqstruct\ (Current\_Vvar))$$

as required.

8.3.7 Implementing the backup and restore operations

The implementation of *rec_backup* gets the values of the tokens for both sequences, and then uses *Resource_CPY_SEQ_OBJ* to replace the saved version by the current version.

```
rec_backup =
  VAR
    bb, cpp, bpp
  IN
    cpp ⟵ Current_VAL_VAR ;
    bpp ⟵ Backup_VAL_VAR ;
    bb ⟵ Resource_CPY_SEQ_OBJ (cpp, bpp)
  END
```

The implementation of *rec_restore* gets the values of the tokens for both sequences, and then uses *Resource_CPY_SEQ_OBJ* to replace the current version by the saved version.

```
rec_restore =
  VAR
    bb, cpp, bpp
  IN
    cpp ⟵ Current_VAL_VAR ;
```

$$bpp \longleftarrow Backup\_VAL\_VAR\ ;$$
$$bb \longleftarrow Resource\_CPY\_SEQ\_OBJ\ (bpp,\ cpp)$$
END

8.3.8 The END clause

The implementation ends with an END clause, which consists of the END keyword.

8.3.9 Implementations with parameters

The implementation *RRManI* has parameters *RESOURCE* and *max_res*, just like the machine *RRMan* which it implements. Before the implementation *RRManI* can be used to generate software for a resource manager, the contents of the set *RESOURCE* and the value of *max_res* have to be decided. In the next chapter we shall look at one technique for incorporating *RRManI* into a resource manager implementation that can be used for generating code.

8.3.10 Other clauses in implementations

You can introduce sets and constants into an implementation with the SETS and CONSTANTS clauses. The values of the sets and constants must be fixed in the PROPERTIES clause.

Operations of imported machines can be made operations of the implementation by naming them in a PROMOTES clause. Since a machine and the implementation that refines it must have the same operations, the name of the promoted operation must be the name of an operation of the machine being refined.

To help with the presentation of an implementation, you can use a DEFINITIONS clause to give short names to long expressions, just as you can in a machine definition.

8.3.11 Implementing mathematical context machines and the machines that see them

In Chapter 5 we saw how large machines could be constructed from smaller machines, and we saw how the SEES clause could be used in the construction process. One of the classes of machines at which a SEES clause could be directed was the mathematical context machine *Mathfac*, defined on page 73. We now present an implementation of this machine, and of the machine *Myfac* that was dependent on it.

First the implementation of *Mathfac*:

IMPLEMENTATION

   Mathfac_imp

REFINES

Mathfac

END

This implementation is very simple, but it throws the burden of implementing the mathematical factorial function on to the machines that depend on it through the SEES clause. Here is a skeleton of the implementation of *Myfac*, which computes the mathematical factorial by using a loop. The loop invariant refers to the mathematical factorial function *mathfac*, and since this function is defined in the machine *Mathfac*, the implementation mentions *Mathfac* in its SEES clause.

IMPLEMENTATION

Myfac_imp

REFINES

Myfac

SEES

Mathfac

OPERATIONS

```
nn ⟵ fac (mm) =
  VAR
    answer, ctr, ...
  IN
    answer := 0 ;
    ctr := 0 ;
    WHILE
      ...
    DO
      ...
    VARIANT
      ...
    INVARIANT
      ... ∧ answer = mathfac (ctr) ∧ ...
    END
  END
```

END

8.4 Code and interface generation

In this section we see how the B-Toolkit generates C code from an analysed implementation.

8.4.1 Generating code from an implementation

Once an implementation has been analysed, the B-Toolkit **code translator** can be used to generate and compile C statements and header files. The B-Toolkit **linker** can then be used to link the output of the compiler with the code provided for the library machines. The analysed implementation does not need to have been proved correct, so a bad implementation of a machine can nevertheless be translated and linked into an executable object.

8.4.2 Generating a sample application for a machine

Once a machine has an analysed implementation, the B-Toolkit **interface generator** can be used to generate a sample application that uses the machine. The sample application can be compiled, and uses code generated from the analysed implementation. The generated sample application has an operator interface that allows you to use the operations of the machine. It differs from animation in the following ways:

- The generated code, not the machine specification, is being executed. If your implementation has errors, perhaps because you risked leaving some proof obligations unproved, the sample application will end abnormally.

- You cannot choose the parameters, or the deferred or enumerated sets. Choice of parameters is made when the sample application is generated; choice of deferred and enumerated sets is made in the implementation.

- The preconditions of operations are not displayed. You are expected to remember them, and to provide inputs that satisfy them.

- The state is not displayed after an operation that changes it. If you wish to examine the contents of the program variables, you should use a debugging tool.

The first step in generating the sample application is to create the interface definition. The B-Toolkit provides a facility for generating a standard interface definition from an analysed machine. The interface consists of an **INTERFACE clause**, derived from the MACHINE clause, an OPERATIONS clause that lists the operations of the machine, and ends with an END clause. Figure 8.5 shows the standard interface definition for the machine *RRMan*.

INTERFACE

RRMan (/* RESOURCE */ SCALAR, /* max_res */ ?)

OPERATIONS

rec_alloc,
is_any_free,
rec_free,
is_free,
rec_backup,
rec_restore

END

Figure 8.5 A standard interface definition.

You change this definition before generating the sample application in the following ways:

• You must supply a value for any numeric parameters in the MACHINE clause. Each numeric parameter is marked with a question mark, and is preceded by a comment to say which machine parameter it is.

• You may change the set parameters to any finite number range that is a subset of *SCALAR* (0 to 2 147 483 646).

• You may delete operations from the OPERATIONS clause.

Once you have committed the interface definition, you can generate the sample application from it. The generation process:

• Creates and analyses several new machines, all of which are consistent, and need no proving.

• Creates and analyses the implementations of the machines. The implementations are correct implementations of the machines, and need no proving.

• Generates code from the implementations, and from the implementation of the original machine, if that has not already been done.

• Links the whole together into an executable object.

Once the generation process is complete, the sample application can be invoked for testing.

8.4.3 Running a sample application

You can run the sample application from the B-Toolkit's generators environment. The sample application offers you a menu of operations. Figure 8.6 shows the menu for *RRMan* with the cursor set for you to enter an operation number.

```
0 RRMan Menu

1 rec_alloc
2 is_any_free
3 rec_free
4 is_free
5 rec_backup
6 rec_restore

7 Quit

RRMan operation number? █
```

Figure 8.6   Menu for an operator interface.

When you select an operation, the sample application asks you for the inputs to the operation. There is some elementary type checking in the interface, but no checking of other preconditions. The sample application displays the outputs, and then asks you to make another selection. As execution progresses, the oldest lines are lost from the execution window, but you can always display the menu with option 0.

8.5 Summary and outlook

In this chapter we have learnt:

- how the design decisions studied in Chapter 7 can be recorded in implementations;
- the format of an implementation, and the restrictions on its construction;
- how to import library machines into an implementation;
- how to use the B-Toolkit to generate code from an analysed implementation;

• how to use the B-Toolkit to generate a sample application for a machine that has an analysed implementation.

We can now conduct a complete development from machine to C code, including a sample application for testing the functions of the machine.

8.6 Exercises

(8.1)   Construct an implementation of *Student_array* using an instance of the library machine *Varr*, which is one of the library machines in Appendix C. Draw the dependency diagram for the implementation.

(8.2)   Construct an implementation *CMA_imp_seq* of *CMA* using two instances of the library machine *Vseq* which is one of the library machines in Appendix C. Draw the dependency diagram for the implementation.

(8.3)   Construct an implementation *CMA_imp_arr* of *CMA* using *Student_array* and two counters *Enrol_Nvar* and *Test_Nvar* from the library machine *Nvar*. The retrieve relation is to be as follows: the set *tested* is to be the students in the cells of the array from 1 up to *Test_Nvar*, and the set *enrolled* is to be the students in the cells of the array from 1 up to *Enrol_Nvar*. Draw the dependency diagram for the implementation.

(8.4)   Construct an implementation of *Storman*, fixing the value of *maxblocks* at 1000 and using the numbers from 1 to 100 for the users.

Chapter 9
API-layer machines and their implementations

9.1 Machines at the API layer	**9.3 Using the string type**
9.2 Implementing API-layer machines	**9.4 Using complex data structures**

Summary: API-layer machines — animation — using the PROPERTIES clause — initialization — dependencies — strings — API-layer machine for the class manager's assistant — machine for student records — dependencies — complex data structures — system definitions — generated machines.

In this chapter we study the general form of machines in the API layer, and see how to implement them. We meet the string type, and explore the B-Toolkit's facilities for defining general data structures and generating machines and implementations that embody them.

9.1 Machines at the API layer

9.1.1 A robust recoverable resource manager

The requirement described informally in Table 5.1 on page 64 will be met by an API-layer machine *RRRMan* (robust recoverable resource manager). The specification at this level is typical of an API-layer machine: the syntax of the interface is precisely expressed, but the semantics is only informally described. A precise semantics could be supplied in abstract machine notation, or in a specification language like Z or VDM, but at the API layer this is not usual, unless formal verification of the application programs is desired.

We have chosen not to parameterize the machine *RRRMan*, but have used a SETS clause to introduce a deferred set *MYRESOURCE* and an enumerated set *RESPONSE*.

MACHINE

RRRMan

SETS

MYRESOURCE;
RESPONSE = {*success, nomorefree, alreadyfree*}

The machine has none of the clauses that create dependencies, so there are none. The machine has no variables, so there can be no invariant and no initialization. There is no state here, and the operations change nothing, merely accepting the correct number of inputs and outputs. However, the operations are not quite vacuous, and their specification provides important information about the interface.

The *allocate* operation has no inputs, and produces two outputs. The specification guarantees that *rr* will be a resource, and that *resp* will be *success* or *nomorefree*. The definition is a multiple substitution, but as there are no variables and no invariant, there is nothing to prove for invariant preservation. The individual substitutions are instances of choice-from-a-set.

```
rr, resp ⟵ allocate =
  BEGIN
    rr :∈ MYRESOURCE ||
    resp :∈ {success, nomorefree}
  END
```

The *deallocate* operation has only a trivial precondition to fix the type of the input *rr*. The output *resp* will be *success* or *alreadyfree*.

$$resp \longleftarrow deallocate\ (rr) =$$
$$\mathsf{PRE}$$
$$rr \in MYRESOURCE$$
$$\mathsf{THEN}$$
$$resp :\in \{success,\ alreadyfree\}$$
$$\mathsf{END}$$

As for *backup* and *restore*, since there is no model, and since they have neither inputs nor outputs, *skip* is the only specification that will do, since *skip* is the substitution that does nothing.

$$backup = skip$$

and

$$restore = skip$$

9.1.2 Proof obligations

Proof obligation generation for this machine produces no obligations.

9.1.3 Animation

Once this machine has been analysed, it can be animated, but the animation is not very interesting. The user is asked to resolve the non-determinism of the choice-from-a-set substitutions.

9.1.4 API-layer machines and full-function machines

The machine *RRRMan* just specified and the full-function machine *FFCMA* discussed in Chapter 6 stand at opposite ends of a spectrum of machines for the API layer. The function of *RRRMan* can be understood from the informal descriptions given in Table 5.1 on page 64. The function of *FFCMA* can be understood from the machine definition on page 87. The main practical difference between the two styles of specification is not in the user's understanding, but in the possibilities of formal reasoning about the properties of the machines.

With *RRRMan*, very little useful formal reasoning is possible. If you wished to develop an application with a formal specification that contained a state, you could use *RRRMan* to implement it, but you would not be able to verify your implementation.

With *FFCMA*, much formal reasoning is possible. The formal part of the specification contains a model that is rich enough to allow precise expression of all the informal ideas described in Table 3.1 on page 38. If you wished to develop an application with a formal specification that contained a state, you could use *FFCMA* to implement it, and you would be able to verify your implementation, if it were correct.

The choice of specification style for a machine at the API layer is dictated by external circumstances. If the requirements are for an API for applications that will not be formally specified, the style of *RRRMan* might be preferred, but if applications are formally specified, the API must be specified as a full-function machine like *FFCMA*. In between these extremes it is possible to define machines that contain state enough to guarantee only certain parts of their behaviour.

9.2 Implementing API-layer machines

9.2.1 The robust recoverable resource manager

The implementation *RRRManI* is to implement *RRRMan*. This implementation needs *TRUE* and *FALSE*, so it has a SEES clause that names the *Bool_TYPE* machine.

IMPLEMENTATION

   RRRManI

REFINES

   RRRMan

SEES

   Bool_TYPE

We import only the machine *RRMan*. Since *RRMan* has two parameters, we supply the set *MYRESOURCE* for the *RESOURCE* parameter and 100 for the *max_res* parameter.

The PROPERTIES clause explains that we have chosen to represent the resources by natural numbers in the range 1 to 100.

IMPORTS

   RRMan (*MYRESOURCE*, 100)

PROPERTIES

   $MYRESOURCE = 1 .. 100$

We need specify no constraints on *rfree* and *bkup.rfree*, and since the machine being refined had no variables, there is no retrieve relation. Therefore we need no INVARIANT clause in this implementation.

The INITIALISATION clause allows us to decide how the robust recoverable resource manager is to be initialized. The machine *RRRMan*, having no variables, gives us no guidance — it does not care what initialization we choose. The imported machines are initialized with *rfree* and *bkup.rfree* both empty, that is, with all the resources allocated. We could accept this if we wish, but have chosen to begin with all the resources free, and that means that initialization has work to do. We present the initialization substitution first, and then comment on its structure.

INITIALISATION

```
VAR
  nn
IN
  nn := 0 ;
  WHILE
    nn < 100
  DO
    nn := nn + 1 ;
    rec_free (nn)
  VARIANT
    100 − nn
  INVARIANT
    rfree = 1 .. nn ∧ nn ∈ ℕ ∧ nn ≤ 100
  END ;
  rec_backup
END
```

The loop invariant expresses the intention that the counter *nn* will represent the number of resources so far added to *rfree*. It also emphasizes the type of *nn*, and that *nn* will never exceed 100.

We choose an initialization of the loop to establish the invariant. We have to show that

$$[nn := 0] \ (rfree = 1 .. nn \land nn \in \mathbb{N} \land nn \leq 100)$$

Making the substitution gives

$$rfree = \varnothing \land 0 \in \mathbb{N} \land 0 \leq 100$$

The first conjunct is true because of the initialization of the imported machine, and the others are theorems of set theory and arithmetic.

Next we turn our attention to the while-test. The loop ends with the while-test false and the invariant true, so

$$\neg P \land Q \Rightarrow R$$

In this case we have a private intention to establish *rfree* = *MYRESOURCE*. Because *RRRMan* has no state and no initialization, the initialization of *RRRManI* could establish any predicate we choose, but we have chosen *rfree* = *MYRESOURCE*. We need to show that

$$\neg \mathbf{P} \wedge \textit{rfree} = 1 \mathrel{..} \textit{nn} \wedge \textit{nn} \in \mathbb{N} \wedge \textit{nn} \leq 100 \Rightarrow$$
$$\textit{rfree} = \textit{MYRESOURCE}$$

so by choosing *nn* ≠ 100 for **P** we get

$$\textit{nn} = 100 \wedge \textit{rfree} = 1 \mathrel{..} \textit{nn} \wedge \textit{nn} \in \mathbb{N} \wedge \textit{nn} \leq 100 \Rightarrow$$
$$\textit{rfree} = 1 \mathrel{..} 100$$

which is a simple result.

For the loop variant we choose $100 - nn$. Using the previously established notation we must show that

$$\mathbf{Q} \Rightarrow \mathbf{E} \in \mathbb{N}$$

In this case we do not need all the invariant in the antecedent, because

$$\textit{nn} \in \mathbb{N} \wedge \textit{nn} \leq 100 \Rightarrow 100 - \textit{nn} \in \mathbb{N}$$

To ensure loop termination, the loop body must decrease the variant. In this case the only part of the loop body that affects *nn* is the simple substitution $nn := nn + 1$, so we have to show that

$$\textit{rfree} = 1 \mathrel{..} \textit{nn} \wedge \textit{nn} \in \mathbb{N} \wedge \textit{nn} \leq 100 \wedge \textit{nn} \neq 100 \Rightarrow$$
$$[\textit{yy} := 100 - \textit{nn}] \, [\textit{nn} := \textit{nn} + 1] \, 100 - \textit{nn} < \textit{yy}$$

Applying the substitutions in the consequent gives

$$[\textit{yy} := 100 - \textit{nn}] \, 100 - (\textit{nn} + 1) < \textit{yy}$$

and then

$$100 - (\textit{nn} + 1) < 100 - \textit{nn}$$

which simplifies to

$$99 < 100$$

which is a theorem of arithmetic.

Lastly we have to satisfy the P-rule, and show that the loop body preserves the invariant. In this case we have

$$nn \neq 100 \wedge rfree = 1 .. nn \wedge nn \in \mathbb{N} \wedge nn \leq 100 \Rightarrow$$
$$[nn := nn + 1 \ ; \ rec\_free \ (nn)]$$
$$(rfree = 1 .. nn \wedge nn \in \mathbb{N} \wedge nn \leq 100)$$

Working on the consequent, we apply the sequence rule and replace *rec_free (nn)* by its definition.

$$[nn := nn + 1]$$
$$[\text{PRE } nn \in (1 .. 100 - rfree)$$
$$\text{THEN } rfree := rfree \cup \{nn\}$$
$$\text{END}] \ (rfree = 1 .. nn \wedge nn \in \mathbb{N} \wedge nn \leq 100)$$

Applying the PRE-THEN-END rule and making the substitution gives

$$[nn := nn + 1]$$
$$(nn \in (1 .. 100 - rfree) \wedge$$
$$rfree \cup \{nn\} = 1 .. nn \wedge$$
$$nn \in \mathbb{N} \wedge$$
$$nn \leq 100)$$

Now we make the last substitution to give

$$nn + 1 \in (1 .. 100 - rfree) \wedge$$
$$rfree \cup \{nn + 1\} = 1 .. nn + 1 \wedge$$
$$nn + 1 \in \mathbb{N} \wedge$$
$$nn + 1 \leq 100$$

To implement the *allocate* operation we introduce a local variable *ans*. The body of the pseudo-program is a sequence of substitutions. In the first, the local variable is used to hold the output of *is_any_free*, and in the second, an IF-THEN-ELSE substitution uses the values of the local variable to decide whether to use the *rec_alloc* operation of *RRMan* and return *success*, or to return *nomorefree*. When the response is *nomorefree*, we can return any value for *rr*, and in this case the value 1 is returned.

```
rr, resp ⟵ allocate =
  VAR
    ans
  IN
    ans ⟵ is_any_free ;
    IF
      ans = TRUE
    THEN
      resp := success ;
      rr ⟵ rec_alloc
    ELSE
```

$resp := nomorefree$;
$rr := 1$
  END
END

The *deallocate* operation is structured in the same way, but here we use the operation *is_free* of *RRMan* before freeing the input resource.

$resp \longleftarrow$ *deallocate* $(rr) =$
  VAR
   ans
  IN
   ans $\longleftarrow$ *is_free* (rr) ;
   IF
    $ans = FALSE$
   THEN
    rec_free (rr) ;
    $resp := success$
   ELSE
    $resp := alreadyfree$
   END
  END

The last two operations are the same as existing operations of *RRMan*.

$backup =$
  rec_backup

and

$restore =$
  rec_restore

Figure 9.1 illustrates the dependencies of this implementation.

9.3 Using the string type

9.3.1 A class manager's assistant with names

For our next example of an API-layer machine, we revisit the class manager's assistant. As well as making the interface robust, we shall fix the nature of the parametric set *STUDENT*. We shall use the names of students as the inputs to the operations that take inputs of type *STUDENT* and to do this we shall use the B-Toolkit library machine *String_TYPE*, whose definition is in Appendix C.

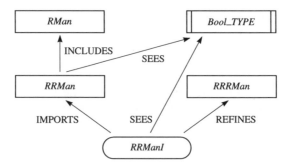

Figure 9.1 Dependency diagram for *RRRManI*.

The B-Toolkit supports the use of notations to represent the character literals of programming languages. In the abstract machine notation a **character** is a number in the range 0 to 255, and a **string** is a finite sequence of characters. There are no special notations for characters apart from the numbers 0 to 255, but strings can be specified in a familiar notation. Thus *"Artichoke"* is a sequence of natural numbers in the range 0 to 255 of length nine. The signs "" and "" are the **string delimiters**. The **empty string** is denoted by "". The correspondence between the character symbols and the natural numbers in the sequence is not defined in the B-Toolkit, but when code is generated from an implementation that contains such notations, the correspondence supported by the compiler becomes effective.

MACHINE

   CMA_names

SEES

   String_TYPE

As before, we need to introduce a set of responses as an enumerated set.

SETS

   CMA_RESPONSE =
   {already_enrolled,
   not_enrolled,
   already_tested,
   no_room,
   certificate,
   no_certificate,
   student_enrolled,

test_noted,
student_tested,
enrolled_but_not_tested}

The CONSTANTS and PROPERTIES clauses introduce two values that are of no significance in the machine itself, but will be used in the implementation.

CONSTANTS

max_students, name_length

PROPERTIES

max_students = 50 ∧ *name_length* = 25

The operations give only the barest information about the types of the inputs and outputs.

OPERATIONS

resp ⟵ *Enrol* (*name*) =
  PRE
    name ∈ *STRING* ∧
    size (*name*) ≤ *name_length*
  THEN
    resp :∈ *CMA_RESPONSE*
  END
;
resp ⟵ *Test* (*name*) =
  PRE
    name ∈ *STRING* ∧
    size (*name*) ≤ *name_length*
  THEN
    resp :∈ *CMA_RESPONSE*
  END
;
resp ⟵ *Leave* (*name*) =
  PRE
    name ∈ *STRING* ∧
    size (*name*) ≤ *name_length*
  THEN
    resp :∈ *CMA_RESPONSE*
  END
;

$resp \longleftarrow Enquire\ (name) =$
  PRE
    $name \in STRING \land$
    size $(name) \leq name\_length$
  THEN
    $resp :\in CMA\_RESPONSE$
  END

END

Figure 9.2 is the dependency diagram for this machine.

9.3.2 Implementing the class manager's assistant with names

When we defined the API-layer machine *CMA_names*, we said that the students were to be represented by strings, and it is in the implementation *CMA_names_imp* defined below that the identification will be made. In this implementation we will need to store the names of the enrolled students, that is, we need a database of strings, which is defined next.

We shall call the string database machine *Student_record*. It needs two parameters:

- the maximum number of strings we need to keep

- the maximum length of a string.

  MACHINE

    Student_record (max_recs, string_length)

  SEES

    String_TYPE, Bool_TYPE

The deferred set *STUDENT_RECORD* gives us tokens by which we can refer to the strings after they have been stored in the database.

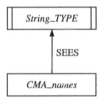

Figure 9.2 Dependency diagram for *CMA_names*.

SETS

STUDENT_RECORD

There are two variables:

- *student_file* is a relation between tokens and strings. Each string may be stored at most once in the database.

- *known_students* is the set of tokens for which we have strings stored in the database.

VARIABLES

student_file, known_students

INVARIANT

student_file $\in$ *known_students* $\rightarrowtail$ *STRING* $\land$
known_students $\subseteq$ *STUDENT_RECORD* $\land$
card (*known_students*) $\leq$ *max_recs* $\land$
$\forall ss$ • ($ss \in$ ran (*student_file*) $\Rightarrow$ size (ss) $\leq$ *string_length*)

We begin with no strings.

INITIALISATION

student_file, known_students $:= \varnothing, \varnothing$

There are few operations:

- *New* will take a string as input, and return a token to identify it. The user of the machine is responsible for making sure that the string is not already in the database, and for looking after the returned token.

- *Search* will take a string as input, say whether it is in the database, and return its token if it is.

- *Del* will take a valid token as input, and delete it and the corresponding string from the database.

OPERATIONS

$st \longleftarrow$ *New* (*name*) =
  PRE
    name $\in$ *STRING* $\land$
    size (*name*) $\leq$ *string_length* $\land$
    name $\notin$ ran (*student_file*) $\land$
    card (*known_students*) $<$ *max_recs*

```
    THEN
      ANY
        st1
      WHERE
        st1 ∈ STUDENT_RECORD − known_students
      THEN
        st := st1 ||
        known_students := known_students ∪ {st1} ||
        student_file (st1) := name
      END
    END
  ;
  ans, st ⟵ Search (nam) =
    PRE
      nam ∈ STRING
    THEN
      IF
        nam ∈ ran (student_file)
      THEN
        ans := TRUE ||
        st := student_file ⁻¹ (nam)
      ELSE
        ans := FALSE ||
        st :∈ STUDENT_RECORD
      END
    END
  ;
  Del (st) =
    PRE
      st ∈ known_students
    THEN
      known_students := known_students − {st} ||
      student_file := {st} ⊲ student_file
    END

END
```

Now we can present the implementation of *CMA_names*.

IMPLEMENTATION

   CMA_names_imp

REFINES

   CMA_names

SEES

String_TYPE, Bool_TYPE

We build up the state of the implementation from *Student_record*, which looks after the strings, and from *CMA*, which uses the tokens from *STUDENT_RECORD* to represent the students.

IMPORTS

CMA (max_students, STUDENT_RECORD),
Student_record (max_students, name_length)

Since *CMA_names* has no state, the invariant is only about the variables of the imported machines. The *enrolled* set in *CMA* will be kept in step with *known_students*, the set of strings in *Student_record*.

INVARIANT

enrolled = known_students

OPERATIONS

```
resp ⟵ Enrol (name) =
  VAR
    os, st, fn, cm, sf
  IN
    cm, sf ⟵ howmany ;
    IF
      cm = sf
    THEN
      resp := no_room
    ELSE
      fn, os ⟵ Search (name) ;
      IF
        fn = TRUE
      THEN
        resp := already_enrolled
      ELSE
        st ⟵ New (name) ;
        enrol (st);
        resp := student_enrolled
      END
    END
  END
  ;
```

```
resp ⟵ Test (name) =
VAR
  st, fn, ft
IN
  fn, st ⟵ Search (name) ;
  IF
    fn = FALSE
  THEN
    resp := not_enrolled
  ELSE
    ft ⟵ istested (st) ;
    IF
      ft = TRUE
    THEN
      resp := already_tested
    ELSE
      test (st) ;
      resp := test_noted
    END
  END
END
;
resp ⟵ Leave (name) =
VAR
  st, fn, ft
IN
  fn, st ⟵ Search (name) ;
  IF
    fn = FALSE
  THEN
    resp := not_enrolled
  ELSE
    ft ⟵ istested (st) ;
    IF
      ft = TRUE
    THEN
      resp := certificate
    ELSE
      resp := no_certificate
    END
    ;
    leave (st) ;
    Del (st)
  END
END
```

```
;
resp ⟵ Enquire (name) =
   VAR
     st, fn, ft
   IN
     fn, st ⟵ Search (name) ;
     IF
       fn = FALSE
     THEN
       resp := not_enrolled
     ELSE
       ft ⟵ istested (st) ;
       IF
         ft = TRUE
       THEN
         resp := student_tested
       ELSE
         resp := enrolled_but_not_tested
       END
     END
   END
```

END

Figure 9.3 is the dependency diagram for this implementation.

9.4 Using complex data structures

We now study machines whose implementations need complex data structures. The B-Toolkit allows you to define a data structure, and to generate a machine whose state is the data structure, and whose operations are all the operations you need to handle it.

We begin with a simple example of a requirement only slightly more complicated that the requirement met by *CMA_names*. We shall present:

- the informal requirement

- an API-layer machine for the requirement

- a definition of the data structure required to implement it

- an outline of the machine generated by the B-Toolkit from the data structure definition

- an implementation of the API-layer machine that imports the generated machine.

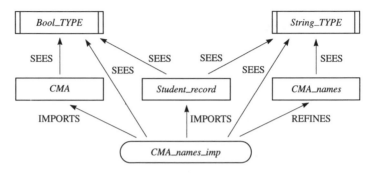

Figure 9.3 Dependency diagram for *CMA_names_imp*.

9.4.1 Informal requirement

The requirement is for a customer database that will be part of a banking system (See Table 9.1). Each customer has a number, a name and perhaps a credit rating.

Table 9.1 Informal state machine for a customer database.

Inputs	Processing	Outputs
Add a new customer		
number name	If the number is already in use, the response is 'Customer number in use'. If there is no room to add another customer, the response is 'No room'. Otherwise the customer number and name are stored in the database, and the response is 'Customer added'. The newly created customer record has no credit rating.	response
Add (or change) a credit rating		
number rating	If the customer number is not in the database, the response is 'Customer not found'. If there is no room to add a credit rating, the response is 'No room'. Otherwise the customer's record is updated by adding or changing the credit rating, and the response is 'Credit rating noted'.	response

Inputs	Processing	Outputs
Display customer details		

Inputs	Processing	Outputs
number	If the customer number is not in the database, the response is 'Customer not found'. Otherwise the customer's number and name are displayed. If the customer has a credit rating, it is displayed, and the response is 'Credit displayed'; but if there is no credit rating, the response is 'No credit displayed'.	response number name rating

Initially there are no records in the database.

You might think that this machine should have more operations, and you will be invited to supply some in the exercises.

9.4.2 The API-layer machine

The following API-layer machine is suggested for this informal state machine.

MACHINE

    CustomersAPI

DEFINITIONS

    $CUSTNAM == \{ss \mid ss \in STRING \wedge \text{size}(ss) \le 32\}$

SEES

    String_TYPE

SETS

    CUSTNO;
    $CUSTRESP = \{customer\_number\_in\_use,$
    no_room, customer_added, customer_not_found,
    credit_rating_noted, credit_displayed,
    no_credit_displayed}

OPERATIONS

    resp ⟵ *add_customer* (*custno, custnam*) =
      PRE
        $custno \in CUSTNO \wedge$
        $custnam \in CUSTNAM$

```
        THEN
          resp :∈ {customer_number_in_use,
          no_room, customer_added}
        END
      ;
      resp ⟵ add_cred (custno, custcred) =
        PRE
          custno ∈ CUSTNO ∧
          custcred ∈ 0 .. 100
        THEN
          resp :∈ {customer_not_found,
          no_room, credit_rating_noted}
        END
      ;
      resp, custnam, custcred ⟵ display_cust (custno) =
        PRE
          custno ∈ CUSTNO
        THEN
          resp :∈ {customer_not_found,
          credit_displayed, no_credit_displayed} ||
          custnam :∈ CUSTNAM ||
          custcred :∈ 0 .. 100
        END

    END
```

The DEFINITIONS clause fixes the type of customer names as strings of length up to 32. The type of customer number is the deferred set *CUSTNO*. Credit ratings are natural numbers in the range 1 to 100.

9.4.3 Informal approach to implementation

To implement this machine we propose to use a database consisting of a set of numbers (for customer numbers) and a set of records (for customer records). Each record will contain a customer number and a customer name, and some records might contain a credit rating. We have chosen to represent customer numbers by natural numbers. Figure 9.4 on page 175 shows a typical state of the database.

Customer number 173 is allocated to M. A. Ward, who has a credit rating of 50. Customer number 9587 is allocated to H. J. H. Sutcliffe, who has no credit rating. Customer number 530 is allocated to S. D. Hammett, who has a credit rating of 85.

cnum	173
cnam	M. A. Ward
ccred	50

cnum	9587
cnam	H. J. H. Sutcliffe

cnum	530
cnam	S. D. Hammett
ccred	85

Figure 9.4 Records in the customer database.

9.4.4 Defining the data structure

The **system definition** is the B-Toolkit construct for defining data structures for implementations. The definition consists of:

- a **SYSTEM clause**, which names the definition
- an **IS clause**, which contains the data structure definition
- an END clause, which ends the definition.

Figure 9.5 shows the system definition for the database described informally above.

The **GLOBAL part** defines the components of the system definition. We define:

- *customers*, a set of numbers for the customer numbers. We have chosen 100 as the maximum number of customer numbers that we need to store in the database.

- *custdb*, a set of database records for the customer records. We have chosen 100 for the maximum number of customer records that we need to store in the database. The contents of a database record are elaborated in the **BASE part**.

The keywords NAT and SET are two of a number of type constructors that can be used in the GLOBAL section. Other possibilities are explained later.

The BASE part has a **MANDATORY section** and an **OPTIONAL section**. In the MANDATORY section we define the two mandatory fields:

SYSTEM

CustomersDB

IS

```
GLOBAL
  customers : SET (NAT) [100] ;
  custdb : SET (custrec) [100]
END ;
BASE
  custrec
MANDATORY
  cnum : NAT ;
  cnam : STRING [32]
OPTIONAL
  ccred : NAT
END
```

END

Figure 9.5 System definition for the customer database.

- *cnum* is a number for the customer number

- *cnam* is a string for the customer name.

The keyword STRING is another type constructor we can use in system definitions.

In the OPTIONAL section we define the optional field *ccred*, a number for the credit rating.

9.4.5 Generating the machine

The B-Toolkit's **base generator** operates in two stages. In the first stage, the tool produces a list of all possible operations on the data structure you have defined in the system definition. You are unlikely to need all the operations provided, so at the end of the first stage you can delete operations from the list. In the second stage the tool produces the machine for the data structure, and a correct implementation of it.

The generated machine has the same name as the system definition from which it was generated. In the model of the generated machine, the database records are represented by **abstract objects**. These abstract objects are drawn from *custrec_ABSOBJ*, which is a

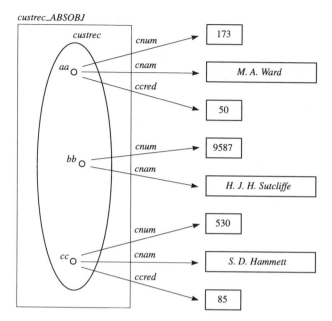

Figure 9.6 State of the generated machine.

deferred set of the machine. Each of the fields of the record is modelled by a function that relates abstract objects to the corresponding
numbers and strings. *custrec*, which was the type of records in the
database, becomes a set of abstract objects. Figure 9.6 shows the
state of the generated machine that corresponds to the state illustrated in Figure 9.4.

In this case there are three abstract objects in *custrec*, and we have
called them *aa*, *bb* and *cc*. The function *cnum*, relating abstract
objects to customer numbers, is

$$\{aa \mapsto 173, bb \mapsto 9587, cc \mapsto 530\}$$

The function *cnam*, relating abstract objects to customer names, is

$$\{aa \mapsto \text{"M. A. Ward"}, bb \mapsto \text{"H. J. H. Sutcliffe"},$$
$$cc \mapsto \text{"S. D. Hammett"}\}$$

The function *ccred*, relating abstract objects to credit ratings, is

$$\{aa \mapsto 50, cc \mapsto 85\}$$

9.4.6 The operations of the generated machine

The generated machine *CustomersDB* has operations to change and enquire on *customers*, the set of customer numbers, and on *custdb*, the set of abstract objects representing the customer records in the database. In addition there are operations for creating, destroying and updating the fields in the records identified by the abstract objects. There are far more operations provided than we need to implement *CustomersAPI*, so we concentrate on the few that we need here and in the exercises.

The operation to add a member to the set *customers* is as follows:

```
rep ⟵ add_customers (nat) =
  PRE
    nat ∈ SCALAR
  THEN
    CHOICE
      customers := customers ∪ {nat} ||
      rep := TRUE
    OR
      resp := FALSE
    END
  END
```

The B-Toolkit library type *SCALAR* (0 to 2 147 483 646) is used for the components that were declared with the keyword NAT in the system definitions. Operations that add things are always cast in the non-deterministic form illustrated above. Either the operation works, and the response is *TRUE*, or it fails, and the response is *FALSE*.

The operation to delete a member of *customers* is as follows:

```
del_customers (nat) =
  PRE
    nat ∈ customers
  THEN
    customers := customers − {nat}
  END
```

The operation to report whether a number is a customer number is as follows:

```
rep ⟵ member_customers (nat) =
  PRE
    nat ∈ SCALAR
  THEN
    rep := bool (nat ∈ customers)
  END
```

The operation to add a customer record to the database is as follows:

```
rep ⟵ add_custdb (Elem_custrec) =
  PRE
    Elem_custrec ∈ custrec
  THEN
    CHOICE
      custdb := custdb ∪ {Elem_custrec} ||
      rep := TRUE
    OR
      rep := FALSE
    END
  END
```

The operation to delete a customer record from the database is as follows:

```
del_custdb (Elem_custrec) =
  PRE
    Elem_custrec ∈ custdb
  THEN
    custdb := custdb − {Elem_custrec}
  END
```

The operation to create a customer record is as follows:

```
rep, Base_custrec ⟵ make_custrec (Val_cnum) =
  PRE
    Val_cnum ∈ SCALAR ∧
    card (custrec) < max_custrec
  THEN
    CHOICE
      ANY
        Base_custrecx, loc
      WHERE
        Base_custrecx ∈ custrec_ABSOBJ − custrec ∧
        loc ∈ 1 .. card (custrec) + 1 ⤖ custrec ∪ {Base_custrecx}
      THEN
        custrec := custrec ∪ {Base_custrecx} ||
        cnum (Base_custrecx) := Val_cnum ||
        cnam (Base_custrecx) := [] ||
        Base_custrec := Base_custrecx ||
        locate_custrec := loc ||
        rep := TRUE
      END
```

```
    OR
      ANY
        Base_custrecx
      WHERE
        Base_custrecx ∈ custrec_ABSOBJ
      THEN
        Base_custrec := Base_custrecx ||
        rep := FALSE
      END
    END
  END
```

The operation to destroy a customer record is as follows:

```
kill_custrec (Base_custrec) =
  PRE
    Base_custrec ∈ custrec
  THEN
    custrec := custrec − {Base_custrec} ||
    cnum := {Base_custrec} ◁ cnum ||
    cnam := {Base_custrec} ◁ cnam ||
    ccred := {Base_custrec} ◁ ccred ||
    locate_custrec :∈ 1 .. card (custrec − {Base_custrec}) ↣
    custrec − {Base_custrec}
  END
```

The operation to find out how many customer records thefe are is as follows:

```
tot ⟵ nbr_custrec =
  BEGIN
    tot := card (custrec)
  END
```

The operation to find the customer record for a particular customer number is as follows:

```
rep, Base_custrec ⟵ key_search_cnum (nat) =
  PRE
    nat ∈ SCALAR
  THEN
    IF
      nat ∈ ran (cnum)
```

```
THEN
  ANY
    Base_custrecx
  WHERE
    Base_custrecx ∈ custrec ∧ cnum (Base_custrecx) = nat
  THEN
    Base_custrec := Base_custrecx | |
    rep := TRUE
  END
ELSE
  Base_custrec :∈ custrec_ABSOBJ | |
  rep := FALSE
END
END
```

If there are several customer records with the input customer number, the operation will pick one of them. In the design we use for *CustomersAPI*, we ensure that there is only one record.

The operation to find the customer name for a customer record is as follows:

```
Str ⟵ xtr_cnam (Base_custrec) =
PRE
  Base_custrec ∈ custrec
THEN
  Str := cnam (Base_custrec)
END
```

The operation to change the customer name in a customer record is as follows:

```
rep ⟵ mod_cnam (Base_custrec, Str) =
PRE
  Base_custrec ∈ custrec ∧
  Str ∈ STRING
THEN
  CHOICE
    cnam (Base_custrec) := Str | |
    rep := TRUE
  OR
    rep := FALSE
  END
END
```

The operation to add a credit rating to a record that has not got one already is as follows:

cre_ccred ($Base\_custrec, nat$) =
  PRE
    $Base\_custrec \in custrec -$ dom ($ccred$) $\wedge nat \in SCALAR$
  THEN
    $ccred$ ($Base\_custrec$) := nat
  END

The operation to find out whether a record has got a credit rating is as follows:

$rep \longleftarrow def\_ccred$ ($Base\_custrec$) =
  PRE
    $Base\_custrec \in custrec$
  THEN
    rep := bool ($Base\_custrec \in$ dom ($ccred$))
  END

The operation to find the credit rating in a record that has a credit rating is as follows:

$nat \longleftarrow val\_ccred$ ($Base\_custrec$) =
  PRE
    $Base\_custrec \in$ dom ($ccred$)
  THEN
    nat := $ccred$ ($Base\_custrec$)
  END

The operation to change the credit rating in a record that has a credit rating is as follows:

mod_ccred ($Base\_custrec, nat$) =
  PRE
    $Base\_custrec \in$ dom ($ccred$) $\wedge nat \in SCALAR$
  THEN
    $ccred$ ($Base\_custrec$) := nat
  END

9.4.7 Implementing the API-layer machine

The implementation of *CustomersAPI* needs a SEES clause that mentions all the library machines for the types used in the *CustomersDB* machine: *String_TYPE*, *Scalar_TYPE* and *Bool_TYPE*. The SEES clause must also mention the machine *CustomersDBCtx* that is generated to define the deferred set of abstract objects *custrec_ABSOBJ*. It imports the generated machine *CustomersDB*.

IMPLEMENTATION

CustomersAPI_imp

REFINES

CustomersAPI

SEES

String_TYPE,
Scalar_TYPE,
Bool_TYPE,
CustomersDBCtx

IMPORTS

CustomersDB (100)

In the PROPERTIES clause we fix the value of the deferred set *CUSTNO*.

PROPERTIES

$CUSTNO = 1 .. 999999$

We add an invariant to say that we intend the set *customers* to be exactly the set of customer numbers appearing in the database records.

INVARIANT

customers = ran (*cnum*)

The implementation of *add_customer* shows the style of programming needed with machines generated from system definitions. There is a lot of work to do sorting out the error cases, and since many of the operations can fail unpredictably, there is a lot of backtracking to do. The operation is presented in full, and there are explanatory notes afterwards.

```
resp ⟵ add_customer (custno, custnam) =
  VAR
    knowncust, canmake, canaddcust, canadddb,
    canaddnam, numcustrec, maderec
  IN
    numcustrec ⟵ nbr_custrec ;                        (1)
    knowncust ⟵ member_customers (custno) ;           (2)
```

```
IF
  numcustrec = 100
THEN
  resp := no_room                                        (3)
ELSIF
  knowncust = TRUE
THEN
  resp := customer_number_in_use                         (4)
ELSE
  canmake, maderec ⟵  make_custrec (custno) ;            (5)
  IF
    canmake = FALSE
  THEN
    resp := no_room                                      (6)
  ELSE
    canaddnam ⟵  mod_cnam (maderec, custnam) ;           (7)
    IF
      canaddnam = FALSE
    THEN
      resp := no_room ;                                  (8)
      kill_custrec (maderec)
    ELSE
      canaddcust ⟵  add_customers (custno) ;             (9)
      IF
        canaddcust = FALSE
      THEN
        resp := no_room ;                                (10)
        kill_custrec (maderec)
      ELSE
        canadddb ⟵  add_custdb (maderec) ;               (11)
        IF
          canadddb = FALSE
        THEN
          resp := no_room ;                              (12)
          kill_custrec (maderec) ;
          del_customers (custno)
        ELSE
          resp := customer_added                         (13)
        END
      END
    END
  END
END
END
```

(1) We find out how many customer records there are already.

(2) We find out if the customer number is already in use.

(3) If there are 100 records, the response is *no_room*.

(4) If the customer number is already in use, the response is *customer_number_in_use*.

(5) We make a new customer record. The output *canmake* tells us whether the operation succeeds. If *canmake* is *TRUE*, *maderec* is the abstract object for the new record.

(6) If we cannot make a customer record, the response is *no_room*.

(7) If the record is made, we try to put the customer name into the record. (A newly created record has a null string for the customer name.) The output *canaddnam* tells use whether the operation succeeds.

(8) If we cannot add the name, the response is *no_room*.

(9) If we can add the name, we try to add the customer number. This is another operation with feedback.

(10) If we cannot add the customer number, the response is *no_room*, and we destroy the customer record created in (5).

(11) We try to add the record, now complete, to the database.

(12) If we fail, the response is *no_room*, and we destroy the customer record, and remove the customer number from *customers*.

(13) If we succeed, the response is *customer_added*.

The implementation of *display_cust* begins by searching the database for the input customer number. If the number is not found, we use *CPY_STR*, an operation of the library machine *String_TYPE*, to set the output *custnam* to the null string. (The machine allows any member of *CUSTNAM* as output in this case.)

```
resp, custnam, custcred ⟵ display_cust (custno) =
  VAR
    knownrec, foundrec, hascred
  IN
    knownrec, foundrec ⟵ key_search_cnum (custno);
    IF
      knownrec = FALSE
```

```
        THEN
          resp := customer_not_found ;
          custnam ⟵ CPY_STR ("") ;
          custcred := 0
        ELSE
          custnam ⟵ xtr_cnam (foundrec) ;
          hascred ⟵ def_ccred (foundrec) ;
          IF
            hascred = TRUE
          THEN
            resp := credit_displayed ;
            custcred ⟵ val_ccred (foundrec)
          ELSE
            resp := no_credit_displayed ;
            custcred := 0
          END
        END
      END
```

9.4.8 System definitions

In the GLOBAL part of the system definition you declare any number of components. The types allowed for the components are as follows:

- STRING [n] for a string of length up to **n**;

- SEQ (T) [n] for a sequence of values of type defined by **T** with a maximum length of **n**;

- SET (T) [n] for a set of values of type defined by **T** with a maximum size of **n**.

n must be a number. The type **T** can be any of the following:

- NAT, meaning the B-Toolkit library type *SCALAR*;

- the name of a BASE part in this system definition;

- any other name spelled entirely in uppercase letters, meaning a user-defined type that will be a parameter of the generated machine.

A system definition can have any number of BASE parts. In a BASE part you specify first the name of the base being defined, then list the mandatory and optional fields in the MANDATORY and OPTIONAL sections.

In the MANDATORY and OPTIONAL sections, you declare any number of components. The types allowed for the components are as follows:

- STRING [**n**] for a string of length up to **n**;

- SEQ (**T**) [**n**] for a sequence of values of type defined by **T** with a maximum length of **n**;

- SET (**T**) [**n**] for a set of values of type defined by **T** with a maximum size of **n**;

- NAT, meaning the B-Toolkit library type *SCALAR*;

- the name of a BASE part in this system definition;

- any other name spelled entirely in uppercase letters, meaning a user-defined type that will be a parameter of the generated machine.

The meanings of **n** and **T** are as described above for the GLOBAL part.

9.4.9 Generated machines

The generation process produces two machines, the **principal machine** and the **context machine**. If the name of the system definition is **s**, the name of the principal machine is **s**, and the name of the context machine is **s***Ctx*.

The context machine contains a MACHINE clause, a SETS clause and an END clause. The SETS clause contains a deferred set of abstract objects for each BASE part of the system definition. If the name of the base part is **b**, the name of the deferred set is **b**_*ABSOBJ*.

In the MACHINE clause of the principal machine, the name of the machine is the same as the name of the system definition from which it is generated. The parameters of the generated machine are:

- a numeric parameter of the form *max*_**b**, where **b** is the name of a BASE part in the system definition. There is one such parameter for each BASE part.

- a set parameter for each user-defined type.

The CONSTRAINTS clause contains a conjunct for each of the numeric parameters. Each parameter is constrained to be a member of *SCALAR* that is greater than zero.

The SEES clause mentions those library machines that provide the basic types used in the generated machine: *Scalar_TYPE* if the NAT keyword is used, *String_TYPE* if the STRING keyword is used, and *Bool_TYPE*. The SEES clause also mentions the context machine.

The VARIABLES and INVARIANT clauses define the model for the generated machine. The model contains a variable for each name in the GLOBAL part, for each name of a BASE part, and for each name in the MANDATORY and OPTIONAL sections of each BASE part. The names of the variables are the same as the names used in the system definition. Their types are described in Tables 9.2 and 9.3. In these tables, **b** and $\mathbf{b}_1$ are the names of BASE parts, and **u** is the name of a user-defined type.

Table 9.2 Types of names declared in a GLOBAL part.

Declaration	Model
STRING	*STRING*
SEQ (NAT)	seq (*SCALAR*)
SEQ (**b**)	seq (**b**_*ABSOBJ*)
SEQ (**u**)	seq (**u**)
SET (NAT)	$\mathbb{P}$ (*SCALAR*)
SET (**b**)	$\mathbb{P}$ (**b**_*ABSOBJ*)
SET (**u**)	$\mathbb{P}$ (**u**)

Table 9.3 Types of names declared in a MANDATORY section.

Declaration	Model
STRING	**b** $\rightarrow$ *STRING*
SEQ (NAT)	**b** $\rightarrow$ seq (*SCALAR*)
SEQ ($\mathbf{b}_1$)	**b** $\rightarrow$ seq ($\mathbf{b}_1$_*ABSOBJ*)
SEQ (**u**)	**b** $\rightarrow$ seq (**u**)
SET (NAT)	**b** $\rightarrow$ $\mathbb{P}$ (*SCALAR*)
SET ($\mathbf{b}_1$)	**b** $\rightarrow$ $\mathbb{P}$ ($\mathbf{b}_1$_*ABSOBJ*)
SET (**u**)	**b** $\rightarrow$ $\mathbb{P}$ (**u**)
NAT	**b** $\rightarrow$ *SCALAR*
$\mathbf{b}_1$	**b** $\rightarrow$ $\mathbf{b}_1$_*ABSOBJ*
u	**b** $\rightarrow$ **u**

The dimensions given in the system definition are not used in the generated machine, though they are used in its implementation to make sure that the structures allocated are big enough to hold the data.

The name **b** of a BASE section appears in the model as a variable with type $\mathbb{P}$ (**b**_*ABSOBJ*). A second variable *locate_*b is associated with each name **b** of a BASE section. The type of this variable is

1 .. card (**b**) $\rightarrowtail$ **b**

which is an injective sequence of all the values in the set **b**. It is used in the operations of the generated machine that allow you to browse the records.

Names declared in the OPTIONAL section are modelled by partial functions like those used for names in the MANDATORY section.

9.5 Summary and outlook

In this chapter we have learnt:

- how to write machines for the API layer;
- how to implement API-layer machines using component-layer machines;
- how to use the string type provided as a B-Toolkit library machine;
- how to write a system definition for a complex data structure;
- how to use a generated machine in an implementation.

9.6 Exercises

(9.1)   Construct an API-layer machine *RCMA* for the class manager's assistant using *RRRMan* as a model.

(9.2)   Construct an implementation of *RCMA* using *CMA* as an imported machine.

(9.3)   Construct an API-layer machine *OTCSAPI* for the oil terminal control system described informally in Table 1.1 on page 7. Make *TANKER* and *BERTH* deferred sets for this machine, and define *OTCS_RESP* as the enumerated set of responses.

(9.4)   Construct an implementation *OTCSAPI_imp* of *OTCSAPI*. Fix *TANKER* as 1 .. 10000 and *BERTH* as 1 .. 5.

(9.5)   Write an implementation of *Student_record* using the library machine *str_obj*. (Because *str_obj* offers no means of searching on the strings stored in it, you will need to keep the tokens that are in use in an instance of the library machine *set*. The operation *VAL_SET* of this machine allows you to access the stored tokens one by one.)

(9.6)   Write an implementation of the operation *add_cred* of the machine *CustomersAPI*.

(9.7)   Add an operation to *CustomersAPI* to delete a customer record. The input is a customer number. The response is 'Customer not found' or 'Customer deleted'. Write an implementation of the operation.

(9.8)   Write an informal description of an operation to change the customer name associated with a customer number in *CustomersAPI*. Write an implementation of the operation.

Chapter 10
Refinements

10.1 What is a refinement?	**10.3 Implementing a refinement**
10.2 Refining the class	
manager's assistant	

Summary: Refinements — REFINEMENT clause — REFINES clause — VARIABLES clause — INVARIANT clause — initialization and its correctness — operations and their correctness — implementing a refinement.

In this chapter we look at how refinements can be used as intermediate constructs between machines and implementations.

10.1 What is a refinement?

In developing implementations from machines there are two distinct transformations that are made. The data design part of the transformation uses variables of the imported machines to represent the abstract variables of the machine being refined. The algorithm design part of the transformation uses the algorithms of the implementation to give effect to the substitutions of the machine. These two transformations give rise to a number of proof obligations whose complexity depends on the nature of the representation and algorithms used. A **refinement** is an abstract machine that can mediate between machine and implementation, and can allow the two transformations to be separated. There are now two lots of correctness conditions to be dealt with, correctness of refinement with respect to machine and correctness of implementation with respect to refinement, but the complexity of the correctness conditions is much reduced if the refinement is well chosen.

10.2 Refining the class manager's assistant

We now look at a refinement that records a data design for *CMA*. Informally we propose to use two disjoint sets *both* and *only* to represent the sets *tested* and *enrolled*. The set *both* represents the set *tested* directly, while *only* represents the set of students that are enrolled but not tested. A subsequent implementation will use two instances of a set from the library.

The refinement is introduced by a **REFINEMENT clause**, which names the refinement. The REFINES clause names the machine that is being refined, and the SEES clause introduces *Bool_TYPE*.

REFINEMENT

CMA_refined

REFINES

CMA

SEES

Bool_TYPE

The VARIABLES clause introduces the variables of the data representation.

VARIABLES

only, both

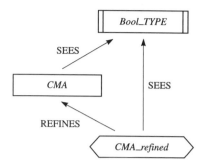

Figure 10.1 Dependencies of a refinement.

Refinements have dependencies that are determined in the same way as the dependencies of a machine and the dependencies of an implementation. The dependencies of this refinement are illustrated in Figure 10.1.

We shall use boxes with pointed ends to represent refinements.

The INVARIANT clause of a refinement has two functions:

- To specify the types of the variables of the refinement, and any constraints that they must satisfy.

- To specify the data design, that is, how the variables of the machine being refined are represented by the variables of the refinement. This is the retrieve relation.

You can supplement the invariant with an ASSERTIONS clause. The predicate in the ASSERTIONS clause of a refinement must be provable from the invariant of the machine being refined and the invariant of the refinement. There is a proof obligation to prove it. The assertions appear in the antecedent of the other proof obligations.

The first two conjuncts fix the types of *only* and *both*. The next conjunct expresses the intention that these sets should be disjoint. The last two conjuncts are the retrieve relation, and they formalize what was expressed informally above.

INVARIANT

$only \subseteq STUDENT \land$
$both \subseteq STUDENT \land$
$only \cap both = \emptyset \land$
$enrolled = only \cup both \land$
$tested = both$

10.2.1 Initializing the refinement

In the INITIALISATION clause we explain how the variables of the refinement are to be initialized. The initialization chosen must conform to the initialization of the variables of *CMA* when viewed through the retrieve relation, so there is a proof obligation here.

INITIALISATION

  only, both := ∅, ∅

10.2.2 Verifying the initialization

First we state the obligation in general, and then apply it to this example. If G_M is the initialization of the machine, G_R the initialization of the refinement, and P_R the invariant of the refinement, we must show that

$$[G_R] \neg [G_M] \neg P_R$$

In this example we have to show the following:

  [*only, both* := ∅, ∅]
  ¬[*tested, enrolled* := ∅, ∅]
  ¬(*only* ⊆ *STUDENT* ∧
  both ⊆ *STUDENT* ∧
  only ∩ *both* = ∅ ∧
  enrolled = *only* ∪ *both* ∧
  tested = *both*)

Making the first substitution gives the following:

  [*only, both* := ∅, ∅]
  ¬¬(*only* ⊆ *STUDENT* ∧
  both ⊆ *STUDENT* ∧
  only ∩ *both* = ∅ ∧
  ∅ = *only* ∪ *both* ∧
  ∅ = *both*)

Using the law of double negation and making the remaining substitution gives the following:

  ∅ ⊆ *STUDENT* ∧
  ∅ ⊆ *STUDENT* ∧
  ∅ ∩ ∅ = ∅ ∧
  ∅ = ∅ ∪ ∅ ∧
  ∅ = ∅

The conjuncts here are all theorems of set theory.

10.2.3 Operations of the refinement

In the OPERATIONS clause we rewrite the operations of the machine in terms of the variables of the refinement. The names of the operations and the numbers and types of inputs and outputs must be the same in the refinement as they were in the machine being refined. The B-Toolkit provides an operation to generate a template of a refinement for an analysed machine. None of the operations need preconditions, since the preconditions of the abstract operations are enough to guarantee that the operations of the refinement will preserve the invariant of the refinement.

OPERATIONS

```
enrol (st) =
  BEGIN
    only := only ∪ {st}
  END
;
ans ⟵ isenrolled (st) =
  BEGIN
    ans := bool (st ∈ only ∨ st ∈ both)
  END
;
test (st) =
  BEGIN
    only := only − {st} ||
    both := both ∪ {st}
  END
;
ans ⟵ istested (st) =
  BEGIN
    ans := bool (st ∈ both)
  END
;
leave (st) =
  BEGIN
    only := only − {st} ||
    both := both − {st}
  END
;
clmax, sofar ⟵ howmany =
  BEGIN
    clmax := class_size ||
    sofar := card (only) + card (both)
  END
```

Like other abstract machines, a refinement ends with an END clause.

10.2.4 Verifying the operations

First we state the obligation in general, and then apply it to the operation *test*. If P_M is the invariant of the machine, P_R the invariant of the refinement, Q_M the precondition of the machine operation, Q_R the precondition of the refinement operation, H_M the then-part of the machine operation, and H_R the then-part of the refinement operation, we must show that

$$P_M \wedge P_R \wedge Q_M \Rightarrow Q_R \wedge [H_R] \neg [H_M] \neg P_R$$

In the case of the operation *test*, we have to show that

> *enrolled* ⊆ *STUDENT* ∧
> *tested* ⊆ *STUDENT* ∧
> *tested* ⊆ *enrolled* ∧
> card (*enrolled*) ≤ *class_size* ∧
> *only* ⊆ *STUDENT* ∧
> *both* ⊆ *STUDENT* ∧
> *only* ∩ *both* = Ø ∧
> *enrolled* = *only* ∪ *both* ∧
> *tested* = *both* ∧
> *st* ∈ *enrolled* ∧
> *st* ∉ *tested*
> ⇒
> [*only, both* := *only* − {*st*}, *both* ∪ {*st*}]
> ¬[*tested* := *tested* ∪ {*st*}]
> ¬(*only* ⊆ *STUDENT* ∧
>   *both* ⊆ *STUDENT* ∧
>   *only* ∩ *both* = Ø ∧
>   *enrolled* = *only* ∪ *both* ∧
>   *tested* = *both*)

Making the first substitution gives the following:

> [*only, both* := *only* − {*st*}, *both* ∪ {*st*}]
> ¬¬(*only* ⊆ *STUDENT* ∧
>   *both* ⊆ *STUDENT* ∧
>   *only* ∩ *both* = Ø ∧
>   *enrolled* = *only* ∪ *both* ∧
>   *tested* = *both*)

Using the law of double negation and making the remaining substitution gives the following:

$$only - \{st\} \subseteq STUDENT \wedge$$
$$both \cup \{st\} \subseteq STUDENT \wedge$$
$$(only - \{st\}) \cap (both \cup \{st\}) = \emptyset \wedge$$
$$enrolled = (only - \{st\}) \cup (both \cup \{st\}) \wedge$$
$$tested \cup \{st\} = both \cup \{st\}$$

The conjuncts here follow from the antecedent by theorems of set theory.

10.2.5 Verifying operations with outputs

When an operation has outputs, the verification condition is slightly different. As before, supposing that P_M is the invariant of the machine, P_R the invariant of the refinement, Q_M the precondition of the machine operation, Q_R the precondition of the refinement operation, H_M the then-part of the machine operation, H_R the then-part of the refinement operation, and **y** the output of the operation, then we must show that

$$\mathbf{P_M} \wedge \mathbf{P_R} \wedge \mathbf{Q_M} \Rightarrow \mathbf{Q_R} \wedge [\mathbf{H'_R}] \neg [\mathbf{H_M}] \neg (\mathbf{P_R} \wedge \mathbf{y'} = \mathbf{y})$$

where $\mathbf{H'_R}$ is the same as $\mathbf{H_R}$ but with the output renamed $\mathbf{y'}$.

10.2.6 Other clauses of a refinement

Refinements are very similar to machines in their construction. The SETS, CONSTANTS and PROPERTIES clauses can be used in refinements in the same way in which they are used in machines. The SEES clause can be used to introduce machines that do not contribute to the state of the refinement, and the INCLUDES clause can be used to introduce machines whose state is to be used as part of the refined state.

To help with the presentation of a refinement, you can use a DEFINITIONS clause to give short names to long expressions, just as you can in a machine definition.

10.3 Implementing a refinement

Refinements can be refined by implementations just as machines can. For an example we present a refinement of *CMA_refined* using two instances of a library machine *set* to represent the sets *both* and *only*. The library machines are imported as *Both_set* and *Only_set*, and each has two parameters, one for the values in the set and the other for the maximum size of the set.

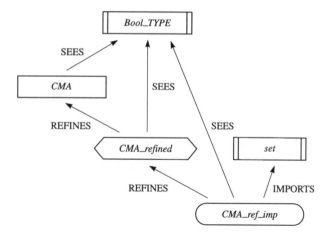

Figure 10.2 Dependencies of an implementation of a refinement.

IMPLEMENTATION

  CMA_ref_imp

REFINES

  CMA_refined

SEES

  Bool_TYPE

IMPORTS

  Both_set (STUDENT, class_size),
  Only_set (STUDENT, class_size)

The dependencies of this implementation are illustrated in Figure 10.2.

The only invariant we need is the retrieve relation.

INVARIANT

  both = Both_sset ∧
  only = Only_sset

The initializations of the imported machines are just what we need — both sets are empty.

INITIALISATION

   skip

10.3.1 Verifying the initialization

The rule for verifying the initialization of the implementation is the same as before, but now the refinement plays the part of the machine. If $\mathbf{G_R}$ is the initialization of the refinement, $\mathbf{G_I}$ the initialization of the implementation, and $\mathbf{P_I}$ the invariant of the implementation, then the proof obligation is

$$[\mathbf{G_I}] \neg [\mathbf{G_R}] \neg \mathbf{P_I}$$

In this case we have to show the following:

[*Both_sset* := Ø ; *Only_sset* := Ø]
¬[*only, both* := Ø, Ø]
¬(*both* = *Both_sset* ∧ *only* = *Only_sset*)

Making the rightmost substitution gives the following:

[*Both_sset* := Ø ; *Only_sset* := Ø]
¬¬(Ø = *Both_sset* ∧ Ø = *Only_sset*)

Making the second substitution of the sequence gives the following:

[*Both_sset* := Ø]
(Ø = *Both_sset* ∧ Ø = Ø)

Making the remaining substitution gives the following:

Ø = Ø ∧ Ø = Ø

The last conjunction is a theorem of set theory.

10.3.2 Implementing the operations

The *enrol* operation of *CMA_refined* is refined by the single operation *Only_ENT_SET*.

   enrol (*st*) =
    BEGIN
      Only_ENT_SET (*st*)
    END

For *isenrolled*, we use two local variables from the set *BOOL* to record whether the input is a member of either set, and then incorporate the substitution of the refinement with appropriate translations.

```
ans ⟵  isenrolled (st) =
  VAR
    bm, om
  IN
    bm ⟵  Both_MBR_SET (st) ;
    om ⟵  Only_MBR_SET (st) ;
    ans ⟵  DIS_BOOL (om, bm)
  END
```

The *test* operation of *CMA_refined* is translated easily into two operations of the imported machines.

```
test (st) =
  BEGIN
    Only_RMV_SET (st) ;
    Both_ENT_SET (st)
  END
```

The remaining operations are straightforward.

```
ans ⟵  istested (st) =
  BEGIN
    ans ⟵  Both_MBR_SET (st)
  END
```

```
leave (st) =
  BEGIN
    Only_RMV_SET (st) ;
    Both_RMV_SET (st)
  END
```

```
clmax, sofar ⟵  howmany =
  VAR
    oc, bc
  IN
    oc ⟵  Only_CRD_SET ;
    bc ⟵  Both_CRD_SET ;
    clmax := class_size ;
    sofar := oc + bc
  END
```

10.3.3 Verifying the operations

The rule for verifying operations of implementations with respect to refinements is analogous to the rule for verifying operations of implementations with respect to machines. If $\mathbf{P_R}$ is the invariant of the refinement, $\mathbf{P_I}$ the invariant of the implementation, $\mathbf{Q_R}$ the precondition of the refinement operation, $\mathbf{Q_I}$ the precondition of the implementation operation, $\mathbf{H_R}$ the then-part of the refinement operation, and $\mathbf{H_I}$ the then-part of the implementation operation, we must show that

$$\mathbf{P_R} \wedge \mathbf{P_I} \wedge \mathbf{Q_R} \Rightarrow \mathbf{Q_I} \wedge [\mathbf{H_I}] \neg [\mathbf{H_R}] \neg \mathbf{P_I}$$

In the case of *enrol*, the desired result is the following:

> *only* ⊆ *STUDENT* ∧
> *both* ⊆ *STUDENT* ∧
> *only* ∩ *both* = Ø ∧
> *enrolled* = *only* ∪ *both* ∧
> *tested* = *both* ∧
> *both* = *Both_sset* ∧
> *only* = *Only_sset* ∧
> *st* ∈ *STUDENT* ∧
> *st* ∉ *only* ∧
> *st* ∉ *both* ∧
> card (*only*) + card (*both*) < *class_size*
> ⇒
> *st* ∈ *STUDENT* ∧
> card (*Both_sset*) < *maxsize* ∧
> [*Only_sset* := *Only_sset* ∪ {*st*}]
> ¬[*only* := *only* ∪ {*st*}]
> ¬(*both* = *Both_sset* ∧ *only* = *Only_sset*)

The consequent can be simplified by making the two substitutions. First we get

> *st* ∈ *STUDENT* ∧
> card (*Both_sset*) < *maxsize* ∧
> [*Only_sset* := *Only_sset* ∪ {*st*}]
> ¬¬(*both* = *Both_sset* ∧ *only* ∪ {*st*} = *Only_sset*)

and finally

> *st* ∈ *STUDENT* ∧
> card (*Both_sset*) < *maxsize* ∧
> *both* = *Both_sset* ∧ *only* ∪ {*st*} = *Only_sset* ∪ {*st*}

The deduction of these conjuncts from the antecedent is straightforward.

10.3.4 Verifying operations with outputs

The rule is a simple adaptation of the rule for implementations of machines. Suppose that $\mathbf{P_R}$ is the invariant of the refinement, $\mathbf{P_I}$ the invariant of the implementation, $\mathbf{Q_R}$ the precondition of the refinement operation, $\mathbf{Q_I}$ the precondition of the implementation operation, $\mathbf{H_R}$ the then-part of the refinement operation, $\mathbf{H_I}$ the then-part of the implementation operation, and $\mathbf{y}$ the output of the operation, then we must show that

$$\mathbf{P_R} \wedge \mathbf{P_I} \wedge \mathbf{Q_R} \Rightarrow \mathbf{Q_I} \wedge [\mathbf{H'_I}] \neg [\mathbf{H_R}] \neg (\mathbf{P_I} \wedge \mathbf{y'} = \mathbf{y})$$

where $\mathbf{H'_I}$ is the same as $\mathbf{H_I}$ but with the output renamed $\mathbf{y'}$.

10.4 Summary and outlook

In this chapter we have learnt:

- how to write a refinement that records the data design aspects of the development of a machine;

- how to write an implementation of a refinement.

This chapter completes our study of the B-Method.

10.5 Exercises

(10.1)   Write a refinement *Server_refined* of *Server* where the model is a single natural number that is initially zero. The operation will output the next natural number, and save it. Write down the proof obligations for your refinement.

(10.2)   Write a refinement of *Nat_SET*, using an instance of *Array* and a counter to keep track of how many of the array cells are in use.

(10.3)   Write an implementation of *Server_refined* that imports an instance of the library machine *Nvar* to represent the natural number of the refinement.

Appendix A
Review of discrete mathematics

Summary: Natural numbers − arithmetic functions − arithmetic predicates − propositions − propositional functions − tautology − sets − membership − enumeration − comprehension − free and bound variables − generalized sum − generalized product − given sets − singleton − empty set − number range − universal quantifier − existential quantifier − subset − equality − powerset − union, intersection and difference − generalized union − generalized intersection − finiteness − ordered pairs − Cartesian product − binary relations − identity − inverse − relational image − domain − range − relational composition − restriction and subtraction − overriding − functions − function application − total functions − injections − surjections − bijections − lambda abstraction − sequences − injective sequences − size − first − last − tail − front − restriction − reverse − concatenation − generalized concatenation − append − prepend − permutation.

In this section of the book we review the mathematical ideas and notations that are used in constructing abstract machines, implementations and refinements. This chapter is provided mainly to supplement the examples and exercises given in the body of the book, and the reader is referred from there to sections of this chapter. It might be read on its own as a primer in discrete mathematics, and could be used before studying the rest of the book.

The language developed here is used to make statements about things of interest in software development. In this language we introduce **terms**, notations that represent the things to be spoken about, and **predicates**, notations that represent the statements made about the things.

A.1 Natural numbers

By the **natural numbers** we mean the set of whole numbers from zero upwards, familiar to readers from elementary arithmetic. We use the signs '1', '2', and so on as **proper names** for natural numbers, and we use the ordinary decimal notation for numbers greater than nine. We use the signs '+', '−', '×', '/', and 'mod' for the usual arithmetic functions of addition, subtraction, multiplication, division, and remainder. Subtraction is only possible if the first number is not less than the second, and division always gives a whole number as quotient.

In building up **arithmetic expressions** using these functions we can sometimes use parentheses to show how the expression is evaluated. We also use **precedence rules** that give '×', '/', and 'mod' greater precedence than '+' and '−', so

$$3 \times 4 - 2 = (3 \times 4) - 2 = 10$$

In a sequence of symbols of the same precedence, association is to the left, so

$$3 \times 4 / 3 \times 2 = ((3 \times 4) / 3) \times 2 = 8$$

and

$$5 + 6 - 7 + 1 = ((5 + 6) - 7) + 1 = 5$$

Natural numbers and expressions that denote natural numbers are terms in the mathematical language.

The signs '=', '≠', '<', '>', '≤', and '≥' are used for the relations of equality, inequality, less than, greater than, less than or equal, and greater than or equal. These arithmetic relations allow us to write predicates in the mathematical language.

A.1.1 Variables

From elementary algebra the reader is familiar with the use of letters like x and y to represent numbers. Names like x and y are called **variables** to distinguish them from proper names like 5 and 132. Variables denote values just as proper names denote values, but we do not always know which particular values they denote. The use of variables has two important conveniences: we can use notation to solve problems, and we can state general or universal truths. Elementary algebra provides many examples of these two uses of variables.

It is often convenient to use as variables names with more than one letter, and to use the underscore character '_' to break up long names. In this book we use variables with names like xy and *flight_departure_time*. (The convention of elementary algebra that an expression like xy denotes the product of x and y is not used in this book.)

Readers who would like a formal treatment of elementary arithmetic should consult Abrial (1993).

A.2 Propositions

Predicates like $x > 5$ denote true or false, depending on the circumstances. (In this case, the only circumstance is the value chosen for x.) Just as in arithmetic we study natural numbers, their combinations (by addition, and so on) and their laws, so too in the **propositional calculus** we study laws about truth and falseness.

In the propositional calculus, a **proposition** is a variable that denotes either true or false. We use bold capital letters **P**, **Q**, **R** as propositions. Informally we can think of propositions as abstractions from predicates where we consider only the trueness or falseness of the predicate, not what it asserts about things.

Propositions, like arithmetic variables, can be combined into **propositional expressions** that also denote true or false. There are five propositional functions that we use in our mathematical language.

The first function is **negation**, a function of one proposition only. The negation of **P** is written $\neg$**P**, and '$\neg$' is the **negation sign**. If **P** denotes true, then $\neg$**P** denotes false, and if **P** denotes false, then $\neg$**P** denotes true.

The rules for determining the values of the four other functions when we know the values of the propositions in it are given by the following **truth table**.

P	Q	P ∧ Q	P ∨ Q	P ⇒ Q	P ⇔ Q
true	true	true	true	true	true
true	false	false	true	false	false
false	true	false	true	true	false
false	false	false	false	true	true

The propositional functions can be summarized as follows:

- **P ∧ Q** is the **conjunction** of P and Q, which are the **conjuncts** of the expression. Conjunction formalizes the informal idea of '... and ...'. The sign '∧' is the **conjunction sign**.

- **P ∨ Q** is the **disjunction** of P and Q, which are the **disjuncts** of the expression. Disjunction formalizes the informal idea of '... or ...'. The sign '∨' is the **disjunction sign**.

- **P ⇒ Q** is an **implication** in which P is the **antecedent** and Q the **consequent**. Implication formalizes some aspects of the informal idea of 'if ... then ...'. The sign '⇒' is the **implication sign**.

- **P ⇔ Q** is the **equivalence** of P and Q. Equivalence formalizes the informal idea of '... if and only if ...', and serves the same purpose among propositions that equality serves among terms. The sign '⇔' is the **equivalence sign**.

In building larger propositional expressions we sometimes use parentheses to show how the propositional operations are to be performed. We also use precedence rules as follows. Highest precedence is accorded to ¬, then ∧ and ∨ are next with equal precedence. Next comes ⇒, and ⇔ is lowest of all. A rule of left-association is used where there are several uses of ∧ and ∨ together.

A.2.1 Laws of propositional functions

We can derive truth tables for more extended propositional expressions, and with the help of these truth tables we can derive laws of propositional calculus like the following.

The commutative law for conjunction is

$$P \wedge Q \Leftrightarrow Q \wedge P$$

Similarly there are commutative laws for disjunction and equivalence, though not for implication.

The associative law for disjunction is

$$(P \vee Q) \vee R \Leftrightarrow P \vee (Q \vee R)$$

The distributive law for disjunction over conjunction is

$$\mathbf{P} \lor (\mathbf{Q} \land \mathbf{R}) \Leftrightarrow (\mathbf{P} \lor \mathbf{Q}) \land (\mathbf{P} \lor \mathbf{R})$$

and the distributive law for conjunction over disjunction is

$$\mathbf{P} \land (\mathbf{Q} \lor \mathbf{R}) \Leftrightarrow (\mathbf{P} \land \mathbf{Q}) \lor (\mathbf{P} \land \mathbf{R})$$

The law of double negation is

$$\neg\neg\mathbf{P} \Leftrightarrow \mathbf{P}$$

There are laws about the negation of other functions. De Morgan's law is

$$\neg(\mathbf{P} \land \mathbf{Q}) \Leftrightarrow \neg\mathbf{P} \lor \neg\mathbf{Q}$$

and De Morgan's other law is

$$\neg(\mathbf{P} \lor \mathbf{Q}) \Leftrightarrow \neg\mathbf{P} \land \neg\mathbf{Q}$$

The law about negating an implication is

$$\neg(\mathbf{P} \Rightarrow \mathbf{Q}) \Leftrightarrow \mathbf{P} \land \neg\mathbf{Q}$$

There is a law about consolidating antecedents:

$$\mathbf{P} \Rightarrow (\mathbf{Q} \Rightarrow \mathbf{R}) \Leftrightarrow \mathbf{P} \land \mathbf{Q} \Rightarrow \mathbf{R}$$

A.2.2 Tautologies

A propositional function, like $\mathbf{P} \Rightarrow \mathbf{P}$, that is true for any truth values of its components is called a **tautology**. Tautologies are very useful in reasoning with predicates, since if a predicate has the form of a tautology, we need not concern ourselves about the truth values of its components, since it is always true.

A.3 Sets of numbers

A **set** is a well-defined, unordered collection of values. We use the expression 'well-defined' to mean that, given any value, we can determine in a finite time by some unambiguous test whether it is a member of the set. We use the sign '$\mathbb{N}$' as a proper name for the whole set of natural numbers from 0 upwards. We use the sign '$\mathbb{N}_1$' for the set of natural numbers from 1 upwards. We can of course use variables to denote sets, and if S is a set of natural numbers and x is a natural number, the predicate

$$x \in S$$

means that x is a member of the set S. The sign '$\in$' is the **membership sign.**

The negation of a membership predicate has a sign of its own, the **non-membership sign '$\notin$'.** The predicate

$$x \notin S$$

means that x is not a member of S.

A set of natural numbers could be defined by a list of the numbers in it:

$$\{1, 5, 78, 329\}$$

The list of numbers is enclosed in braces '{', '}', and the elements of the list are separated by commas. Given a natural number, we can tell if it is a member of the set or not. If it is one of the four numbers listed, it is, otherwise it is not. This method of defining a set is called **set enumeration.** The elements of a set have no order. The same set could be defined by the enumeration

$$\{5, 1, 329, 78\}$$

without any change to the set being defined. There is no notion of how many times a value is a member of a set. A value is either a member or it is not a member. The enumeration

$$\{1, 5, 1, 329, 78, 5\}$$

defines the same set as before.

The other method of defining a set is called **set comprehension,** and it involves stating a property that defines the members of the set.

$$\{x \mid x \in \mathbb{N} \wedge x > 5\}$$

Informally we read the definition as 'the set of xs where x is a natural number and x is greater than 5'. The set comprehension is bounded by braces and is divided into two parts by the | sign. The first part is a list of variables separated by commas (in this case we have only one variable), and the second part is a predicate for the property that determines which values are members of the set.

A.3.1 Free and bound variables

The value of the natural number expression

$$x + 1$$

depends on the value chosen for x. We can imagine choosing different values for x, and evaluating the expression.

The truth value of the predicate

$$x \in \mathbb{N} \wedge x > 5$$

also depends on the value chosen for x. We call a variable like x a **free variable** of the expression or predicate in which it occurs, and we say that x is free in the expression or predicate.

We have already met expressions that contained variables that were not free. For instance the expression

$$\{x \mid x \in \mathbb{N} \wedge x < 5\}$$

denotes the set $\{0, 1, 2, 3, 4\}$. In this expression we cannot choose a value of x and then evaluate the expression. In a set comprehension term we are obliged to take all possible values of x at once, allowing those that satisfy the predicate to fall into the set. In an expression like this, the variable x is called a **bound variable**.

It is always possible to change the name of a bound variable without changing the value of the expression, so

$$\{y \mid y \in \mathbb{N} \wedge y < 5\}$$

has a different bound variable, but denotes the same set. Sometimes, however, care must be exercised. Consider the expression

$$\{x \mid x \in \mathbb{N} \wedge x < y\}$$

This contains a free variable y and a bound variable x. If y is 0, it denotes an empty set of natural numbers. If y is 5, it denotes the set described above. We can change the bound variable without changing the value of the expression as follows:

$$\{z \mid z \in \mathbb{N} \wedge z < y\}$$

However, if we had chosen to replace the name x by the name y, the result would have been quite different, because

$$\{y \mid y \in \mathbb{N} \wedge y < y\}$$

has no free variable, and denotes an empty set of natural numbers.

A.3.2 Generalized sum

The expression

$$\Sigma x \bullet (x \in 1 .. 3 \mid x \times x)$$

is intended to denote the sum of the squares of the numbers in the set 1 .. 3. The sign 'Σ' is the **generalized sum sign,** and x is a variable bound by it. The predicate $x \in 1 .. 3$ fixes the values of x that are to be considered, and the expression $x \times x$ after the vertical bar is the typical expression whose values are to be summed. In this case we are summing the squares of 1, 2 and 3, and the expression therefore denotes $1 + 4 + 9$, which is 14.

We can make the definition of generalized sum precise as follows. Consider the expression

$$\Sigma \mathbf{x} \bullet (\mathbf{P} \mid \mathbf{E})$$

where $\mathbf{x}$ is a list of variables, $\mathbf{P}$ is a predicate that constrains the variables in $\mathbf{x}$, and $\mathbf{E}$ is a natural number expression that depends on the variables in $\mathbf{x}$.

(1) If $\{\mathbf{x} \mid \mathbf{P}\}$ is empty, the generalized sum is zero.

(2) If $\{\mathbf{x} \mid \mathbf{P}\}$ contains a member $\mathbf{y}$, and $\mathbf{E_y}$ is the value of $\mathbf{E}$ for the values in $\mathbf{y}$, then the value of the generalized sum is

$$\mathbf{E_y} + \Sigma \mathbf{x} \bullet (\mathbf{P} \wedge \mathbf{x} \neq \mathbf{y} \mid \mathbf{E})$$

A.3.3 Generalized product

The expression

$$\Pi x \bullet (x \in 1 .. 3 \mid x \times x)$$

is intended to denote the product of the squares of the numbers in the set 1 .. 3. The sign 'Π' is the **generalized product sign,** and x is a variable bound by it. The predicate $x \in 1 .. 3$ fixes the values of x that are to be considered, and the expression $x \times x$ after the vertical bar is the typical expression whose values are to be multiplied. In this case we are multiplying the squares of 1, 2 and 3, and the expression therefore denotes $1 \times 4 \times 9$, which is 36.

We can make the definition of generalized product precise as follows. Consider the expression

$$\Pi \mathbf{x} \bullet (\mathbf{P} \mid \mathbf{E})$$

where **x** is a list of variables, **P** is a predicate that constrains the variables in **x**, and **E** is a natural number expression that depends on the variables in **x**.

(1) If $\{\mathbf{x} \mid \mathbf{P}\}$ is empty, the generalized product is one.

(2) If $\{\mathbf{x} \mid \mathbf{P}\}$ contains a member **y**, and $\mathbf{E_y}$ is the value of **E** for the values in **y**, then the value of the generalized product is

$$\mathbf{E_y} \times \Pi\mathbf{x} \bullet (\mathbf{P} \wedge \mathbf{x} \neq \mathbf{y} \mid \mathbf{E})$$

A.4 Abstract sets

In describing and developing software systems, we need to talk about sets whose members are not natural numbers, but are closely related to the real-world things that the software models. Sets of this kind are called **abstract sets**. They are introduced as needed to formalize informal ideas about software with a view to correct development. Formalizing the oil terminal control system described in Chapter 1 demands the introduction of sets whose members are tankers and berths.

A.4.1 Given sets

The set comprehension notation is a very powerful way of defining collections of values. The **set comprehension principle** says that if **P** is a predicate that establishes some property of a variable x, the value y is a member of the set

$$\{x \mid \mathbf{P}\}$$

if and only if y has the property **P**. In the early history of set theory it was found that this principle led to contradictions. The use of set comprehension for constructing sets had to be revised in various ways, and the most appropriate of these revisions is the use of **given sets**. Given sets are sets introduced into mathematical discussions to constrain the kinds of values that can be collected together by set comprehension. The given sets form the basis for the **constraining sets** of a mathematical discussion. Every given set is a constraining set, and there are three more rules about constraining sets to come later. The only kinds of set comprehensions that are allowed are of the following form:

$$\{x \mid x \in S \wedge \mathbf{P}\}$$

where S must be a constraining set. This set comprehension defines the set of members of S that satisfy the property **P**. The set comprehension

$$\{x \mid x \in \mathbb{N} \wedge x > 5\}$$

on page 208 was of this form, with $\mathbb{N}$ as the given set. Any finite set can serve as a given set, and in the abstract machine notation we use $\mathbb{N}$ and various finite sets as given sets.

A.4.2 Singleton sets and enumerations

If S is a given set, we can define the **singleton set** of any member of S as a set comprehension thus:

$$\{y\} = \{x \mid x \in S \wedge x = y\}$$

Any set enumeration of values from the same given set can be defined, with patience, as a set comprehension. For instance

$$\{1, 6, 4\} = \{x \mid x \in \mathbb{N} \wedge (x = 1 \vee x = 6 \vee x = 4)\}$$

A.4.3 Empty sets

If S is a given set, then the following set comprehension

$$\{x \mid x \in S \wedge x \neq x\}$$

defines a set with no members. This is an **empty set**, though strictly we should call it the S-empty set, since S is the given set from which its members would have been drawn had there been any. The sign '$\varnothing$' is the **empty set sign**, and it is used to denote any empty set. In every case it must be possible to determine the relevant given set from the context in which the notation is used.

A.4.4 Number range

We define a **number range** by a set comprehension as follows:

$$m \mathinner{.\,.} n = \{x \mid x \in \mathbb{N} \wedge x \geq m \wedge x \leq n\}$$

If $m = n$, this is a singleton set. If $m > n$, this set is empty.

A.5 Quantifiers

There are two quantifiers, the universal quantifier ('for all', or 'for each'), and the existential quantifier ('there is a', or 'for some').

A.5.1 Universal quantifier

If we wish to formalize the true statement that every natural number greater than 5 is greater than 4, we can take the predicate

$$x \in \mathbb{N} \wedge x > 5 \Rightarrow x > 4$$

and form from it a **universal quantification** thus:

$$\forall x \bullet (\ x \in \mathbb{N} \wedge x > 5 \Rightarrow x > 4)$$

The sign '∀' is the **universal quantifier**. The variable x, which is free in the first predicate, is bound in the second. The form of a universal quantification is always

$$\forall \mathbf{x} \bullet (\mathbf{P} \Rightarrow \mathbf{Q})$$

where $\mathbf{x}$ is a list of variables, $\mathbf{P}$ is a predicate that constrains all the variables in $\mathbf{x}$, and $\mathbf{Q}$ is another predicate.

The predicate $\forall \mathbf{x} \bullet (\mathbf{P} \Rightarrow \mathbf{Q})$ is true if and only if $\mathbf{P} \Rightarrow \mathbf{Q}$ is true for an arbitrary value of $\mathbf{x}$.

A.5.2 Existential quantifier

If we wish to formalize the true statement that there is a natural number greater than 5, we can take the predicate

$$x \in \mathbb{N} \wedge x > 5$$

and form from it an **existential quantification** thus:

$$\exists x \bullet (x \in \mathbb{N} \wedge x > 5)$$

The sign '∃' is the **existential quantifier**. The variable x, which is free in the first predicate, is bound in the second. The form of an existential quantification is always

$$\exists \mathbf{x} \bullet (\mathbf{P} \wedge \mathbf{Q})$$

where $\mathbf{x}$ is a list of variables, $\mathbf{P}$ is a predicate that constrains all the variables in $\mathbf{x}$, and $\mathbf{Q}$ is another predicate.

The existential quantification can be shown to be true by exhibiting a value that satisfies $\mathbf{P} \wedge \mathbf{Q}$. When the predicate $\mathbf{P} \wedge \mathbf{Q}$ contains an equality predicate that fixes the value to be used, all we have to do is to show that the value satisfies the rest of $\mathbf{P} \wedge \mathbf{Q}$. So to show that

$$\exists x \bullet (x \in \mathbb{N} \wedge x = 5 \wedge x > 3)$$

all we have to show is

$$5 \in \mathbb{N} \wedge 5 > 3$$

which is true. This observation is the basis of the **one-point rule** as follows:

$$\exists x \bullet (x = E \land P) \Leftrightarrow P_E$$

where **x** is a variable, **E** an expression, **P** a predicate, and P_E the predicate **P** with all the free occurrences of the variable **x** replaced by the expression **E**.

A.5.3 Negation of quantifications

There are two useful rules about the negation of quantifications. The rule for negating a universal quantification is as follows:

$$\neg \forall x \bullet (P \Rightarrow Q) \Leftrightarrow \exists x \bullet (P \land \neg Q)$$

The rule for negating an existential quantification is as follows:

$$\neg \exists x \bullet (P \land Q) \Leftrightarrow \forall x \bullet (P \Rightarrow \neg Q)$$

A.6 Set theory

One set is a **subset** of another if all the members of the first are members of the second. We can use the following predicate to define this notion.

$$X \subseteq Y \Leftrightarrow \forall x \bullet (x \in X \Rightarrow x \in Y)$$

The subsets of a constraining set are also constraining sets.

If X and Y are both subsets of a given set S, but X is not a subset of Y, we can use the following notation:

$$X \nsubseteq Y \Leftrightarrow \neg X \subseteq Y$$

The sign '$\nsubseteq$' is the **not-subset sign**.

Two subsets of a given set are equal if and only if they have the same members, and we use the equals sign for **set equality**.

$$X = Y \Leftrightarrow \forall x \bullet (x \in X \Leftrightarrow x \in Y)$$

The not-equals sign is used for **set inequality**.

A set X is a **proper subset** of Y, if X is a subset of Y, but X is not equal to Y.

$$X \subseteq S \land Y \subseteq S \Rightarrow (X \subset Y \Leftrightarrow X \subseteq Y \land X \neq Y)$$

The sign '$\subset$' is the **proper subset sign**.

The proper subset sign also has its negation, the **not-proper-subset sign**, '$\not\subset$'.

The **powerset** of a set is the set of all its subsets.

$$Y \in \mathbb{P}(X) \Leftrightarrow Y \subseteq X$$

The sign '$\mathbb{P}$' is the **powerset sign**.

There is another rule about constraining sets here. If S is a constraining set, then so is $\mathbb{P}(S)$.

The X-empty set is a subset of X, so it is a member of $\mathbb{P}(X)$. We have a notation for the non-empty subsets of X:

$$Y \in \mathbb{P}_1(X) \Leftrightarrow Y \subseteq X \wedge Y \neq \emptyset$$

The sign '$\mathbb{P}_1$' is the **non-empty subsets sign**.

Suppose S is a given set and X and Y are subsets of it. We can define the **union** of two sets by the predicate

$$X \cup Y = \{x \mid x \in X \vee x \in Y\}$$

The union of two sets is the set of values that are members of either set. The sign '$\cup$' is the **union sign**.

We can define the **intersection** of two sets by the predicate

$$X \cap Y = \{x \mid x \in X \wedge x \in Y\}$$

The intersection of two sets is the set of values that are members of both sets. The sign '$\cap$' is the **intersection sign**.

Two sets are called **disjoint** if their intersection is the empty set of appropriate type.

We can define the **difference** of two sets by the predicate

$$X - Y = \{x \mid x \in X \wedge x \notin Y\}$$

The difference of two sets is the set of values that are members of the first but not of the second. The sign '$-$' is the **difference sign**.

In evaluating set expressions, the precedence rules are as follows. Difference takes the highest priority, and intersection and union take the same lower priority. A rule of left-association is used where there are several uses of union and intersection together.

A.6.1 Generalized union and intersection

The **generalized union** of a set of sets is the set formed from the members of the sets. It can be defined as follows:

$$\text{union}(U) = \{x \mid \exists y \bullet (y \in U \wedge x \in y)\}$$

Thus

$$\text{union}(\{1, 2\}, \{2, 3\}) = \{1, 2, 3\}$$

Another form of the generalized union allows us to use a predicate to specify which sets are to be considered. In the following definition, z is a list of variables, **P** is a predicate that must constrain all the variables in the list, **E** is a set expression.

$$\bigcup z \bullet (P \mid E) = \{x \mid \exists z \bullet (P \wedge x \in E)\}$$

Thus

$$\bigcup x \bullet (x \in 1 \, ..2 \mid \{x, x + 1\}) = \{1, 2, 3\}$$

The sign '$\bigcup$' is the **generalized union sign**.

The **generalized intersection** of a set of sets is the set of elements common to all the members of the sets. It can be defined as follows:

$$\mathsf{inter}\ (U) = \{x \mid \forall y \bullet (y \in U \Rightarrow x \in y)\}$$

Thus

$$\mathsf{inter}\ (\{1, 2\}, \{2, 3\}) = \{2\}$$

Another form of the generalized intersection allows us to use a predicate to specify which sets are to be considered. In the following definition, z is a list of variables, **P** is a predicate that must constrain all the variables in the list, **E** is a set expression.

$$\bigcap z \bullet (P \mid E) = \{x \mid \forall z \bullet (P \Rightarrow x \in E)\}$$

Thus

$$\bigcap x \bullet (x \in 1 \, ..2 \mid \{x, x + 1\}) = \{2\}$$

The sign '$\bigcap$' is the **generalized intersection sign**.

A.6.2 Finite sets and cardinality

Apart from $\mathbb{N}$ and sets derived from it, all the sets we use in this book are **finite** sets. The members of a finite set can be counted, and the number of members of a finite set is a natural number called its **cardinality**. The notation for the cardinality of a finite set X is card (X). The following predicates express important properties of cardinality.

$$\mathsf{card}\ (\emptyset) = 0$$

$$x \in S \wedge X \subseteq S \wedge x \notin X \Rightarrow \mathsf{card}\ (X \cup \{x\}) = \mathsf{card}\ (X) + 1$$

We use the notation $\mathbb{F}\ (S)$ for the **finite powerset** of a set S, that is, the set of all its finite subsets. '$\mathbb{F}$' is the **finite powerset sign**.

We use the notation $\mathbb{F}_1$ (S) for the non-empty finite subsets of a set S. '$\mathbb{F}_1$' is the **non-empty finite subsets sign**.

If S is a non-empty finite set of natural numbers, we denote the smallest number in the set by min (S). The definition of min is a definition by cases as follows:

$$\min (\{x\}) = x$$

$$\min (\{x\} \cup S) = x \text{ if } x \le \min (S)$$

$$\min (\{x\} \cup S) = \min (S) \text{ if } \min (S) \le x$$

This definition by cases works as follows:

(1) If the set is a singleton, its minimum is the number in the set.

(2) If the set is not a singleton, we construct a recursive definition as follows: we choose one of its members, x, and call the rest of the set S. There are now two cases:

   (a) x is less than or equal to the least number in S, then x is the least number in the set.

   (b) x is not less than or equal to the least number in S, then the minimum is the least member of the smaller set S.

If S is a non-empty finite set of natural numbers, we denote the largest number in the set by max (S). The definition of max is a definition by cases as follows:

$$\max (\{x\}) = x$$

$$\max (\{x\} \cup S) = x \text{ if } x \ge \max (S)$$

$$\max (\{x\} \cup S) = \max (S) \text{ if } \max (S) \ge x$$

Readers who would like a formal treatment of finiteness and cardinality should consult Abrial (1993).

A.7 Ordered pairs, Cartesian products and relations

A.7.1 Ordered pairs

An **ordered pair** is a means of bringing together two values from sets that are possibly different, distinguishing one as the first member of the ordered pair and one as the second. If x and y are values, the ordered pair whose first member is x and whose second member is y is denoted by

$$x \mapsto y$$

The sign '$\mapsto$' is the **ordered pair sign**. The ordered pair is the basis of describing relations between subsets of different given sets.

We extend the set comprehension notation introduced on page 208 to a case in which there are two variables in the first part of the set comprehension. The notation

$$\{x, y \mid x \in \mathbb{N} \wedge y \in \mathbb{N} \wedge x < 3 \wedge y < x\}$$

denotes the following set of ordered pairs:

$$\{1 \mapsto 0, 2 \mapsto 0, 2 \mapsto 1\}$$

A.7.2 Cartesian products

The set of all ordered pairs whose first members are members of set X and whose second members are members of set Y is called the **Cartesian product** of the two sets, and it is denoted by

$$X \times Y$$

where '$\times$' is the **Cartesian product sign.**

We can define the Cartesian product of two sets with a set comprehension term as follows:

$$X \times Y = \{x, y \mid x \in X \wedge y \in Y\}$$

If the sets in a Cartesian product are constraining sets, then their Cartesian product is also a constraining set. The Cartesian product completes the repertoire of constructions that generate constraining sets.

A.7.3 Binary relations

A **binary relation** between two sets is a set of ordered pairs whose first elements are drawn from the first set (the **from-set**), and whose second elements are drawn from the second set (the **to-set**).

If X is a subset of a given set S, and Y is a subset of a given set T, the set of all binary relations between X and Y is defined as follows.

$$X \leftrightarrow Y = \mathbb{P} (X \times Y)$$

The sign '$\leftrightarrow$' is the **relation sign.**

If r is a relation between X and Y, and $x \mapsto y$ is a pair in r, we can use either of the predicates

$$x \mapsto y \in r$$

or

$$x \, r \, y$$

to express this. The latter is an instance of **infix notation** for expressing relations. It corresponds to the grammatical form of predicates like 'x is a parent of y', in which 'is a parent of' serves as the name of a relation.

The smallest relation between X and Y is the **empty relation**, which contains no ordered pairs, and the largest such relation is $X \times Y$, in which each member of X is related to every member of Y.

The two sets X and Y do not have to be different, so we can define a binary relation on a single set X, or more properly between X and X. Thus the relation denoted by the sign '$\leq$' is a relation on natural numbers, and it could be defined as a set of ordered pairs as follows:

$$`\leq` = \{x, y \mid x \in \mathbb{N} \wedge y \in \mathbb{N} \wedge \exists z \bullet (z \in \mathbb{N} \wedge y = x + z)\}$$

This set comprehension has two bound variables, and is intended to denote a set of ordered pairs. The first named variable is intended to be the first member of the pair, and the second named to be the second member of the pair. The set comprehension principle is extended in an obvious way to cover this new form of set comprehension.

The **identity relation** on a set X is the relation in which each member of X is paired with itself. It can be defined as follows.

$$\mathsf{id}\,(X) = \{x, y \mid x \in X \wedge y \in X \wedge x = y\}$$

The **inverse** of a binary relation is the relation with its pairs reversed.

$$r \in (X \leftrightarrow Y) \Rightarrow r^{-1} = \{y, x \mid x \mapsto y \in r\}$$

The sign '$^{-1}$' is the **inverse sign**.

If r is a relation between X and Y, the **relational image** of a subset Z of X is the set of members of Y that correspond to members of Z under r.

$$Z \subseteq X \wedge r \in (X \leftrightarrow Y) \Rightarrow$$
$$r\,[Z] = \{y \mid y \in Y \wedge \exists x \bullet x \in Z \wedge x \mapsto y \in r\}$$

The **domain** of a relation is the set of first members of its pairs.

$$r \in (X \leftrightarrow Y) \Rightarrow \mathsf{dom}\,(r) = \{x \mid \exists y \bullet (y \in Y \wedge x \mapsto y \in r)\}$$

The **range** of a relation is the set of second members of its pairs.

$$r \in (X \leftrightarrow Y) \Rightarrow \text{ran } (r) = r [X]$$

A relation r from X to Y and a relation s from Y to Z can be used to generate a new relation from X to Z by **relational composition**. The composition of r and s is defined as follows.

$$r \in X \leftrightarrow Y \wedge s \in Y \leftrightarrow Z \Rightarrow$$
$$r \,;\, s = \{x, z \mid x \in X \wedge z \in Z \wedge \exists y \bullet (y \in Y \wedge x \, r \, y \wedge y \, s \, z)\}$$

The sign ';' is the **relational composition** sign. Relational composition relates any member of X to some member of Z provided that there is some intermediate member of Y.

The **backward composition** of two relations is defined as follows.

$$r \circ s = s \,;\, r$$

The sign 'o' is the **backward composition** sign.

A relation can be restricted in various ways by confining attention to those pairs whose first (or second) members are in some subset of the from-set (or to-set) of the relation. The **domain restriction** of a relation r by some subset of its from-set is those pairs of r whose first members are in the subset.

$$r \in X \leftrightarrow Y \wedge Z \subseteq X \Rightarrow Z \lhd r = \text{id } (Z) \,;\, r$$

The sign '$\lhd$' is the **domain restriction sign**.

The **range restriction** of a relation r by some subset of its to-set is those pairs of r whose second members are in the subset.

$$r \in X \leftrightarrow Y \wedge Z \subseteq Y \Rightarrow r \rhd Z = r \,;\, \text{id } (Z)$$

The sign '$\rhd$' is the **range restriction sign**.

The **domain subtraction** of a relation r by some subset of its from-set is those pairs of r whose first members are not in the subset.

$$r \in X \leftrightarrow Y \wedge Z \subseteq X \Rightarrow Z \lhd\!\!\!- \, r = (X - Z) \lhd r$$

The sign '$\lhd\!\!\!-$' is the **domain subtraction sign**.

The **range subtraction** of a relation r by some subset of its to-set is those pairs of r whose second members are not in the subset.

$$r \in X \leftrightarrow Y \wedge Z \subseteq Y \Rightarrow r \,-\!\!\!\rhd Z = r \rhd (Y - Z)$$

The sign '$-\!\!\!\rhd$' is the **range subtraction sign**.

Another way of constructing new relations involves combining two relations of the same kind. If r and s are relations from X to Y the **right override** of r by s defines a new relation that contains the whole of s and such of r as do not conflict with it.

$$r \lhd\!\!\!- s = (\text{dom } (s) \lhd\!\!\!- r) \cup s$$

The sign '$\lhd$' is the **right override sign**.
   The **left override** is defined as follows.

$$r \rhd s = s \lhd r$$

The sign '$\rhd$' is the **left override sign**.

A.8 Functions

The **functions** from X to Y are the binary relations with a special property: each member of X is related to at most one member of Y. In pictorial terms, each member of X has at most one arrow connecting it to a member of Y. The set of all functions from X to Y is defined as follows.

$$X \nrightarrow Y =$$
$$\{r \mid r \in (X \leftrightarrow Y) \wedge$$
$$\forall x, y, z \bullet (x \mapsto z \in r \wedge y \mapsto z \in r \Rightarrow y = z)\}$$

Since functions are binary relations, the concepts of relational image, domain, range and so on can be carried over to functions from relations. Also we might note that the empty relation between two sets is a function.

Since each member of the domain of a function is related to exactly one member of the range, we use the **function application** notation to denote that member of the range. If x is in the domain of function f, then the corresponding element of the range is denoted by $f(x)$.

$$f \in (X \nrightarrow Y) \wedge x \in \text{dom}(f) \Rightarrow f[\{x\}] = \{f(x)\}$$

The **total functions** from X to Y are those functions from X to Y whose domain is the whole of X.

$$X \rightarrow Y = \{f \mid f \in X \nrightarrow Y \wedge \text{dom}(f) = X\}$$

The sign '$\rightarrow$' is the **total function sign**. The total functions from X to Y are a subset of the functions from X to Y.
   A function is an **injection** if its inverse is a function.

$$X \nrightarrowtail Y = \{f \mid f \in X \nrightarrow Y \wedge f^{-1} \in Y \nrightarrow X\}$$

The sign '$\nrightarrowtail$' is the **injection sign**.
   The **total injections** from X to Y are the total functions from X to Y that are injections.

$$X \rightarrowtail Y = (X \rightarrow Y) \cap (X \nrightarrowtail Y)$$

The sign '$\rightarrowtail$' is the **total injection sign**.

The **surjections** from X to Y are those functions from X to Y whose range is the whole of Y.

$$X \twoheadrightarrow Y = \{f \mid f \in X \to Y \wedge \text{ran}\ (f) = Y\}$$

The sign '$\twoheadrightarrow$' is the **surjection sign**.

The **total surjections** from X to Y are the total functions from X to Y that are surjections.

$$X \twoheadrightarrow Y = (X \to Y) \cap (X \twoheadrightarrow Y)$$

The sign '$\twoheadrightarrow$' is the **total surjection sign**.

The **bijections** from X to Y are the total injections from X to Y that are surjections.

$$X \rightarrowtail\!\!\!\twoheadrightarrow Y = (X \rightarrowtail Y) \cap (X \twoheadrightarrow Y)$$

The sign '$\rightarrowtail\!\!\!\twoheadrightarrow$' is the **bijection sign**.

A.8.1 Lambda abstraction

Sometimes it is useful to define a function by showing how the range element (the value) is calculated when the domain element is given. The notation for doing this is called **lambda abstraction**.

The notation

$$\lambda x \bullet (x \in \mathbb{N} \mid x + 1)$$

denotes a function that can be applied to a single natural number x, and denotes the next number $x + 1$. So

$$\lambda x \bullet (x \in \mathbb{N} \mid x + 1)\ (4)$$

denotes 5.

The general form of a lambda abstraction is as follows:

$$\lambda \mathbf{x} \bullet (\mathbf{P} \mid \mathbf{E})$$

where $\mathbf{x}$ is a list of variables (for a function of several arguments), $\mathbf{P}$ is a predicate that constrains all the variables in $\mathbf{x}$, and $\mathbf{E}$ is an expression. Provided that a list of values $\mathbf{z}$ satisfies $\mathbf{P}$, the value of the function applied to $\mathbf{z}$ is $\mathbf{E}$ with the variables of $\mathbf{x}$ replaced by the values of $\mathbf{z}$. We can formalize this idea as follows:

$$\mathbf{P_z} \Rightarrow \lambda \mathbf{x} \bullet (\mathbf{P} \mid \mathbf{E})\ (\mathbf{z}) = \mathbf{E_z}$$

In this predicate, $\mathbf{P_z}$ is the predicate $\mathbf{P}$ with the variables of $\mathbf{x}$ replaced by the values of $\mathbf{z}$, and $\mathbf{E_z}$ is the expression $\mathbf{E}$ with the variables of $\mathbf{x}$ replaced by the values of $\mathbf{z}$.

A.9 Sequences

The informal notion of a **sequence** is a collection of values in which there is an idea of order. We use as a mathematical model for sequences a function that relates the natural numbers from one up to some maximum to the values in the corresponding positions in the sequence. The following predicate defines the notion of the sequences of values drawn from the set S.

$$\text{seq} (S) = \{s \mid s \in \mathbb{N} \nrightarrow S \wedge \exists n \bullet (n \in \mathbb{N} \wedge \text{dom} (s) = 1 \mathrel{..} n)\}$$

An instance of a sequence of the natural numbers 5, 3, 5, 8, in that order, could be displayed as a set enumeration as follows.

$$\{1 \mapsto 5, 2 \mapsto 3, 3 \mapsto 5, 4 \mapsto 8\}$$

There is also a notation for **sequence enumeration**, using square brackets as **sequence brackets**, and the same sequence would be displayed as follows.

$$[5, 3, 5, 8]$$

In general, the same value might be repeated many times in a sequence, and we have a special notation for sequences that have no repetitions. Such a sequence is called an **injective sequence**, and the definition is as follows.

$$\text{iseq} (S) = \{s \mid s \in \text{seq} (S) \wedge \text{card} (\text{dom} (s)) = \text{card} (\text{ran} (s))\}$$

An **empty sequence** (we should say an S-empty sequence) is possible.

$$[\,] = \varnothing$$

When the empty sequence notation is used, it must always be clear from the context which set the members would have been drawn from, had there been any.

The set of all **non-empty sequences** of values from a set S is defined as follows.

$$\text{seq1} (S) = \{s \mid s \in \text{seq} (S) \wedge s \neq [\,]\}$$

The **non-empty injective sequences** of values from a set S are defined as follows.

$$\text{iseq1} (S) = \text{iseq} (S) \cap \text{seq1} (S)$$

A **singleton sequence** is a sequence with only one element.

$$[x] = \{1 \mapsto x\}$$

A.9.1 Operations on sequences

The **size** of a sequence is the number of elements in it.

$$s \in \text{seq}\ (S) \Rightarrow \text{size}\ (s) = \text{card}\ (\text{dom}\ (s))$$

If a sequence is not empty, the **first** of the sequence is its first element.

$$s \in \text{seq1}\ (S) \Rightarrow \text{first}\ (s) = s\ (1)$$

Similarly, the **last** of the sequence is its last element.

$$s \in \text{seq1}\ (S) \Rightarrow \text{last}\ (s) = s\ (\text{size}\ (s))$$

If a sequence is not empty, the **tail** of the sequence is the sequence without its first element.

$$s \in \text{seq1}\ (S) \Rightarrow$$
$$\text{tail}\ (s) = \{n, x \mid n \in 1\ ..\ (\text{size}\ (s) - 1) \wedge x = s\ (n + 1)\}$$

Similarly, the **front** of the sequence is the sequence without its last element.

$$s \in \text{seq1}\ (S) \Rightarrow \text{front}\ (s) = (1\ ..\ (\text{size}\ (s) - 1)) \triangleleft s$$

There are other ways of restricting the number of elements of a sequence. The first n elements of a sequence with at least n elements is denoted by $s \uparrow n$, and its definition is as follows.

$$s \in \text{seq}\ (S) \wedge n \le \text{size}\ (s) \Rightarrow s \uparrow n = (1\ ..\ n) \triangleleft s$$

Similarly, all but the first n elements of a sequence with at least n elements is denoted by $s \downarrow n$, and its definition is as follows.

$$s \in \text{seq}\ (S) \wedge n \le \text{size}\ (s) \Rightarrow$$
$$s \downarrow n = \{i, x \mid i \in 1\ ..\ (\text{size}\ (s) - n) \wedge x = s\ (i + n)\}$$

The **reverse** of a (not necessarily non-empty) sequence is the sequence backwards.

$$s \in \text{seq}\ (S) \Rightarrow$$
$$\text{rev}\ (s) = \{n, x \mid n \in 1\ ..\ \text{size}\ (s) \wedge x = s\ (\text{size}\ (s) - n + 1)\}$$

The informal meaning of **concatenation** is the joining together of two sequences into a single sequence, so

$$[1, 5, 0, 7] \,\char`\^\, [3, 2] = [1, 5, 0, 7, 3, 2]$$

where '$\char`\^$' is the **concatenation sign**. Concatenation can be formally defined as follows.

$$s \in \text{seq } (S) \wedge t \in \text{seq } (S) \Rightarrow$$
$$s \,\char`\^\, t = s \cup \{x, y \mid x \in (\text{size } (s) + 1) \,..\, (\text{size } (s) + \text{size } (t))$$
$$\wedge \; y = t \, (x - \text{size } (s))\}$$

In **generalized concatenation**, we take a sequence of sequences, and concatenate them in order. The definition is a recursive definition as follows:

$$\text{conc } ([]) = []$$

$$\text{conc } ([s]) \,\char`\^\, S) = s \,\char`\^\, \text{conc } (S)$$

An element of the right type can be added to the end of a sequence with the **append** operator.

$$s \in \text{seq } (S) \wedge x \in S \Rightarrow s \leftarrow x = s \,\char`\^\, [x]$$

Similarly, an element of the right type can be added to the beginning of a sequence with the **prepend** operator.

$$s \in \text{seq } (S) \wedge x \in S \Rightarrow x \rightarrow s = [x] \,\char`\^\, s$$

For a finite set S we can define a set of sequences called the **permutations** of S. The permutations of S are all the arrangements of the members of S, and can be defined as follows.

$$\text{perm } (S) = \{p \mid p \in \text{iseq } (S) \wedge \text{ran } (p) = S\}$$

Appendix B
Summary tables

226

B.1 Summary of mathematical notation

The following summary illustrates all the mathematical notation supported by the B-Toolkit for writing abstract machines, refinements and implementations. The symbols used for various syntactic categories are as follows: **P**, **Q** are predicates, **z** is a list of variables, **G**, **H**, **I** are substitutions, **E**, **F** are expressions, **S**, **T** are expressions that denote sets, **U** is an expression denoting a set of sets, **m**, **n** are expressions denoting integers, **p**, **q**, **r** are expressions denoting relations, **f** is an expression denoting a function, **j**, **k** are expressions denoting sequences, and **l** is an expression denoting a sequence of sequences.

In each table the first column (**Maths**) gives the mathematical notation that is used in this book. The second column (**B**) gives the notation used to enter the mathematics into the B-Toolkit. The third column gives an informal explanation of what the notation means. The fourth column gives a page reference to where the notation is introduced.

B.1.1 Logic

Maths	B	Explanation	Page
$P \wedge Q$	P & Q	conjunction	206
$P \vee Q$	P or Q	disjunction	206
$P \Rightarrow Q$	P => Q	implication	206
$P \Leftrightarrow Q$	P <=> Q	equivalence	206
$\neg P$	not P	negation	205
$\forall z \bullet P$	!(z).P	universal quantification	212
$\exists z \bullet P$	#(z).P	existential quantification	213
$[G] P$	[G] P	substitution	24

B.1.2 Equality and inequality

Maths	B	Explanation	Page
$E = F$	E = F	equality	204, 214
$E \neq F$	E /= F	inequality	204, 214

B.1.3 Set predicates

Maths	B	Explanation	Page
E ∈ S	E : S	membership	208
E ∉ S	E /: S	non-membership	208
S ⊆ T	S <: T	subset	214
S ⊈ T	S /<: T	not a subset	214
S ⊂ T	S <<: T	proper subset	214
S ⊄ T	S /<<: T	not a proper subset	214

B.1.4 Sets

Maths	B	Explanation	Page
{z | P}	{z | P}	set comprehension	208
E ↦ F	E |-> F	ordered pair	217
S × T	S * T	Cartesian product	218
$\mathbb{P}$ (S)	POW (S)	powerset	215
S ∪ T	S \/ T	union	215
S ∩ T	S /\ T	intersection	215
S − T	S - T	difference	215
∅	{}	empty set	212
$\mathbb{P}_1$ (S)	POW1 (S)	non-empty subsets	215
$\mathbb{F}$ (S)	FIN (S)	finite powerset	216
$\mathbb{F}_1$ (S)	FIN1 (S)	non-empty finite subsets	217
{E}	{E}	singleton set	212
union (U)	union (U)	generalized union	215
inter (U)	inter (U)	generalized intersection	216
$\bigcup$z • (P | E)	UNION (z).(P | E)	generalized union	216
$\bigcap$z • (P | E)	INTER (z).(P | E)	generalized intersection	216

B.1.5 Number predicates

Maths	B	Explanation	Page
m > n	m > n	greater	204
m < n	m < n	less	204
m ≥ n	m >= n	greater or equal	204
m ≤ n	m <= n	less or equal	204

B.1.6 Numbers

Maths	B	Explanation	Page
$\mathbb{N}$	NAT	natural numbers	207
$\mathbb{N}_1$	NAT1	natural numbers	207
min (**S**)	min (**S**)	minimum	217
max (**S**)	max (**S**)	maximum	217
m + n	m + n	sum	204
m − n	m - n	difference	204
m × n	m * n	product	204
m / n	m / n	quotient	204
m mod n	m mod n	remainder	204
m .. n	m .. n	number range	212
card (**S**)	card (**S**)	size	216
$\Sigma z \bullet (P \mid E)$	SIGMA(z).(P | E)	generalized sum	210
$\Pi z \bullet (P \mid E)$	PI(z).(P | E)	generalized product	210

B.1.7 Relations

Maths	B	Explanation	Page
S ↔ T	S <-> T	relations	218
dom (**r**)	dom (**r**)	domain	219
ran (**r**)	ran (**r**)	range	220
p ; q	p ; q	relational composition	220

Maths	B	Explanation	Page
$p \circ q$	p circ q	backward composition	220
id (S)	id (S)	identity	219
$S \triangleleft r$	S <| r	domain restriction	220
$S \triangleleft\!\!\!\!- r$	S <<| r	domain subtraction	220
$r \triangleright T$	r |> T	range restriction	220
$r \triangleright\!\!\!\!- T$	r |>> T	range subtraction	220
r^{-1}	r~	inverse	219
r [S]	r [S]	image	219
$r_1 \triangleleft\!\!\!- r_2$	r_1 <+ r_2	right overriding	220
$r_1 \triangleright\!\!\!- r_2$	r_1 +> r_2	left overriding	221

B.1.8 Functions

Maths	B	Explanation	Page
$S \rightarrow\!\!\!\!\!\rightarrow T$	S +-> T	functions	221
$S \rightarrow T$	S --> T	total functions	221
$S \rightarrowtail\!\!\!\!\!\rightarrow T$	S >+> T	injections	221
$S \rightarrowtail T$	S >-> T	total injections	221
$S \twoheadrightarrow\!\!\!\!\!\rightarrow T$	S +->> T	surjections	222
$S \twoheadrightarrow T$	S -->> T	total surjections	222
$S \rightarrowtail\!\!\!\!\!\rightarrow T$	S >->> T	bijections	222
$\lambda z \bullet (P \mid E)$	%z.(P|E)	lambda abstraction	222
f (E)	f (E)	function application	221

B.1.9 Sequences

Maths	B	Explanation	Page
[ ]	< >	empty sequence	223
seq (S)	seq (S)	sequences	223
seq1 (S)	seq1 (S)	non-empty sequences	223

Maths	B	Explanation	Page
iseq (**S**)	iseq (**S**)	injective sequences	223
iseq1 (**S**)	iseq1 (**S**)	non-empty injective sequences	223
perm (**S**)	perm (**S**)	permutations	225
j ^ **k**	**j** ^ **k**	concatenation	225
E → **j**	**E** -> **j**	prepend	225
j ← **E**	**j** <- **E**	append	225
[**E**]	[**E**]	singleton sequence	224
size (**j**)	size (**j**)	size	224
rev (**j**)	rev (**j**)	reverse	224
j ↑ **n**	**j** /|\ **n**	first **n** elements of **j**	224
j ↓ **n**	**j** \\\|/ **n**	**j** except the first **n** elements	224
first (**j**)	first (**j**)	first element	224
last (**j**)	last (**j**)	last element	224
tail (**j**)	tail (**j**)	**j** except the first element	224
front (**j**)	front (**j**)	**j** except the last element	224
conc (**l**)	conc (**l**)	generalized concatenation	225
" "	" "	string delimiters	164

B.1.10 Substitutions

Maths	B	Explanation	Page
x := **E**	x := E	simple substitution	24
x, y := **E, F**	x, y := E, F	multiple substitution	41
G ; **H**	G ; H	sequence	106
skip	skip	skip	82
x := bool (**P**)	x := bool (**P**)	Boolean substitution	68

Maths	B	Explanation	Page
x :∈ S	x :: S	choice from a set	57
x : P	x : P	choice by predicate	84
f (x) := E	f (x) := E	functional over-riding	55
x ⟵ op (z)	x <-- op (z)	operation with output	43

B.2 Substitutions

The following tables show the notations for simple and generalized substitutions, the axioms defining the meanings of the substitutions, abbreviated substitutions and the pseudo-programming notations. The symbols used for various syntactic categories are as follows: **x**, **y** are variables, **E**, **F** are expressions, **P**, **Q** are predicates, **z** is a list of variables, **G**, **H**, **I** are substitutions, **S** is an expression that denotes a set, and **f** is an expression that denotes a function.

B.2.1 Rules for selected substitutions

Pseudo-program	Rule	Note	Page
[BEGIN G END] Q	[G] Q		46
[PRE P THEN G END] Q	P ∧ [G] Q		26
[IF P THEN G ELSE H END] Q	$(P \Rightarrow [G]\,Q) \wedge$ $(\neg P \Rightarrow [H]\,Q)$		44
[ANY x WHERE P THEN G END] Q	$\forall x \bullet (P \Rightarrow [G]\,Q)$	(1)	57
[CHOICE G OR H END] Q	[G] Q ∧ [H] Q		55
[SELECT P₁ THEN G₁ WHEN P₂ THEN G₂ END] Q	$(P_1 \Rightarrow [G_1]\,Q) \wedge$ $(P_2 \Rightarrow [G_2]\,Q)$		85
[skip] Q	Q		82
[VAR x IN G END] Q	$\forall x \bullet (P \Rightarrow [G]\,Q)$	(1)	142
[LET x BE x = E IN G END] Q	$\forall x \bullet (x = E \Rightarrow [G]\,Q)$	(1)	87
[G ; H] P	[G] [H] P		106

Pseudo-program	Rule	Note	Page
[**G** ; WHILE **P** DO **H** VARIANT **E** INVARIANT **I** END] **Q**	([**G**] **I**) ∧ (**I** ∧ ¬**P** ∧ ⇒ **Q**) ∧ (**I** ⇒ **E** ∈ ℕ) ∧ (**I** ∧ **P** ⇒ [**y** := **E**] [**H**] **E** < **y**) ∧ (**I** ∧ **P** ⇒ [**H**] **I**)	(2)	114

Notes:

(1) **x** is not free in **Q**.

(2) **y** is not free in **H**.

B.2.2 Substitutions defined by other substitutions

Notation	Expansion	Page
x := bool (**P**)	IF **P** THEN **x** := *TRUE* ELSE **x** := *FALSE* END	68
x :∈ **E**	ANY **y** WHERE **y** ∈ **E** THEN **x** := **y** END	62
x : **P**	ANY **y** WHERE [**x** := **y**] **P** THEN **x** := **y** END	92
f (**x**) := **E**	**f** := **f** ⊲ {**x** ↦ **E**}	55
IF **P** THEN **G** END	IF **P** THEN **G** ELSE *skip* END	82
IF **P** THEN **G** ELSIF **Q** THEN **H** ELSE **I** END	IF **P** THEN **G** ELSE (IF **Q** THEN **H** ELSE **I** END) END	83
CASE **E** OF EITHER **S** THEN **G** OR **T** THEN **H** END END	SELECT **E** ∈ **S** THEN **G** WHEN **E** ∈ **T** THEN **H** END	86

B.2.3 Parallel substitution rules

Parallel form	Simplification
x := **E** | | **y** := **F**	**x**, **y** := **E**, **F**
G | | **H**	**H** | | **G**
BEGIN **G** END | | **H**	**G** | | **H**

Parallel form	Simplification
G || *skip*	G
PRE **P** THEN **G** END || **H**	PRE **P** THEN **G** || **H** END
IF **P** THEN **G**$_1$ ELSE **G**$_2$ END || **H**	IF **P** THEN **G**$_1$ || **H** ELSE **G**$_2$ || **H** END
CHOICE **G**$_1$ OR **G**$_2$ END || **H**	CHOICE **G**$_1$ || **H** OR **G**$_2$ || **H** END
SELECT **P**$_1$ THEN **G**$_1$ WHEN **P**$_2$ THEN **G**$_2$ END || **H**	SELECT **P**$_1$ THEN **G**$_1$ || **H** WHEN **P**$_2$ THEN **G**$_2$ || **H** END

B.3 Proof obligations

B.3.1 Machine

In the following machine definition, **x**, **y**, **z** are lists of names, **P**, **Q**, **R**, **L** are predicates, **G**, **H** are substitutions, and *machine* and *opname* are names.

MACHINE

  machine (**x**)

CONSTRAINTS

  P

CONSTANTS

  y

PROPERTIES

  Q

VARIABLES

  z

INVARIANT

  R

INITIALISATION

  H

OPERATIONS

  opname = PRE **L** THEN **G** END

END

The following theorems should be proved.

∃**x** • **P**

There are values **x** that satisfy the constraints. This is the test of the consistency of the constraints.

P ⇒ ∀**y** • **Q**

Given the constraints, there are constants **y** that satisfy the properties. This is the test of consistency of the properties.

P ∧ **Q** ⇒ ∃**z** • **R**

Given the constraints and properties, there are values **z** that establish the invariant. This is the test of implementability.

P ∧ **Q** ⇒ [**H**] **R**

Given the constraints and properties, the initialization substitution **H** serves to establish the invariant **R**. This is the test of correctness of the initialization.

P ∧ **Q** ∧ **R** ∧ **L** ⇒ [**G**] **R**

Given the constraints, properties, invariant and operation precondition, the operation substitution **G** preserves the invariant **R**. This is the test of correctness of an operation, and it is repeated for each operation.

B.3.2 Refinement and implementation

	Abstract	Concrete
variables	X_A	X_C
invariant	P_A	P_C
initialization	G_A	G_C
operation output	y	y
operation precondition	Q_A	Q_C
operation substitution	H_A	H_C

Correctness of initialization

$$[G_C] \neg [G_A] \neg P_C$$

Correctness of operation

$$P_A \wedge P_C \wedge Q_A \Rightarrow Q_C \wedge [H'_C] \neg [H_A] \neg (P_C \wedge y' = y)$$

where H'_C is H_C with y replaced by y'.

B.4 Clauses of machines, refinements and implementations

The table on the next two pages shows the clauses that can appear in each kind of abstract machine.

Machine	Refinement	Implementation
MACHINE name (parameter list)	REFINEMENT name	IMPLEMENTATION name
CONSTRAINTS predicate		
	REFINES name	REFINES name
USES (renamed) instantiated machines		
SEES (renamed) instantiated machines	SEES (renamed) instantiated machines	SEES (renamed) instantiated machines
INCLUDES (renamed) instantiated machines	INCLUDES (renamed) instantiated machines	
		IMPORTS (renamed) instantiated machines
PROMOTES (renamed) operations		PROMOTES (renamed) operations
EXTENDS (renamed) instantiated machines		
SETS names	SETS names	SETS names

Machine	Refinement	Implementation
	CONSTANTS names	CONSTANTS names
	PROPERTIES predicate	PROPERTIES predicate
CONSTANTS names	VARIABLES names	
PROPERTIES predicate	INVARIANT predicate	INVARIANT predicate
VARIABLES names	ASSERTIONS predicate	ASSERTIONS predicate
INVARIANT predicate	DEFINITIONS definitions	DEFINITIONS definitions
ASSERTIONS predicate	INITIALISATION substitution	INITIALISATION substitution
DEFINITIONS definitions	OPERATIONS substitutions	OPERATIONS substitutions
INITIALISATION substitution	END	END
OPERATIONS substitutions		
END		

Appendix C
Library machines

The following machine definitions are a selection from the B-Toolkit library, and are reproduced here by kind permission of B-Core UK Ltd. Each machine definition is preceded by an informal explanation of its purpose. Some of the definitions have been abridged by removing operations, but the operations required for solving the exercises are all believed to be present. B-Core (1994) contains a summary of all the machines in the B-Toolkit Reusable Module Library.

C.1 The Boolean type

This machine is a type machine with no state. It establishes the set *BOOL*, the values *TRUE* and *FALSE*, and operations on them. This definition is given in its entirety.

MACHINE

    Bool_TYPE

SETS

    BOOL = {FALSE, TRUE}

OPERATIONS

    bb ⟵ *CNJ_BOOL (cc, dd)* =
      PRE
        cc ∈ *BOOL* ∧
        dd ∈ *BOOL*
      THEN
        bb := bool *(cc = TRUE ∧ dd = TRUE)*
      END
    ;
    bb ⟵ *DIS_BOOL (cc, dd)* =
      PRE
        cc ∈ *BOOL* ∧
        dd ∈ *BOOL*
      THEN
        bb := bool *(cc = TRUE ∨ dd = TRUE)*
      END
    ;
    bb ⟵ *NEG_BOOL (cc)* =
      PRE
        cc ∈ *BOOL*
      THEN
        bb := bool *(cc = FALSE)*
      END
    ;
    vv ⟵ *BTS_BOOL (bb)* =
      PRE
        bb ∈ *BOOL*
      THEN
        IF
          bb = TRUE
        THEN
          vv := 1

```
   ELSE
      vv := 0
   END
 END
```

END

C.2 The variable machine

A complete definition of *Vvar* is to be found in Figure 8.2 on page 138.

C.3 The natural number machine

The *Nvar* machine models a natural number in the range 0 .. *maxint*, where *maxint* is the machine's only parameter. The machine has a constraint that *maxint* must not exceed 2 147 483 646. The value stored in the machine is initialized to zero. The definition of this machine has been abridged.

MACHINE

   Nvar (*maxint*)

CONSTRAINTS

   $maxint \leq 2147483646$

SEES

   Bool_TYPE

VARIABLES

   Nvar

INVARIANT

   $Nvar \in 0. .. maxint$

INITIALISATION

   $Nvar := 0$

OPERATIONS

$vv \longleftarrow VAL\_NVAR =$
  BEGIN
    $vv := Nvar$
  END
;
$STO\_NVAR\ (vv) =$
  PRE
    $vv \in 0\ ..\ maxint$
  THEN
    $Nvar := vv$
  END
;
$INC\_NVAR =$
  PRE
    $Nvar + 1 \in 0\ ..\ maxint$
  THEN
    $Nvar := Nvar + 1$
  END
;
$DEC\_NVAR =$
  PRE
    $Nvar \in 1\ ..\ maxint$
  THEN
    $Nvar := Nvar - 1$
  END
;
$bb \longleftarrow EQL\_NVAR\ (vv) =$
  PRE
    $vv \in 0\ ..\ maxint$
  THEN
    $bb := $ bool $(Nvar = vv)$
  END

END

C.4 The scalar type

This machine is a type machine with no state. It establishes the set *SCALAR*, and operations on the values in it. This definition is given in its entirety.

MACHINE

Scalar_TYPE

SEES

  Bool_TYPE

SETS

  SCALAR

CONSTANTS

  MaxScalar

PROPERTIES

  $MaxScalar = 2147483646 \land$
  $SCALAR = 0 \mathinner{\ldotp\ldotp} 2147483646 \land$
  $\text{card}\,(SCALAR) = 2147483647$

OPERATIONS

  $uu \longleftarrow SCL\,(vv) =$
    PRE
      $vv \in 0 \mathinner{\ldotp\ldotp} MaxScalar$
    THEN
      $uu := vv$
    END
  ;
  $uu \longleftarrow MIN\,(vv, ww) =$
    PRE
      $vv \in 0 \mathinner{\ldotp\ldotp} MaxScalar \land$
      $ww \in 0 \mathinner{\ldotp\ldotp} MaxScalar$
    THEN
      $uu := \min\,(\{vv, ww\})$
    END
  ;
  $uu \longleftarrow MAX\,(vv, ww) =$
    PRE
      $vv \in 0 \mathinner{\ldotp\ldotp} MaxScalar \land$
      $ww \in 0 \mathinner{\ldotp\ldotp} MaxScalar$
    THEN
      $uu := \max\,(\{vv, ww\})$
    END
  ;
  $uu \longleftarrow INC\,(vv) =$
    PRE
      $vv \in 0 \mathinner{\ldotp\ldotp} MaxScalar \land$
      $vv + 1 \leq MaxScalar$

```
    THEN
      uu := vv + 1
    END
  ;
  uu ⟵ DEC (vv) =
    PRE
      vv ∈ 1 .. MaxScalar
    THEN
      uu := vv − 1
    END
  ;
  uu ⟵ ADD (vv, ww) =
    PRE
      vv ∈ 0 .. MaxScalar ∧
      ww ∈ 0 .. MaxScalar ∧
      vv + ww ≤ MaxScalar
    THEN
      uu := vv + ww
    END
  ;
  uu ⟵ MUL (vv, ww) =
    PRE
      vv ∈ 0 .. MaxScalar ∧
      ww ∈ 0 .. MaxScalar ∧
      vv × ww ≤ MaxScalar
    THEN
      uu := vv × ww
    END
  ;
  uu ⟵ SUB (vv, ww) =
    PRE
      vv ∈ 0 .. MaxScalar ∧
      ww ∈ 0 .. MaxScalar ∧
      vv ≥ ww
    THEN
      uu := vv − ww
    END
  ;
  uu ⟵ DIV (vv, ww) =
    PRE
      vv ∈ 0 .. MaxScalar ∧
      ww ∈ 1 .. MaxScalar
    THEN
      uu := vv / ww
    END
```

;
$uu \longleftarrow MOD \; (vv, ww) =$
   PRE
     $vv \in 0 \; .. \; MaxScalar \; \wedge$
     $ww \in 1 \; .. \; MaxScalar$
   THEN
     $uu := vv - ww \times (vv \; / \; ww)$
   END
;
$bb \longleftarrow EQL \; (vv, ww) =$
   PRE
     $vv \in 0 \; .. \; MaxScalar \; \wedge$
     $ww \in 0 \; .. \; MaxScalar$
   THEN
     $bb := \mathsf{bool} \; (vv = ww)$
   END
;
$bb \longleftarrow NEQ \; (vv, ww) =$
   PRE
     $vv \in 0 \; .. \; MaxScalar \; \wedge$
     $ww \in 0 \; .. \; MaxScalar$
   THEN
     $bb := \mathsf{bool} \; (vv \neq ww)$
   END
;
$bb \longleftarrow GTR \; (vv, ww) =$
   PRE
     $vv \in 0 \; .. \; MaxScalar \; \wedge$
     $ww \in 0 \; .. \; MaxScalar$
   THEN
     $bb := \mathsf{bool} \; (vv > ww)$
   END
;
$bb \longleftarrow GEQ \; (vv, ww) =$
   PRE
     $vv \in 0 \; .. \; MaxScalar \; \wedge$
     $ww \in 0 \; .. \; MaxScalar$
   THEN
     $bb := \mathsf{bool} \; (vv \geq ww)$
   END
;
$bb \longleftarrow SMR \; (vv, ww) =$
   PRE
     $vv \in 0 \; .. \; MaxScalar \; \wedge$
     $ww \in 0 \; .. \; MaxScalar$

```
      THEN
        bb := bool (vv < ww)
      END
    ;
    bb ⟵ LEQ (vv, ww) =
      PRE
        vv ∈ 0 .. MaxScalar ∧
        ww ∈ 0 .. MaxScalar
      THEN
        bb := bool (vv ≤ ww)
      END
    ;
    bb ⟵ EQZ (vv) =
      PRE
        vv ∈ 0 .. MaxScalar
      THEN
        bb := bool (vv = 0)
      END
```

END

C.5 The sequence machine

The machine *Vseq* provides a sequence. The parameters are *VALUE* for the values in the sequence, and *maxsize* for the maximum length of the sequence. Initially the sequence is empty. The definition of this machine has been abridged.

MACHINE

   Vseq (VALUE, maxsize)

SEES

   Bool_TYPE

VARIABLES

   Vseq

INVARIANT

   Vseq ∈ seq *(VALUE)* ∧
   size *(Vseq)* ≤ *maxsize*

INITIALISATION

$Vseq := [\ ]$

OPERATIONS

$STO\_SEQ \ (ii, \ vv) =$
  PRE
    $vv \in VALUE \ \wedge$
    $ii \in 1 \ .. \ \text{size} \ (Vseq)$
  THEN
    $Vseq \ (ii) := vv$
  END
;
$CLR\_SEQ =$
  BEGIN
    $Vseq := [\ ]$
  END
;
$PSH\_SEQ \ (vv) =$
  PRE
    $vv \in VALUE \ \wedge$
    $\text{size} \ (Vseq) < maxsize$
  THEN
    $Vseq := Vseq \leftarrow vv$
  END
;
$POP\_SEQ =$
  PRE
    $\text{size} \ (Vseq) \neq 0$
  THEN
    $Vseq := \text{front} \ (Vseq)$
  END
;
$vv \longleftarrow FST\_SEQ =$
  PRE
    $\text{size} \ (Vseq \ ) \neq 0$
  THEN
    $vv := Vseq \ (1)$
  END
;
$vv \longleftarrow LST\_SEQ =$
  PRE
    $\text{size} \ (Vseq) \neq 0$

```
    THEN
      vv := Vseq (size (Vseq))
    END
  ;
  TAL_SEQ =
    PRE
      size (Vseq) ≠ 0
    THEN
      Vseq := tail (Vseq)
    END
  ;
  SWP_SEQ (ii, jj) =
    PRE
      ii ∈ 1 .. size (Vseq) ∧
      jj ∈ 1 .. size (Vseq)
    THEN
      Vseq :=
        Vseq ◁ {ii ↦ Vseq (jj), jj ↦ Vseq (ii)}
    END
  ;
  vv ⟵ VAL_SEQ (ii) =
    PRE
      ii ∈ 1 .. size (Vseq)
    THEN
      vv := Vseq (ii)
    END
  ;
  nn ⟵ LEN_SEQ =
    BEGIN
      nn := size (Vseq)
    END
  ;
  bb, ii ⟵ SCH_LO_EQL_SEQ (jj, kk, vv) =
    PRE
      vv ∈ VALUE ∧
      jj ∈ dom (Vseq) ∧
      kk ∈ dom (Vseq)
    THEN
      LET
        ss
      BE
        ss = jj .. kk ∩ Vseq ⁻¹ [{vv}]
```

```
  IN
    bb := bool (ss ≠ Ø) | |
    ii := min (ss ∪ {maxsize})
  END
 END

END
```

C.6 The sequence object machine

An abridged definition of *seq_obj* is to be found in Chapter 8.

C.7 The set machine

The *set* machine implements a finite set. The two parameters are a set *VALUE* to fix the kind of values to be kept in the set, and a natural number *maxcrd*, the maximum size of the set. The model includes *sset*, which is the set itself, and *ordn*, a sequence of the members of the set that can be used for browsing.

There are operations to make the set empty (*CLR_SET*), add a member to the set if it is not full (*ENT_SET*), and remove a member from the set if it is not empty (*RMV_SET*). The operations to add and remove a member might change the sequence in an unpredictable way.

There are enquiry operations for the preconditions of these operations, one to find out if the set is full (*FUL_SET*) and one to find out if it is empty (*EMP_SET*).

There are also enquiry operations to find out whether a natural number is a valid index into the sequence (*XST_IDX_SET*), to find out the size of the set (*CRD_SET*), to retrieve the value from the sequence at a given valid index (*VAL_SET*), and to decide whether a value is a member of the set (*MBR_SET*).

Lastly there is an operation to extract any member of the set if it is not empty (*ANY_SET*).

This definition is given in its entirety.

MACHINE

   set (*VALUE, maxcrd*)

SEES

   Bool_TYPE

VARIABLES

   sset, ordn

INVARIANT

$sset \in \mathbb{F}\ (VALUE) \land$
$ordn \in \text{perm}\ (sset) \land$
$\text{card}\ (sset) \leq maxcrd$

INITIALISATION

$sset, ordn := \emptyset, [\ ]$

OPERATIONS

```
bb ⟵ FUL_SET =
  BEGIN
    bb := bool (card (sset) = maxcrd)
  END
;
bb ⟵ XST_IDX_SET (ii) =
  PRE
    ii ∈ 1 .. maxcrd
  THEN
    bb := bool (ii ∈ 1 .. card (sset))
  END
;
nn ⟵ CRD_SET =
  BEGIN
    nn := card (sset)
  END
;
vv ⟵ VAL_SET (ii) =
  PRE
    ii ∈ 1 .. card (sset)
  THEN
    vv := ordn (ii)
  END
;
vv ⟵ ANY_SET =
  PRE
    ¬(sset = ∅)
  THEN
    vv :∈ sset
  END
;
```

```
CLR_SET =
  BEGIN
    sset := Ø ||
    ordn := [ ]
  END
;
ENT_SET (vv) =
  PRE
    vv ∈ VALUE ∧
    card (sset) < maxcrd
  THEN
    sset := sset ∪ {vv} ||
    ordn :∈ perm (sset ∪ {vv})
  END
;
RMV_SET (vv) =
  PRE
    vv ∈ VALUE
  THEN
    sset := sset − {vv} ||
    ordn :∈ perm (sset − {vv})
  END
;
bb ⟵ MBR_SET (vv) =
  PRE
    vv ∈ VALUE
  THEN
    bb := bool (vv ∈ sset)
  END
;
bb ⟵ EMP_SET =
  BEGIN
    bb := bool (sset = Ø)
  END

END
```

C.8 The string type

This machine is a type machine with no state. It establishes the sets *STRING* and *CHAR*. This definition is given in its entirety.

MACHINE

String_TYPE

CONSTANTS

> STRING, EmptyString, CHAR,
> CHARperWORD,
> UnPack

PROPERTIES

> $STRING = $ seq $(0 .. 255) \wedge$
> $CHAR = 0 .. 255 \wedge$
> $UnPack \in \mathbb{N} \nrightarrow \mathbb{N} \rightarrow$ seq $(CHAR) \wedge$
> $EmptyString \in STRING \wedge$
> size $(EmptyString) = 0 \wedge$
> $EmptyString = $ "" $\wedge$
> $CHARperWORD = 4$

OPERATIONS

> $rr \longleftarrow ASSIGN_ANY_STR = $
>   BEGIN
> $rr :\in STRING$
>   END
> ;
> $rr \longleftarrow CPY_STR (ss) = $
>   PRE
> $ss \in STRING \wedge$
>   size $(ss) \le 250$
>   THEN
> $rr := ss$
>   END

END

C.9 The string object machine

Strings are identified by tokens that are members of the given set *STROBJ*. *sstrn* is the set of tokens currently associated with strings, and *sstro* is the relation between the tokens and the strings. *stotstr* is a counter representing the amount of memory used by the strings. *maxobj* is the maximum number of tokens that this machine can cope with. The rôle of *maxmem* is not made explicit in the machine invariant, but it is an upper bound for *stotstr*. Initially no tokens are in use, and the counter *stotstr* is zero. The definition of this machine has been abridged.

MACHINE

   str_obj (*maxobj*, *maxmem*)

CONSTRAINTS

   maxobj > 0

SEES

   Bool_TYPE, *String_TYPE*

SETS

   STROBJ

PROPERTIES

   card (*STROBJ*) = *maxobj*

VARIABLES

   strtok, *strstruct*, *strmem*

INVARIANT

   strtok ⊆ *STROBJ* ∧
   strstruct ∈ *strtok* → *STRING* ∧
   strmem ∈ ℕ

INITIALISATION

   strtok, *strstruct*, *strmem* := ∅, ∅, 0

OPERATIONS

   pp ⟵ *ANY_STR_OBJ* =
    BEGIN
     pp :∈ *STROBJ*
    END
   ;
   bb, *pp* ⟵ *NEW_STR_OBJ* (*nn*) =
    PRE
     strtok ≠ *STROBJ* ∧
     nn ∈ *STRING*
    THEN
     IF
      strmem + size (*nn*) ≤ *maxmem*

```
        THEN
          ANY
            qq
          WHERE
            qq ∈ STROBJ − strtok
          THEN
            strstruct (qq) := nn ||
            strtok := strtok ∪ {qq} ||
            strmem := strmem + size (nn) ||
            pp := qq ||
            bb := TRUE
          END
        ELSE
          bb := FALSE ||
          pp :∈ STROBJ
        END
      END
    ;
    KIL_STR_OBJ (pp) =
      PRE
        pp ∈ strtok
      THEN
        strstruct := {pp} ◁ strstruct ||
        strtok := strtok − {pp} ||
        strmem := strmem − size (strstruct (pp))
      END
    ;
    bb ⟵ EQL_LIT_STR_OBJ (tt, nn) =
      PRE
        tt ∈ strtok ∧
        nn ∈ STRING
      THEN
        bb := bool (strstruct (tt) = nn)
      END

  END
```

C.10 The array machine

The model chosen for an array is a total function from the set of indexes (1 .. *maxidx*) to the set of values (*VALUE*). The array is initialized in an arbitrary way. The definition of this machine has been abridged.

MACHINE

   Varr (*VALUE, maxidx*)

CONSTRAINTS

   maxidx > 0

SEES

   Bool_TYPE

VARIABLES

   Varr

INVARIANT

   Varr $\in 1 \mathrel{..} maxidx \rightarrow VALUE$

INITIALISATION

   Varr $:\in 1 \mathrel{..} maxidx \rightarrow VALUE$

OPERATIONS

```
bb ⟵  TST_IDX_ARR (ii) =
  PRE
    ii ∈ ℕ
  THEN
    bb := bool (ii ∈ 1 .. maxidx)
  END
;
vv ⟵  VAL_ARR (ii) =
  PRE
    ii ∈ 1 .. maxidx
  THEN
    vv := Varr (ii)
  END
;
STO_ARR (ii, vv) =
  PRE
    vv ∈ VALUE ∧
    ii ∈ 1 .. maxidx
  THEN
    Varr (ii) := vv
  END
;
```

```
bb ⟵ EQL_ARR (ii, vv) =
  PRE
    vv ∈ VALUE ∧
    ii ∈ 1 .. maxidx
  THEN
    bb := bool (Varr (ii) = vv)
  END
;
bb ⟵ NEQ_ARR (ii, vv) =
  PRE
    vv ∈ VALUE ∧
    ii ∈ 1 .. maxidx
  THEN
    bb := bool (Varr (ii) ≠ vv)
  END
;
bb, ii ⟵ SCH_LO_EQL_ARR (jj, kk, vv) =
  PRE
    vv ∈ VALUE ∧
    jj ∈ 1 .. maxidx ∧
    kk ∈ 1 .. maxidx
  THEN
    LET ss BE
      ss = jj .. kk ∩ Varr ⁻¹ [{vv}]
    IN
      bb := bool (ss ≠ ∅) ||
      ii := min (ss ∪ {maxidx})
    END
  END
;
SWP_ARR (ii, jj) =
  PRE
    ii ∈ 1 .. maxidx ∧
    jj ∈ 1 .. maxidx
  THEN
    Varr :=
    Varr ⊲ {ii ↦ Varr (jj), jj ↦ Varr (ii)}
  END

END
```

Sample solutions to selected exercises

The following solutions are samples only; many of the problems have other solutions that differ from those given here both in style and content. Some of the exercises have no solution given, and are marked 'For discussion'. The author believes that these exercises have solutions that can be worked out by anyone who has read the appropriate chapters of the book, and readers are encouraged to find a group of people to discuss their solutions with.

The sample solutions are arranged in order of the chapters in the book.

Chapter 2

(2.1)   The theorem is as follows:

$$rfree \subseteq RES \wedge rr \in RES \wedge rr \notin rfree \Rightarrow$$
$$[rfree := rfree \cup \{rr\}] \, rfree \subseteq RES$$

Making the substitution in the consequent gives the following:

$$rfree \subseteq RES \wedge rr \in RES \wedge rr \notin rfree \Rightarrow$$
$$rfree \cup \{rr\} \subseteq RES$$

which is a theorem of set theory.

(2.2)   The theorem is as follows:

$$rfree \subseteq RES \wedge rrs \subseteq RES \Rightarrow$$
$$[rfree := rrs] \, rfree \subseteq RES$$

Making the substitution in the consequent gives the following:

$$rfree \subseteq RES \wedge rrs \subseteq RES \Rightarrow rrs \subseteq RES$$

and the consequent is one of the hypotheses.

(2.3)   The results of the substitutions are as follows:

(a) $1 \neq yy$

(b) $yy = yy$

(c) $\forall xx \bullet (xx \in \mathbb{N} \Rightarrow xx \geq yy) \vee 1 \geq 0$

(d) $yy > 0$

(e) $xx + 1 > 0$

(2.4)   The results of the substitutions are as follows:

(a) $xx > 0 \wedge xx - 1 > yy$

(b) $xx > yy \wedge yy > 0$

(c) $xx \in \mathbb{N} \wedge xs \cup \{xx\} \subseteq \mathbb{N}$

(d) $xx \in \mathbb{N} \wedge \forall ww \bullet (ww \in \mathbb{N} \Rightarrow xx > zz)$

Chapter 3

(3.1) First use the *isenrolled* operation to check that the student is already enrolled. If the output is *FALSE*, then nothing more can be done. If it is *TRUE*, use the *istested* operation to see if the student has done the exercises. If the result is *TRUE*, then nothing more can be done, but if it is false, then it is safe to use the *test* operation to record that this student has done the exercises.

(3.2) First use the *isenrolled* operation to check that the student is already enrolled. If the output is *FALSE*, then nothing more can be done, but otherwise use the *istested* operation to decide whether the student is entitled to a certificate (*TRUE*) or not (*FALSE*). Now use the *leave* operation to record that this student has left the class.

(3.3) The machine *Positive* could be defined as follows.

MACHINE

  Positive (*maxint*)

VARIABLES

  val

INVARIANT

  val ∈ 0 .. *maxint*

INITIALISATION

  val := 0

OPERATIONS

```
set (xx) =
  PRE
    xx ∈ 0 .. maxint
  THEN
    val := xx
  END
;
vv ⟵ read =
  vv := val
;
```

$incr =$
  PRE
    $val < maxint$
  THEN
    $val := val + 1$
  END
;
$decr =$
  PRE
    $val > 0$
  THEN
    $val := val - 1$
  END
;
$add\ (xx) =$
  PRE
    $xx \in \mathbb{N} \wedge xx + val \leq maxint$
  THEN
    $val := xx + val$
  END
;
$subtract\ (xx) =$
  PRE
    $xx \in \mathbb{N} \wedge val - xx \geq 0$
  THEN
    $val := val - xx$
  END
;
$mult\ (xx) =$
  PRE
    $xx \in \mathbb{N} \wedge val \times xx \leq maxint$
  THEN
    $val := val \times xx$
  END

END

(3.4)   The machine *Array* could be defined as follows.

MACHINE

Array (maxindex, TYPE)

VARIABLES

arr

INVARIANT

$arr \in 1 \ .. \ maxindex \nrightarrow TYPE$

INITIALISATION

$arr := \emptyset$

OPERATIONS

$set \ (ix, \ tt) =$
  PRE
    $ix \in 1 \ .. \ maxindex \ \wedge \ tt \in TYPE$
  THEN
    $arr := arr \vartriangleleft \{ix \mapsto tt\}$
  END
;
$tt \longleftarrow read \ (ix) =$
  PRE
    $ix \in \mathrm{dom} \ (arr)$
  THEN
    $tt := arr \ (ix)$
  END
;
$swap \ (ix, \ jx) =$
  PRE
    $ix \in \mathrm{dom} \ (arr) \ \wedge$
    $jx \in \mathrm{dom} \ (arr)$
  THEN
    $arr := arr \vartriangleleft \{ix \mapsto arr \ (jx), jx \mapsto arr \ (ix)\}$
  END

END

(3.5)   The machine *Nat_SET* could be defined as follows:

MACHINE

Nat_SET (max_card, max_nat)

CONSTRAINTS

$max\_nat \geq max\_card$

VARIABLES

nat_set

INVARIANT

$nat\_set \subseteq 0 \mathrel{..} max\_nat \wedge$
$\mathsf{card}\,(nat\_set) \le max\_card$

INITIALISATION

$nat\_set := \varnothing$

OPERATIONS

$nn \longleftarrow howbig =$
  BEGIN
    $nn := \mathsf{card}\,(nat\_set)$
  END
;
$add\,(nn) =$
  PRE
    $nn \in 0 \mathrel{..} max\_nat \wedge$
    $\mathsf{card}\,(nat\_set) < max\_card$
  THEN
    $nat\_set := nat\_set \cup \{nn\}$
  END
;
$remove\,(nn) =$
  PRE
    $nn \in 0 \mathrel{..} max\_nat$
  THEN
    $nat\_set := nat\_set - \{nn\}$
  END
;
$bb \longleftarrow find\,(nn) =$
  PRE
    $nn \in 0 \mathrel{..} max\_nat$
  THEN
    IF
      $nn \in nat\_set$
    THEN
      $bb := 1$
    ELSE
      $bb := 0$
    END
  END

END

(3.6)   The results of the substitutions are as follows:

(a) $1 + 2 \geq zz$

(b) $\forall xx \bullet (xx \in \mathbb{N} \Rightarrow xx \geq 1)$

(c) $yy > xx$

(3.7)   The results of the substitutions are as follows:

(a) $(x > 0 \Rightarrow 1 = 1) \wedge (x = 0 \Rightarrow x + 1 = 1)$

(b) $(x < 5 \Rightarrow x + 4 \geq 4) \wedge (x \geq 5 \Rightarrow x - 1 \geq 4)$

(c) $(x \in S \Rightarrow x \in S \cap (T \cup \{x\})) \wedge$
       $(x \notin S \Rightarrow x \in (S \cup \{x\}) \cap T)$

(3.8)   The proof obligation is as follows:

$enrolled \subseteq STUDENT \wedge$
$tested \subseteq STUDENT \wedge$
$tested \subseteq enrolled \wedge$
card $(enrolled) \leq class\_size \wedge$
$st \in enrolled$
$\Rightarrow$
[IF
  $st \in tested$
THEN
  $tested := tested - \{st\} \;||$
  $enrolled := enrolled - \{st\}$
ELSE
  $enrolled := enrolled - \{st\}$
END]
$(enrolled \subseteq STUDENT \wedge$
$tested \subseteq STUDENT \wedge$
$tested \subseteq enrolled \wedge$
card $(enrolled) \leq class\_size)$

For the moment we ignore the antecedent, and concentrate on simplifying the consequent. First we use the IF-THEN-ELSE-END rule.

$(st \in tested \;\Rightarrow$
$[tested := tested - \{st\} \;||$
$enrolled := enrolled - \{st\}]$
$(enrolled \subseteq STUDENT \wedge$
$tested \subseteq STUDENT \wedge$
$tested \subseteq enrolled \wedge$
card $(enrolled) \leq class\_size)) \wedge$

$(st \notin tested \Rightarrow$
$[enrolled := enrolled - \{st\}]$
$(enrolled \subseteq STUDENT \wedge$
$tested \subseteq STUDENT \wedge$
$tested \subseteq enrolled \wedge$
$card\ (enrolled) \leq class\_size))$

Now we make the remaining substitutions to give the following:

$(st \in tested \Rightarrow$
$enrolled - \{st\} \subseteq STUDENT \wedge$
$tested - \{st\} \subseteq STUDENT \wedge$
$tested - \{st\} \subseteq enrolled - \{st\} \wedge$
$card\ (enrolled - \{st\}) \leq class\_size) \wedge$
$(st \notin tested \Rightarrow$
$enrolled - \{st\} \subseteq STUDENT \wedge$
$tested \subseteq STUDENT \wedge$
$tested \subseteq enrolled - \{st\} \wedge$
$card\ (enrolled - \{st\}) \leq class\_size)$

The consequent can be deduced from the antecedent by the laws of set theory.

Chapter 4

(4.1) For discussion.

(4.2) The first obligation is to do with the initialization.

$\emptyset \subseteq 1\ ..\ 100$

and it is a theorem of set theory.
The second obligation is for the operation.

$gone \subseteq 1\ ..\ 100 \Rightarrow$
$(gone = 1\ ..\ 100 \Rightarrow gone \subseteq 1\ ..\ 100) \wedge$
$(gone \neq 1\ ..\ 100 \Rightarrow$
$\forall nn \bullet (nn \in \mathbb{N} \wedge nn \in 1\ ..\ 100 \wedge nn \notin gone \Rightarrow$
$[gone := gone \cup \{nn\}]\ gone \subseteq 1\ ..\ 100))$

The first conjunct in the consequent of the outer implication is a theorem of set theory. The second conjunct can be simplified to give the following simpler obligation.

$gone \subseteq 1\ ..\ 100 \Rightarrow$
$(gone \neq 1\ ..\ 100 \wedge nn \in \mathbb{N} \wedge nn \in 1\ ..\ 100 \wedge nn \notin gone$
$\Rightarrow$
$gone \cup \{nn\} \subseteq 1\ ..\ 100)$

This follows from theorems of set theory.

(4.3)   The rest of the storage manager machine could be defined as follows.

OPERATIONS

$block \longleftarrow get\ (us)$ =
  PRE
    $us \in USER\ \wedge$
    $\text{dom}\ (alloc) \neq 1\ ..\ maxblocks$
  THEN
    ANY
      fb
    WHERE
      $fb \in (1\ ..\ maxblocks) - \text{dom}\ (alloc)$
    THEN
      $block,\ alloc := fb,\ alloc \cup \{fb \mapsto us\}$
    END
  END
;
$free\ (bn,\ us)$ =
  PRE
    $bn \in 1\ ..\ maxblocks\ \wedge$
    $us \in USER\ \wedge$
    $bn \mapsto us \in alloc$
  THEN
    $alloc := \{bn\} \lhd alloc$
  END
;
$fn \longleftarrow askfree$ =
  BEGIN
    $fn := \text{card}\ ((1\ ..\ maxblocks) - \text{dom}\ (alloc))$
  END
;
$freeall\ (us)$ =
  PRE
    $us \in USER$
  THEN
    $alloc := alloc \rhd \{us\}$
  END

END

(4.4) We have to show that

$$[\text{ANY } xx \text{ WHERE } xx \in \mathbb{N} \wedge xx > 5 \text{ THEN } yy := xx \text{ END}]$$
$$yy > 5$$

Applying the ANY-WHERE-THEN-END rule gives

$$\forall xx \bullet (xx \in \mathbb{N} \wedge xx > 5 \Rightarrow [yy := xx] \, yy > 5)$$

Making the simple substitution gives

$$\forall xx \bullet (xx \in \mathbb{N} \wedge xx > 5 \Rightarrow xx > 5)$$

The last predicate is a theorem of arithmetic.

(4.5) We have to show that

$$[\text{ANY } xx \text{ WHERE } xx \in \mathbb{N} \wedge xx > 0$$
$$\text{THEN } yy := xx + 1 \text{ END}] \, yy > 1$$

Applying the ANY-WHERE-THEN-END rule gives

$$\forall xx \bullet (xx \in \mathbb{N} \wedge xx > 0 \Rightarrow [yy := xx + 1] \, yy > 1)$$

Making the simple substitution gives

$$\forall xx \bullet (xx \in \mathbb{N} \wedge xx > 0 \Rightarrow xx + 1 > 1)$$

The last predicate is a theorem of arithmetic.

(4.6) We have to show that

$$[\text{ANY } xx \text{ WHERE } xx \in \mathbb{N} \wedge xx > yy \text{ THEN } zz := xx \text{ END}]$$
$$zz > yy$$

Applying the ANY-WHERE-THEN-END rule gives

$$\forall xx \bullet (xx \in \mathbb{N} \wedge xx > yy \Rightarrow [zz := xx] \, zz > yy)$$

Making the simple substitution gives

$$\forall xx \bullet (xx \in \mathbb{N} \wedge xx > yy \Rightarrow xx > yy)$$

The last predicate is a theorem of arithmetic.

(4.7) We have to show that

$$[\text{CHOICE } xx := 1 \text{ OR } xx := 2 \text{ END}] \, xx > 0$$

Applying the CHOICE-OR-END rule gives

$$[xx := 1] \, xx > 0 \wedge [xx := 2] \, xx > 0$$

Making the simple substitutions gives

$$1 > 0 \wedge 2 > 0$$

The last predicate is a theorem of arithmetic.

(4.8)   We have to show that

$$[\text{CHOICE } xx := yy - 1 \text{ OR } xx := yy + 1 \text{ END}] \; xx \neq yy$$

Applying the CHOICE-OR-END rule gives

$$[xx := yy - 1] \; xx \neq yy \wedge [xx := yy + 1] \; xx \neq yy$$

Making the simple substitutions gives

$$yy - 1 \neq yy \wedge yy + 1 \neq yy$$

The last predicate is a theorem of arithmetic.

(4.9)   We begin with

$$[\text{CHOICE } xx := 1 \text{ OR } xx := 2 \text{ END}] \; xx = 1$$

Applying the CHOICE-OR-END rule gives

$$[xx := 1] \; xx = 1 \wedge [xx := 2] \; xx = 1$$

Making the simple substitutions gives

$$1 = 1 \wedge 2 = 1$$

This is false.
        We begin with

$$[\text{CHOICE } xx := 1 \text{ OR } xx := 2 \text{ END}] \; xx \neq 1$$

Applying the CHOICE-OR-END rule gives

$$[xx := 1] \; xx \neq 1 \wedge [xx := 2] \; xx \neq 1$$

Making the simple substitutions gives

$$1 \neq 1 \wedge 2 \neq 1$$

This is also false.

(4.10)   We have to show that

$$[xx :\in \mathbb{N}] \; xx \in \mathbb{N}$$

Applying the choice-from-a-set rule gives

$$\forall zz \bullet (zz \in \mathbb{N} \Rightarrow [xx := zz] \; xx \in \mathbb{N})$$

Making the simple substitution gives

$$\forall zz \bullet (zz \in \mathbb{N} \Rightarrow zz \in \mathbb{N})$$

The last predicate is a theorem of set theory.

(4.11)   We have to show that

$$[xx :\in \{yy\}] \; xx = yy$$

Applying the choice-from-a-set rule gives

$$\forall zz \bullet (zz \in \{yy\} \Rightarrow [xx := zz] \; xx = yy)$$

Making the simple substitution gives

$$\forall zz \bullet (zz \in \{yy\} \Rightarrow zz = yy)$$

The last predicate is a theorem of set theory.

(4.12)   We have to show that

$$[xx :\in \{0, 1, 2\}] \; xx \neq 3$$

Applying the choice-from-a-set rule gives

$$\forall yy \bullet (yy \in \{0, 1, 2\} \Rightarrow [xx := yy] \; xx \neq 3)$$

Making the simple substitution gives

$$\forall yy \bullet (yy \in \{0, 1, 2\} \Rightarrow yy \neq 3)$$

The last predicate is a theorem of set theory.

(4.13)   We have to show that

$$[xx :\in yy \cap zz] \; xx \in yy$$

Applying the choice-from-a-set rule gives

$$\forall ww \bullet (ww \in yy \cap zz \Rightarrow [xx := ww] \; xx \in yy)$$

Making the simple substitution gives

$$\forall ww \bullet (ww \in yy \cap zz \Rightarrow zz \in yy)$$

The last predicate is a theorem of set theory.

(4.14)   We have to show that

$$[xx :\in yy \cap zz] \; xx \in yy \cup zz$$

Applying the choice-from-a-set rule gives

$$\forall ww \bullet (ww \in yy \cap zz \Rightarrow [xx := ww] \; xx \in yy \cup zz)$$

Making the simple substitution gives

$$\forall ww \bullet (ww \in yy \cap zz \Rightarrow ww \in yy \cup zz)$$

The last predicate is a theorem of set theory.

(4.15)   The predicate

$$[\text{ANY } \mathbf{y} \text{ WHERE } \mathbf{y} \in \mathbf{S} \text{ THEN } \mathbf{x} := \mathbf{y} \text{ END}] \; \mathbf{P}$$

is equivalent, by the ANY-WHERE-THEN-END rule, to

$$\forall \mathbf{y} \bullet (\mathbf{y} \in \mathbf{S} \Rightarrow [\mathbf{x} := \mathbf{y}] \; \mathbf{P})$$

which is the choice-from-a-set rule.

Chapter 5

(5.1)   The new machine could be defined as follows.

    MACHINE

        Student_array (maxsize, STUDENT)

    CONSTRAINTS

        maxsize > 0 ∧
        card (*STUDENT*) ∈ $\mathbb{N}$

    EXTENDS

        Array (maxsize, STUDENT)

    OPERATIONS

        $ix \longleftarrow$ *find (lim, st)* =
          PRE
            lim ∈ 1 .. *maxsize* ∧
            st ∈ *STUDENT* ∧
            1 .. *lim* ⊆ dom (*array*)
          THEN
            IF
              $arr^{-1}\,[\{st\}] \cap 1 .. lim \neq \varnothing$
            THEN
              $ix :\in arr^{-1}\,[\{st\}]$
            ELSE
              $ix := 0$
            END
          END

    END

(5.2)   For discussion.

(5.3)   For discussion.

Chapter 6

(6.1)   We have to show that

$$[\text{IF } xx = 0$$
$$\text{THEN } xx := xx + 1$$
$$\text{END}] \, xx > 0$$

Applying the IF-THEN-END rule gives

$$xx = 0 \Rightarrow [xx := xx + 1] \, xx > 0 \wedge xx \neq 0 \Rightarrow xx > 0$$

Making the remaining substitution gives

$$xx = 0 \Rightarrow xx + 1 > 0 \wedge xx \neq 0 \Rightarrow xx > 0$$

The last conjunction is two theorems of arithmetic.

(6.2)   We have to show that

$$[\text{IF } xx = 0$$
$$\text{THEN } xx := xx + 1$$
$$\text{ELSIF } xx > 1$$
$$\text{THEN } xx := 1$$
$$\text{END}] \, xx = 1$$

Applying a variant of the IF-THEN-ELSIF rule gives

$$(xx = 0 \Rightarrow [xx := xx + 1] \, xx = 1) \wedge$$
$$(xx \neq 0 \wedge xx > 1 \Rightarrow [xx := 1] \, xx = 1) \wedge$$
$$(xx \neq 0 \wedge xx \leq 1 \Rightarrow xx = 1)$$

Making the remaining substitutions gives

$$(xx = 0 \Rightarrow xx + 1 = 1) \wedge$$
$$(xx \neq 0 \wedge xx > 1 \Rightarrow 1 = 1) \wedge$$
$$(xx \neq 0 \wedge xx \leq 1 \Rightarrow xx = 1)$$

These three conjuncts are all theorems of arithmetic.

(6.3)   We have to show that

$$[\text{LET } xx \text{ BE } xx = 5 \text{ IN } yy := xx \text{ END}] \, yy = 5$$

Applying the LET-BE-IN-END rule gives

$$\forall xx \bullet (xx = 5 \Rightarrow [yy := xx] \, yy = 5)$$

Making the remaining substitution gives

$\forall xx \bullet (xx = 5 \Rightarrow xx = 5)$

The last predicate is a tautology.

(6.4)   We have to show that

$$[\text{LET } xx \text{ BE } xx = yy + zz \text{ IN } yy := xx - yy \text{ END}]$$
$$yy = zz$$

Applying the LET-BE-IN-END rule gives

$$\forall xx \bullet (xx = yy + zz \Rightarrow [yy := xx - yy] \, yy = zz)$$

Making the remaining substitution gives

$$\forall xx \bullet (xx = yy + zz \Rightarrow xx - yy = zz)$$

The last predicate is a theorem of arithmetic.

(6.5)   We have to show that

$$[\text{LET } xx \text{ BE } xx = yy \cap zz \text{ IN } ww := xx \text{ END}] \, ww \subseteq yy$$

Applying the LET-BE-IN-END rule gives

$$\forall xx \bullet (xx = yy \cap zz \Rightarrow [ww := xx] \, ww \subseteq yy)$$

Making the remaining substitution gives

$$\forall xx \bullet (xx = yy \cap zz \Rightarrow xx \subseteq yy)$$

The last predicate is a theorem of set theory.

(6.6)   We have to show that

$$[xx : xx \in \mathbb{N} \wedge xx > 0] \, xx > 0$$

Applying the choice-by-predicate rule gives

$$\forall yy \bullet ([xx := yy] \, (xx \in \mathbb{N} \wedge xx > 0) \Rightarrow$$
$$[xx := yy] \, xx > 0)$$

Making the remaining substitution gives

$$\forall yy \bullet (yy \in \mathbb{N} \wedge yy > 0 \Rightarrow yy > 0)$$

The last predicate is a theorem of arithmetic.

(6.7)   We have to show that

$$[xx : xx \in \mathbb{N} \wedge xx = 0] \, xx \neq 1$$

Applying the choice-by-predicate rule gives

$$\forall yy \bullet ([xx := yy] (xx \in \mathbb{N} \land xx = 0) \Rightarrow$$
$$[xx := yy] \, xx \neq 1)$$

Making the remaining substitution gives

$$\forall yy \bullet (yy \in \mathbb{N} \land yy = 0 \Rightarrow yy \neq 1)$$

The last predicate is a theorem of arithmetic.

(6.8)   We have to show that

$$[xx : xx \in \mathbb{N} \land xx > 5] \, xx \neq 0$$

Applying the choice-by-predicate rule gives

$$\forall yy \bullet ([xx := yy] (xx \in \mathbb{N} \land xx > 5) \Rightarrow$$
$$[xx := yy] \, xx \neq 0)$$

Making the remaining substitution gives

$$\forall yy \bullet (yy \in \mathbb{N} \land yy > 5 \Rightarrow yy \neq 0)$$

The last predicate is a theorem of arithmetic.

(6.9)   We have to show that

$$[xx : xx \in \mathbb{N} \land xx < 1] \, xx = 0$$

Applying the choice-by-predicate rule gives

$$\forall yy \bullet ([xx := yy] (xx \in \mathbb{N} \land xx < 1) \Rightarrow$$
$$[xx := yy] \, xx = 0)$$

Making the remaining substitution gives

$$\forall yy \bullet (yy \in \mathbb{N} \land yy < 1 \Rightarrow yy = 0)$$

The last predicate is a theorem of arithmetic.

(6.10)   Applying the SELECT rule to the predicate

$$[\text{SELECT } \mathbf{P} \text{ THEN } \mathbf{G} \text{ WHEN } \neg\mathbf{P} \text{ THEN } \mathbf{H} \text{ END}] \, \mathbf{Q}$$

gives

$$(\mathbf{P} \Rightarrow [\mathbf{G}] \, \mathbf{Q}) \land (\neg\mathbf{P} \Rightarrow [\mathbf{H}] \, \mathbf{Q})$$

which is exactly the IF-THEN-ELSE-END rule.

(6.11)   For discussion.

(6.12)   For discussion.

(6.13)   For discussion.

(6.14)   The machine *Birthday_book* could be defined as follows:

MACHINE

Birthday_book

SETS

NAME; *DATE*;
REPORT = {*birthday_added, already_known,*
name_found, not_known, no_room,
no_more_birthdays, no_birthdays, another_birthday}

VARIABLES

birthday, browsing

INVARIANT

birthday ∈ *NAME* ⇸ *DATE* ∧
browsing ∈ seq (*NAME*)

INITIALISATION

birthday, browsing := ∅, [ ]

OPERATIONS

rep ⟵ *AddBirthday* (*nam, dat*) =
  PRE
    nam ∈ *NAME* ∧ *dat* ∈ *DATE*
  THEN
    CHOICE
      IF
        nam ∈ dom (*birthday*)
      THEN
        rep := *already_known*
      ELSE
        rep := *birthday_added* ||
        birthday := *birthday* ◁ {*nam* ↦ *dat*}
      END
    OR
      rep := *no_room*
    END
  END
  ;

```
rep, dat ⟵  FindBirthday (nam) =
  PRE
    nam ∈ NAME
  THEN
    IF
      nam ∈ dom (birthday)
    THEN
      dat := birthday (nam) ||
      rep := name_found
    ELSE
      rep := not_known ||
      dat :∈ DATE
    END
  END
;
rep, nam ⟵  StartRemind (dat) =
  PRE
    dat ∈ DATE
  THEN
    IF
      dat ∉ ran (birthday)
    THEN
      rep := no_birthdays ||
      nam :∈ NAME
    ELSE
      rep := birthdays_found ||
      ANY
        ns
      WHERE
        ns ∈ iseq (NAME) ∧
        ran (ns) = dom (birthday ▷ {dat})
      THEN
        browsing := tail (ns) ||
        nam := first (ns)
      END
    END
  END
;
rep, nam ⟵  NextRemind =
  IF
    browsing = [ ]
  THEN
    rep := no_more_birthdays ||
    nam :∈ NAME
```

```
        ELSE
          browsing := tail (browsing) ||
          nam := first (browsing) ||
          rep := another_birthday
        END

    END
```

Chapter 7

(7.1)   We have to show that

$$[xx := 0 \ ; \ xx := xx + 1] \ xx = 1$$

Applying the sequence rule gives

$$[xx := 0] \ [xx := xx + 1] \ xx = 1$$

Making the second substitution gives

$$[xx := 0] \ xx + 1 = 1$$

Making the remaining substitution gives

$$0 + 1 = 1$$

which is a theorem of arithmetic.

(7.2)   We have to show that

$$[xx := 5 \ ; \ yy := 3 \ ; \ zz := xx \times yy] \ zz = 15$$

Applying the sequence rule gives

$$[xx := 5; \ yy := 3 \ ] \ [zz := xx \times yy] \ zz = 15$$

Making the second substitution gives

$$[xx := 5 \ ; \ yy := 3] \ xx \times yy = 15$$

Applying the sequence rule again gives

$$[xx := 5] \ [yy := 3] \ xx \times yy = 15$$

Making the second substitution gives

$$[xx := 5] \ xx \times 3 = 15$$

Making the remaining substitution gives

$$5 \times 3 = 15$$

which is a theorem of arithmetic.

(7.3)   We have to show that

$$[xx := yy \ ; yy := yy + 1] \, yy > xx$$

Applying the sequence rule gives

$$[xx := yy \,] \, [\, yy := yy + 1] \, yy > xx$$

Making the second substitution gives

$$[xx := yy \,] \, yy + 1 > xx$$

Making the remaining substitution gives

$$yy + 1 > yy$$

The last predicate is a theorem of arithmetic.

(7.4)   We have to show that

$$[xx := yy \ ; yy := yy + zz] \, yy \geq xx$$

Applying the sequence rule gives

$$[xx := yy \,] \, [\, yy := yy + zz] \, yy \geq xx$$

Making the second substitution gives

$$[xx := yy \,] \, yy + zz \geq xx$$

Making the remaining substitution gives

$$yy + zz \geq yy$$

The last predicate is a theorem of arithmetic.

(7.5)   We begin with

$$[xx := 0] \, [\text{CHOICE } yy := 0 \text{ OR } yy := 1 \text{ END}]$$
$$(xx \in \mathbb{N} \wedge xx = yy)$$

Applying the CHOICE-OR-END rule gives

$$[xx := 0]$$
$$([yy := 0] \, (xx \in \mathbb{N} \wedge xx = yy) \wedge$$
$$[yy := 1] \, (xx \in \mathbb{N} \wedge xx = yy))$$

Making the simple substitutions for yy gives

$$[xx := 0]$$
$$(xx \in \mathbb{N} \wedge xx = 0 \wedge xx \in \mathbb{N} \wedge xx = 1)$$

Making the remaining substitution gives

$$0 \in \mathbb{N} \wedge 0 = 0 \wedge 0 \in \mathbb{N} \wedge 0 = 1$$

The last of these four conjuncts is false.

Now we do the same to the second conjecture:

$$[xx := 0]$$
$$\neg [\text{CHOICE } yy := 0 \text{ OR } yy := 1 \text{ END}]$$
$$\neg (xx \in \mathbb{N} \wedge xx = yy)$$

Applying the CHOICE-OR-END rule gives

$$[xx := 0]$$
$$\neg ([yy := 0] \; (xx \notin \mathbb{N} \vee xx \neq yy) \wedge$$
$$[yy := 1] \; (xx \notin \mathbb{N} \vee xx \neq yy))$$

Making the simple substitutions for yy gives

$$[xx := 0]$$
$$\neg ((xx \notin \mathbb{N} \vee xx \neq 0) \wedge (xx \notin \mathbb{N} \vee xx \neq 1))$$

Making the remaining substitution gives

$$\neg ((0 \notin \mathbb{N} \vee 0 \neq 0) \wedge (0 \notin \mathbb{N} \vee 0 \neq 1))$$

Using the rule for negating a conjunction (De Morgan) gives

$$(0 \in \mathbb{N} \wedge 0 = 0) \vee (0 \in \mathbb{N} \wedge 0 = 1)$$

The first conjunct is a theorem of arithmetic.

(7.6)   The correctness condition is as follows:

$$[yy := 3] \; \neg [xx := \in 0 .. 5] \; \neg (yy \in \mathbb{N} \wedge yy = xx)$$

We use the choice-from-a-set rule to make the second substitution as follows:

$$[yy := 3]$$
$$\neg \forall zz \bullet (\, zz \in 0 .. 5 \Rightarrow [xx := zz] \; \neg (yy \in \mathbb{N} \wedge yy = xx))$$

Now we make the simple substitution of zz for xx:

$$[yy := 3] \; \neg \forall zz \bullet (\, zz \in 0 .. 5 \Rightarrow \neg (yy \in \mathbb{N} \wedge yy = zz))$$

Next we use the rules for negating a universal quantification and for negating an implication:

$$[yy := 3] \; \exists zz \bullet (\, zz \in 0 .. 5 \wedge yy \in \mathbb{N} \wedge yy = zz)$$

Now we use the one-point rule:

$$[yy := 3] \; (yy \in 0 .. 5 \wedge yy \in \mathbb{N})$$

Making the last substitution gives the following theorem of arithmetic:

$$3 \in 0 .. 5 \wedge 3 \in \mathbb{N}$$

(7.7)   For discussion.

(7.8)   The correctness condition is as follows:

$xx \in \mathbb{N} \wedge yy \in \mathbb{N} \wedge yy = xx \Rightarrow$
$[\text{IF } yy > 5 \text{ THEN } yy := 5 \text{ END}]$
$\neg [xx :\in 0 .. 5] \neg (yy \in \mathbb{N} \wedge yy = xx)$

Simplifying as in the answer to the previous exercise gives the following:

$xx \in \mathbb{N} \wedge yy \in \mathbb{N} \wedge yy = xx \Rightarrow$
$[\text{IF } yy > 5 \text{ THEN } yy := 5 \text{ END}]$
$(yy \in 0 .. 5 \wedge yy \in \mathbb{N})$

Now we apply the IF-THEN-END rule:

$xx \in \mathbb{N} \wedge yy \in \mathbb{N} \wedge yy = xx \Rightarrow$
$(yy > 5 \Rightarrow [yy := 5] (yy \in 0 .. 5 \wedge yy \in \mathbb{N})) \wedge$
$(yy \leq 5 \Rightarrow yy \in 0 .. 5 \wedge yy \in \mathbb{N})$

Making the remaining substitution gives the following theorem of arithmetic:

$xx \in \mathbb{N} \wedge yy \in \mathbb{N} \wedge yy = xx \Rightarrow$
$(yy > 5 \Rightarrow (5 \in 0 .. 5 \wedge yy \in \mathbb{N})) \wedge$
$(yy \leq 5 \Rightarrow yy \in 0 .. 5 \wedge yy \in \mathbb{N})$

(7.9)   For discussion.

(7.10) The I-rule is

$$[xx := 0] (xx \in \mathbb{N} \wedge xx \leq 10)$$

which is equivalent to

$$0 \in \mathbb{N} \wedge 0 \leq 10$$

which is a theorem of arithmetic.
  The F-rule is

$$xx \in \mathbb{N} \wedge xx \leq 10 \wedge xx \geq 10 \Rightarrow xx = 10$$

and this is a theorem of arithmetic.
  The T1-rule is

$$xx \in \mathbb{N} \wedge xx \leq 10 \Rightarrow 10 - xx \in \mathbb{N}$$

and this is a theorem of arithmetic.

The T2-rule is

$$xx \in \mathbb{N} \wedge xx \leq 10 \wedge xx < 10 \Rightarrow$$
$$[yy := 10 - xx\,] \, [xx := xx + 1] \, 10 - xx < yy$$

Making the substitutions gives the following predicate:

$$xx \in \mathbb{N} \wedge xx \leq 10 \wedge xx < 10 \Rightarrow$$
$$10 - (xx + 1) < 10 - xx$$

which is a theorem of arithmetic.

The P-rule is

$$xx \in \mathbb{N} \wedge xx \leq 10 \wedge xx < 10 \Rightarrow$$
$$[xx := xx + 1] \, (xx \in \mathbb{N} \wedge xx \leq 10)$$

and the consequent simplifies to

$$xx + 1 \in \mathbb{N} \wedge xx + 1 \leq 10$$

which can be deduced from the antecedent by the laws of arithmetic.

(7.11)   Each loop fails, and can be improved, as follows:

(a)   This loop fails the I-rule only. It can be improved by correcting the initialization.

(b)   This loop fails the T2-rule only. The loop body is not good enough to decrease the variant.

(c)   This loop fails the T1-rule only. The invariant needs strengthening to constrain xx better.

(d)   This loop fails the P-rule only. This is because the invariant is too strong to be preserved as xx changes.

(e)   This loop fails the F-rule only. The invariant is too weak; it should say that xx can take only even values.

(7.12)   The I-rule is as follows:

$$mm \in \mathbb{N} \wedge$$
$$mm > 0 \wedge$$
$$num \in 1 \mathinner{..} 100 \wedge$$
$$narr \in 1 \mathinner{..} mm \to 1 \mathinner{..} 100 \wedge$$
$$num \in \mathrm{ran}\,(narr) \wedge$$
$$ctr \in \mathbb{N} \Rightarrow$$
$$[ctr := 1\,]$$
$$(num \notin \mathrm{ran}\,(1 \mathinner{..} (ctr - 1) \lhd narr) \wedge ctr \in 1 \mathinner{..} mm)$$

Making the substitution gives

$$mm \in \mathbb{N} \wedge$$
$$mm > 0 \wedge$$
$$num \in 1 .. 100 \wedge$$
$$narr \in 1 .. mm \rightarrow 1 .. 100 \wedge$$
$$num \in \text{ran} \, (narr) \wedge$$
$$ctr \in \mathbb{N} \Rightarrow$$
$$(num \notin \text{ran} \, (1 .. 0 \vartriangleleft narr) \wedge 1 \in 1 .. mm)$$

and this is a theorem of arithmetic.

The F-rule is as follows:

$$narr \, (ctr) = num \wedge$$
$$num \notin \text{ran} \, (1 .. (ctr - 1) \vartriangleleft narr) \wedge$$
$$ctr \in 1 .. mm \Rightarrow$$
$$narr \, (ctr) = num$$

which is a tautology.

The T1-rule is as follows:

$$num \notin \text{ran} \, (1 .. (ctr - 1) \vartriangleleft narr) \wedge ctr \in 1 .. mm \Rightarrow$$
$$mm - ctr \in \mathbb{N}$$

and this is a theorem of arithmetic.

The T2-rule is as follows:

$$num \notin \text{ran} \, (1 .. (ctr - 1) \vartriangleleft narr) \wedge ctr \in 1 .. mm \Rightarrow$$
$$[yy := mm - ctr] \, [\, ctr := ctr + 1]$$
$$mm - ctr < yy$$

Making the second substitution gives:

$$num \notin \text{ran} \, (1 .. (ctr - 1) \vartriangleleft narr) \wedge ctr \in 1 .. mm \Rightarrow$$
$$[yy := mm - ctr]$$
$$mm - (ctr + 1) < yy$$

Making the last substitution gives the following:

$$num \notin \text{ran} \, (1 .. (ctr - 1) \vartriangleleft narr) \wedge ctr \in 1 .. mm \Rightarrow$$
$$mm - (ctr + 1) < mm - ctr$$

and this is a theorem of arithmetic.

The P-rule is as follows:

$$narr \, (ctr) \neq num \wedge$$
$$num \notin \text{ran} \, (1 .. (ctr - 1) \vartriangleleft narr) \wedge$$
$$ctr \in 1 .. mm \Rightarrow$$
$$[ctr := ctr + 1]$$
$$(num \notin \text{ran} \, (1 .. (ctr - 1) \vartriangleleft narr) \wedge ctr \in 1 .. mm)$$

Making the substitution gives the following:

> *narr* (*ctr*) ≠ *num* ∧
> *num* ∉ ran (1 .. (*ctr* − 1) ◁ *narr*) ∧ *ctr* ∈ 1 .. *mm* ⇒
> *num* ∉ ran (1 .. *ctr* ◁ *narr*) ∧ *ctr* + 1 ∈ 1 .. *mm*

and this is a theorem of arithmetic.

(7.13)   We introduce local variables *maxn* to hold the largest number so far and *ctr* to count through the array. The important part of the invariant says that *maxn* contains the largest number of those so far examined, and *where* is an index of an occurrence of *maxn* in the part of the array so far examined. This invariant is illustrated in Figure S7.1.

The loop might be as follows:

```
maxn := narr (1) ;
ctr := 1 ;
where := 1 ;
WHILE
  ctr < nn
DO
  ctr := ctr + 1 ;
  IF
    narr (ctr) > maxn
  THEN
    maxn := narr (ctr) ;
    where := ctr
  END
VARIANT
  nn − ctr
INVARIANT
  ctr ∈ 1 .. nn ∧
  where ∈ 1 .. ctr ∧
  narr (where) = maxn ∧
  maxn = max (ran (1 .. ctr ◁ narr))
END
```

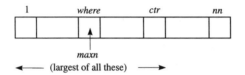

maxn

◄────── (largest of all these) ──────►

Figure S7.1 Invariant for finding a maximum in an array.

We prove that this program establishes the predicate

> *where* ∈ 1 .. *nn* ∧
> *narr* (*where*) = *maxn* ∧
> *maxn* = max (ran (*narr*))

The I-rule is as follows:

> [*maxn* := *narr* (1) ;
> *ctr* := 1 ;
> *where* := 1]
> (*ctr* ∈ 1 .. *nn* ∧
> *where* ∈ 1 .. *ctr* ∧
> *narr* (*where*) = *maxn* ∧
> *maxn* = max (ran (1 .. *ctr* ◁ *narr*)))

Making the substitutions in order gives the following:

> 1∈ 1 .. *nn* ∧
> 1 ∈ 1 .. 1 ∧
> *narr* (1) = *narr* (1) ∧
> *narr* (1) = max (ran (1 .. 1 ◁ *narr*))

and this is a conjunction of theorems of arithmetic and set theory.

The F-rule is as follows:

> *ctr* ≥ *nn* ∧
> *ctr* ∈ 1 .. *nn* ∧
> *where* ∈ 1 .. *ctr* ∧
> *narr* (*where*) = *maxn* ∧
> *maxn* = max (ran (1 .. *ctr* ◁ *narr*))
> ⇒
> *where* ∈ 1 .. *nn* ∧
> *narr* (*where*) = *maxn* ∧
> *maxn* = max (ran (*narr*))

and this is a conjunction of theorems of arithmetic and set theory.

The T-1 rule is as follows:

> *ctr* ∈ 1 .. *nn* ∧
> *where* ∈ 1 .. *ctr* ∧
> *narr* (*where*) = *maxn* ∧
> *maxn* = max (ran (1 .. *ctr* ◁ *narr*))
> ⇒
> *nn* − *ctr* ∈ ℕ

which is a theorem of arithmetic.

The T-2 rule is as follows:

$ctr < nn$ ∧
$ctr \in 1 \, .. \, nn$ ∧
$where \in 1 \, .. \, ctr$ ∧
$narr\,(where) = maxn$ ∧
$maxn = \max\,(\mathrm{ran}\,(1 \, .. \, ctr \lhd narr))$
⇒
$[yy := nn - ctr]\,[ctr := ctr + 1]$
$nn - ctr < yy$

Making the substitutions gives the following:

$ctr < nn$ ∧
$ctr \in 1 \, .. \, nn$ ∧
$where \in 1 \, .. \, ctr$ ∧
$narr\,(where) = maxn$ ∧
$maxn = \max\,(\mathrm{ran}\,(1 \, .. \, ctr \lhd narr))$
⇒
$nn - (ctr + 1) < nn - ctr$

which is a theorem of arithmetic.

Now we have the P-rule:

$ctr < nn$ ∧
$ctr \in 1 \, .. \, nn$ ∧
$where \in 1 \, .. \, ctr$ ∧
$narr\,(where) = maxn$ ∧
$maxn = \max\,(\mathrm{ran}\,(1 \, .. \, ctr \lhd narr))$
⇒
$[ctr := ctr + 1\,;$
IF $narr\,(ctr) > maxn$
THEN $maxn := narr\,(ctr)\,;\ where := ctr$ END$]$
$(ctr \in 1 \, .. \, nn$ ∧
$where \in 1 \, .. \, ctr$ ∧
$narr\,(where) = maxn$ ∧
$maxn = \max\,(\mathrm{ran}\,(1 \, .. \, ctr \lhd narr)))$

For the moment we ignore the antecedent, and concentrate on simplifying the consequent. First we use the IF-THEN-END rule.

$[ctr := ctr + 1]$
$(narr\,(ctr) > maxn \Rightarrow$
$[maxn := narr\,(ctr)\,;\ where := ctr]$
$(ctr \in 1 \, .. \, nn$ ∧

$$
\begin{aligned}
&where \in 1 \,..\, ctr \;\wedge \\
&narr\,(where) = maxn \;\wedge \\
&maxn = \mathrm{max}\,(\mathrm{ran}\,(1 \,..\, ctr \lhd narr))) \;\wedge \\
&(narr\,(ctr) \le maxn
\end{aligned}
$$

$\Rightarrow$

$$
\begin{aligned}
&ctr \in 1 \,..\, nn \;\wedge \\
&where \in 1 \,..\, ctr \;\wedge \\
&narr\,(where) = maxn \;\wedge \\
&maxn = \mathrm{max}\,(\mathrm{ran}\,(1 \,..\, ctr \lhd narr))))
\end{aligned}
$$

This expression has the form of a simple substitution establishing a conjunction, so we can take the parts separately.

The first part is

$$
\begin{aligned}
&[ctr := ctr + 1] \\
&(narr\,(ctr) > maxn \Rightarrow \\
&[maxn := narr\,(ctr) \,; where := ctr] \\
&(ctr \in 1 \,..\, nn \;\wedge \\
&where \in 1 \,..\, ctr \;\wedge \\
&narr\,(where) = maxn \;\wedge \\
&maxn = \mathrm{max}\,(\mathrm{ran}\,(1 \,..\, ctr \lhd narr))))
\end{aligned}
$$

Making the second substitution gives the following:

$$
\begin{aligned}
&[ctr := ctr + 1] \\
&(narr\,(ctr) > maxn \Rightarrow \\
&(ctr \in 1 \,..\, nn \;\wedge \\
&ctr \in 1 \,..\, ctr \;\wedge \\
&narr\,(ctr) = maxn \;\wedge \\
&narr\,(ctr) = \mathrm{max}\,(\mathrm{ran}\,(1 \,..\, ctr \lhd narr))))
\end{aligned}
$$

Making the remaining substitution gives the following:

$$
\begin{aligned}
&[ctr := ctr + 1] \\
&(narr\,(ctr + 1) > maxn \Rightarrow \\
&(ctr + 1 \in 1 \,..\, nn \;\wedge \\
&ctr + 1 \in 1 \,..\, ctr + 1 \;\wedge \\
&narr\,(ctr + 1) = maxn \;\wedge \\
&narr\,(ctr + 1) = \mathrm{max}\,(\mathrm{ran}\,(1 \,..\, (ctr + 1) \lhd narr))))
\end{aligned}
$$

and this follows from the antecedent by the laws of arithmetic and set theory.

The second part is

$$
\begin{aligned}
&[ctr := ctr + 1] \\
&(narr\,(ctr) \le maxn \Rightarrow \\
&ctr \in 1 \,..\, nn \;\wedge \\
&where \in 1 \,..\, ctr \;\wedge
\end{aligned}
$$

$narr \ (where) = maxn \ \wedge$
$maxn = \text{max} \ (\text{ran} \ (1 \ .. \ ctr \lhd narr)))$

Making the simple substitution gives the following:

$(narr \ (ctr \ + \ 1) \le maxn \Rightarrow$
$ctr \ + \ 1 \in 1 \ .. \ nn \ \wedge$
$where \in 1 \ .. \ ctr \ + \ 1 \wedge$
$narr \ (where) = maxn \ \wedge$
$maxn = \text{max} \ (\text{ran} \ (1 \ .. \ (ctr \ + \ 1) \lhd narr)))$

This follows from the antecedent by the laws of arithmetic and set theory.

(7.14) The following loop could be used:

```
sum := 0 ;
ctr := 1 ;
WHILE
  ctr ≤ nn
DO
  sum := sum + numseq (ctr) ;
  ctr := ctr + 1
VARIANT
  nn + 1 − ctr
INVARIANT
  ctr ∈ 1 .. (nn + 1) ∧
  sum = Σii • (ii ∈ 1 .. (ctr − 1) | numseq (ii))
END
```

We show that this program establishes the predicate

$sum = \Sigma ii \bullet (ii \in 1 \ .. \ nn \ | \ numseq \ (ii))$

The I-rule is as follows:

$[sum := 0 \ ; \ ctr := 1]$
$(ctr \in 1 \ .. \ (nn \ + \ 1) \ \wedge$
$sum = \Sigma ii \bullet (ii \in 1 \ .. \ (ctr \ - \ 1) \ | \ numseq \ (ii)))$

Making the substitutions gives the following:

$[sum := 0 \ ; \ ctr := 1]$
$(1 \in 1 \ .. \ (nn \ + \ 1) \ \wedge$
$0 = \Sigma ii \bullet (ii \in 1 \ .. \ (1 \ - \ 1) \ | \ numseq \ (ii)))$

which follows from the laws of arithmetic and the definition of Σ.

The F-rule is as follows:

$$ctr > nn \; \wedge$$
$$ctr \in 1 \; .. \; (nn + 1) \; \wedge$$
$$sum = \Sigma ii \bullet (ii \in 1 \; .. \; (ctr - 1) \mid numseq \; (ii))$$
$$\Rightarrow$$
$$sum = \Sigma ii \bullet (ii \in 1 \; .. \; nn \mid numseq \; (ii))$$

We can extend the antecedent by noting that $ctr = nn + 1$, and then making the consequent appear in the antecedent.

The T-1 rule is as follows:

$$ctr \in 1 \; .. \; (nn + 1) \; \wedge$$
$$sum = \Sigma ii \bullet (ii \in 1 \; .. \; (ctr - 1) \mid numseq \; (ii))$$
$$\Rightarrow$$
$$nn + 1 - ctr \in \mathbb{N}$$

Most of the invariant is irrelevant here, and the consequent follows from the antecedent by the laws of arithmetic.

The T-2 rule is as follows:

$$ctr \leq nn \; \wedge$$
$$ctr \in 1 \; .. \; (nn + 1) \; \wedge$$
$$sum = \Sigma ii \bullet (ii \in 1 \; .. \; (ctr - 1) \mid numseq \; (ii))$$
$$\Rightarrow$$
$$[ww := nn + 1 - ctr]$$
$$[sum := ...] \, [ctr := ctr - 1] \, nn + 1 - ctr < ww$$

Making the substitutions in the consequent gives the following:

$$ctr \leq nn \; \wedge$$
$$ctr \in 1 \; .. \; (nn + 1) \; \wedge$$
$$sum = \Sigma ii \bullet (ii \in 1 \; .. \; (ctr - 1) \mid numseq \; (ii))$$
$$\Rightarrow$$
$$[ww := nn + 1 - ctr] \, [sum := ...] \, [ctr := ctr - 1]$$
$$nn + 1 - (ctr - 1) < nn + 1 - ctr$$

and this is a theorem of arithmetic.

The P-rule is as follows:

$$ctr \leq nn \; \wedge$$
$$ctr \in 1 \; .. \; (nn + 1) \; \wedge$$
$$sum = \Sigma ii \bullet (ii \in 1 \; .. \; (ctr - 1) \mid numseq \; (ii))$$
$$\Rightarrow$$
$$[sum := sum + numseq \; (ctr)] \, [ctr := ctr + 1]$$
$$(ctr \in 1 \; .. \; (nn + 1) \; \wedge$$
$$sum = \Sigma ii \bullet (ii \in 1 \; .. \; (ctr - 1) \mid numseq \; (ii)))$$

Making the rightmost substitution first gives the following:

$ctr \leq nn \; \wedge$
$ctr \in 1 \: .. \: (nn + 1) \; \wedge$
$sum = \Sigma ii \bullet (ii \in 1 \: .. \: (ctr - 1) \mid numseq \: (ii))$
$\Rightarrow$
$[sum := sum + numseq \: (ctr)]$
$(ctr + 1 \in 1 \: .. \: (nn + 1) \; \wedge$
$sum = \Sigma ii \bullet (ii \in 1 \: .. \: (ctr + 1 - 1) \mid numseq \: (ii)))$

Making the remaining substitution gives the following:

$ctr \leq nn \; \wedge$
$ctr \in 1 \: .. \: (nn + 1) \; \wedge$
$sum = \Sigma ii \bullet (ii \in 1 \: .. \: (ctr - 1) \mid numseq \: (ii))$
$\Rightarrow$
$(ctr + 1 \in 1 \: .. \: (nn + 1) \; \wedge$
$sum + numseq \: (ctr) =$
$\Sigma ii \bullet (ii \in 1 \: .. \: (ctr + 1 - 1) \mid numseq \: (ii)))$

and this follows from the laws of arithmetic and the properties of sequences and Σ.

(7.15) For discussion.

(7.16) For discussion.

Chapter 8

(8.1) The machine *Student_array* might be implemented as follows:

IMPLEMENTATION

Student_array_imp

REFINES

Student_array

SEES

Bool_TYPE

IMPORTS

Student_Varr (*STUDENT*, *maxsize*)

INVARIANT

$arr \subseteq Student\_Varr$

INITIALISATION

skip

OPERATIONS

$ix \longleftarrow find\ (lim, st) =$
```
VAR
  bb, ii
IN
  bb, ii ←
  Student_SCH_LO_EQL_ARR (1, lim, st) ;
  IF
    bb = TRUE
  THEN
    ix := ii
  ELSE
    ix := 0
  END
END
```
;
$set\ (ix, tt) =$
  $Student\_STO\_ARR\ (ix, tt)$
;
$tt \longleftarrow read\ (ix) =$
  $tt \longleftarrow Student\_VAL\_ARR\ (ix)$
;
$swap\ (ix, jx) =$
  $Student\_SWP\_ARR\ (ix, jx)$

END

Figure S8.1 on page 289 illustrates the dependencies of this implementation.

(8.2)   The class manager's assistant might be implemented as follows:

IMPLEMENTATION

CMA_imp_seq

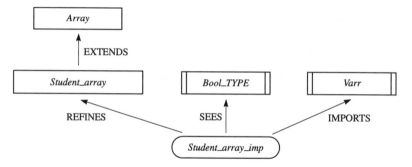

Figure S8.1 Dependencies of the student array implementation.

REFINES

   CMA

SEES

   Bool_TYPE

IMPORTS

   En_Vseq (*STUDENT, class_size*),
   Te_Vseq (*STUDENT, class_size*)

INVARIANT

   enrolled = ran (*En_Vseq*) ∧
   size (*En_Vseq*) = card (*enrolled*) ∧
   tested = ran (*Te_Vseq*)
   size (*Te_Vseq*) = card (*tested*)

INITIALISATION

   skip

OPERATIONS

   enrol (*st*) =
     BEGIN
       En_PSH_SEQ (*st*)
     END
   ;

```
ans ←— isenrolled (st) =
  VAR
    bb, ii, len
  IN
    len ←— En_LEN_SEQ ;
    IF
      len = 0
    THEN
      ans := FALSE
    ELSE
      bb, ii ←—
      En_SCH_LO_EQL_SEQ (1, len, st) ;
      ans := bb
    END
  END
;
test (st) =
  BEGIN
    Te_PSH_SEQ (st)
  END
;
ans ←— istested (st) =
  VAR
    bb, ii, len
  IN
    len ←— Te_LEN_SEQ ;
    IF
      len = 0
    THEN
      ans := FALSE
    ELSE
      bb, ii ←—
      Te_SCH_LO_EQL_SEQ (1, len, st) ;
      ans := bb
    END
  END
;
leave (st) =
  VAR
    tlen, elen, bb, ii
  IN
    tlen ←— Te_LEN_SEQ ;
    elen ←— En_LEN_SEQ ;
    IF
      tlen ≠ 0
```

```
THEN
    bb, ii ⟵
    Te_SCH_LO_EQL_SEQ (1, tlen, st) ;
    IF
        bb = TRUE
    THEN
        Te_SWP_SEQ (ii, tlen) ;
        Te_POP_SEQ
    END
    END ;
    bb, ii ⟵
    En_SCH_LO_EQL_SEQ (1, elen, st) ;
    En_SWP_SEQ (ii, elen) ;
    En_POP_SEQ
    END
;
clmax, sofar ⟵ howmany =
    BEGIN
        clmax := class_size ;
        sofar ⟵ En_LEN_SEQ
    END

END
```

Figure S8.2 is the dependency diagram for this imple-mentation.

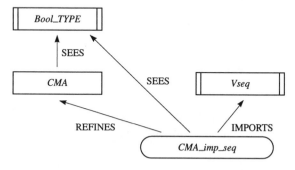

Figure S8.2 Dependency diagram for (8.2).

(8.3)

IMPLEMENTATION

CMA_imp_arr

REFINES

CMA

SEES

Bool_TYPE

IMPORTS

Student_array (class_size, STUDENT),
Enrol_Nvar (class_size),
Test_Nvar (class_size)

INVARIANT

Test_Nvar $\leq$ *Enrol_Nvar* $\wedge$
enrolled = *arr* [1 .. *Enrol_Nvar*] $\wedge$
tested = *arr* [1 .. *Test_Nvar*] $\wedge$
card (*enrolled*) = *Enrol_Nvar* $\wedge$
card (*tested*) = *Test_Nvar*

INITIALISATION

skip

OPERATIONS

enrol (st) =
  VAR
    ee
  IN
    Enrol_INC_NVAR ;
    ee $\longleftarrow$ *Enrol_VAL_NVAR* ;
    set (ee, st)
  END
;
ans $\longleftarrow$ *isenrolled (st)* =
  VAR
    ee, ix

```
IN
  ee ⟵ Enrol_VAL_NVAR ;
  ix ⟵ find (ee, st) ;
  IF
    ix = 0
  THEN
    ans := FALSE
  ELSE
    ans := TRUE
  END
END
;
test (st) =
  VAR
    ee, ix, tt
  IN
    ee ⟵ Enrol_VAL_NVAR ;
    ix ⟵ find (ee, st) ;
    Test_INC_NVAR ;
    tt ⟵ Test_VAL_NVAR ;
    swap (tt, ix)
  END
;
ans ⟵ istested (st) =
  VAR
    tt, ix
  IN
    tt ⟵ Test_VAL_NVAR ;
    ix ⟵ find (tt, st) ;
    IF
      ix = 0
    THEN
      ans := FALSE
    ELSE
      ans := TRUE
    END
  END
;
leave (st) =
  VAR
    tt, ee, ix
  IN
    tt ⟵ Test_VAL_NVAR ;
    ee ⟵ Enrol_VAL_NVAR ;
```

```
                ix ⟵ find (ee, st) ;
                IF
                  ix > tt
                THEN
                  swap (ix, ee) ;
                  Enrol_DEC_NVAR
                ELSE
                  swap (ix, tt) ;
                  Test_DEC_NVAR ;
                  swap (tt, ee) ;
                  Enrol_DEC_NVAR
                END
              END
              ;
              clmax, sofar ⟵ howmany =
                BEGIN
                  clmax := class_size ;
                  sofar ⟵ Enrol_VAL_NVAR
                END

          END
```

Figure S8.3 on page 295 illustrates the dependencies of this implementation.

(8.4)

IMPLEMENTATION

Storman_imp

REFINES

Storman

SEES

Bool_TYPE

IMPORTS

Stor_Varr (0 .. 100, 1000)

PROPERTIES

$USER = 1 .. 100 \wedge$
$maxblocks = 1000$

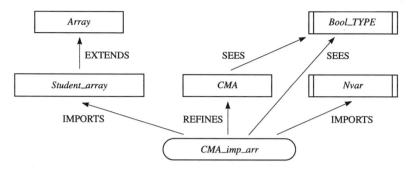

Figure S8.3 Dependencies of the class manager array implementation.

INVARIANT

$alloc = Stor\_Varr \rhd \{0\}$

INITIALISATION

```
VAR
  nn
IN
  nn := 1 ;
  WHILE
    nn ≤ 1000
  DO
    Stor_STO_ARR (nn, 0) ;
    nn := nn + 1
  INVARIANT
    (1 .. nn − 1 ◁ Stor_Varr) ▷ {0} = Ø ∧
    nn ∈ 1 .. 1001
  VARIANT
    1001 − nn
  END
END
```

OPERATIONS

```
block ⟵ get (us) =
  VAR
    bb, ii
  IN
    bb, ii ⟵
    Stor_SCH_LO_EQL_ARR (1, 1000, 0) ;
```

```
            block := ii ;
            Stor_STO_ARR (ii, us)
         END
      ;
      free (bn, us) =
         BEGIN
            Stor_STO_ARR (bn, 0)
         END
      ;
      fn ⟵  askfree =
         VAR
            acc, bb, ii
         IN
            acc := 0 ;
            bb, ii ⟵
            Stor_SCH_LO_EQL_ARR (1, 1000, 0) ;
            WHILE
               bb = TRUE
            DO
               acc := acc + 1 ;
               IF
                  ii = 1000
               THEN
                  bb := FALSE
               ELSE
                  bb, ii ⟵
                  Stor_SCH_LO_EQL_ARR (ii + 1, 1000, 0)
               END
            INVARIANT
               (bb = TRUE ⇒
               acc = card (1 .. ii − 1 ◁ Stor_Varr ▷ {0})) ∧
               (bb = FALSE ⇒
               acc = card (Stor_Varr ▷ {0})) ∧
               acc ∈ 0 .. 1000 ∧
               bb ∈ BOOL ∧
               ii ∈ 1 .. 1000
            VARIANT
               1000 − acc
            END
            ;
            fn := acc
         END
      ;
```

```
freeall (us) =
  VAR
    bb, ii
  IN
    bb, ii ⟵
    Stor_SCH_LO_EQL_ARR (1, 1000, us) ;
    WHILE
      bb = TRUE
    DO
      Stor_STO_ARR (ii, 0) ;
      bb, ii ⟵
      Stor_SCH_LO_EQL_ARR (ii, 1000, us)
    INVARIANT
      1 .. ii − 1 ◁ Stor_Varr ▷ {us} = ∅ ∧
      (bb = TRUE ⟹ Stor_Varr (ii) = us) ∧
      (bb = FALSE ⟹ Stor_Varr ▷ {us} = ∅) ∧
      bb ∈ BOOL ∧
      ii ∈ 1 .. 1000
    VARIANT
      1000 − ii
    END
  END

END
```

Chapter 9

(9.1)

MACHINE

   RCMA

SETS

   STUDENT;
   RCMA_RESP =
     *{no_room, already_enrolled, student_enrolled,
     not_enrolled, already_tested, test_noted,
     certificate, no_certificate, student_tested,
     enrolled_but_not_tested}*

OPERATIONS

$re \longleftarrow Enrol\ (st) =$
  PRE
    $st \in STUDENT$
  THEN
    $re :\in \{no\_room,\ student\_enrolled,\ already\_enrolled\}$
  END
;
$re \longleftarrow Test\ (st) =$
  PRE
    $st \in STUDENT$
  THEN
    $re :\in \{not\_enrolled,\ already\_tested,\ test\_noted\}$
  END
;
$re \longleftarrow Leave\ (st) =$
  PRE
    $st \in STUDENT$
  THEN
    $re :\in \{not\_enrolled,\ certificate,\ no\_certificate\}$
  END
;
$re \longleftarrow Enquire\ (st) =$
  PRE
    $st \in STUDENT$
  THEN
    $re :\in$
    $\{not\_enrolled,\ student\_tested,\ enrolled\_but\_not\_tested\}$
  END

END

(9.2)

IMPLEMENTATION

  $RCMA\_imp$

REFINES

  $RCMA$

SEES

  $Bool\_TYPE$

IMPORTS

   CMA (*class_size*, *STUDENT*)

PROPERTIES

   class_size = 100 ∧
   STUDENT = 0 .. 99999

OPERATIONS

```
re ⟵  Enrol (st) =
  VAR
    bb, mm, nn
  IN
    bb ⟵  isenrolled (st) ;
    IF
      bb = TRUE
    THEN
      re := already_enrolled
    ELSE
      mm, nn ⟵  howmany ;
      IF
        mm < nn
      THEN
        enrol (st) ;
        re := student_enrolled
      ELSE
        re := no_room
      END
    END
  END
;
re ⟵  Test (st) =
  VAR
    bb
  IN
    bb ⟵  isenrolled (st) ;
    IF
      bb = TRUE
    THEN
      bb ⟵  istested (st) ;
      IF
        bb = TRUE
      THEN
        re := already_tested
```

```
            ELSE
              test (st) ;
              re := test_noted
            END
          ELSE
            re := not_enrolled
          END
        END
      ;
      re ⟵ Leave (st) =
        VAR
          bb
        IN
          bb ⟵ isenrolled (st) ;
          IF
            bb = FALSE
          THEN
            re := not_enrolled
          ELSE
            bb ⟵ istested (st) ;
            leave (st) ;
            IF
              bb = TRUE
            THEN
              re := certificate
            ELSE
              re := no_certificate
            END
          END
        END
      ;
      re ⟵ Enquire (st) =
        VAR
          bb
        IN
          bb ⟵ isenrolled (st) ;
          IF
            bb = FALSE
          THEN
            re := not_enrolled
          ELSE
            bb ⟵ istested (st) ;
            IF
              bb = TRUE
```

```
        THEN
          re := student_tested
        ELSE
          re := enrolled_but_not_tested
        END
      END
    END
```

END

(9.3)   For discussion.

(9.4)   For discussion.

(9.5)   For discussion.

(9.6)   For discussion.

(9.7)   For discussion.

(9.8)   For discussion.

Chapter 10

(10.1)

REFINEMENT

Server_refined

REFINES

Server

SEES

Bool_TYPE

VARIABLES

sofar

INVARIANT

$sofar \in 0 .. 100 \land$
$gone = 1 .. sofar$

INITIALISATION

$sofar := 0$

OPERATIONS

$resp, num \longleftarrow go =$
IF
$\quad sofar = 100$
THEN
$\quad resp := FALSE \,||$
$\quad num := 1$
ELSE
$\quad resp := TRUE \,||$
$\quad num := sofar + 1 \,||$
$\quad sofar := sofar + 1$
END

END

The proof obligation for initialization is as follows.

$[sofar := 0]$
$\neg [gone := \varnothing]$
$\neg (sofar \in 0 \,..\, 100 \wedge gone = 1 \,..\, sofar)$

If we make the inner substitution we have the following.

$[sofar := 0]$
$\neg \neg (sofar \in 0 \,..\, 100 \wedge \varnothing = 1 \,..\, sofar)$

This can be simplified to

$$0 \in 0 \,..\, 100 \wedge \varnothing = 1 \,..\, 0$$

both of which are theorems of set theory.

The proof obligation for the operation is left for discussion.

(10.2)

REFINEMENT

Nat_SET_refined

REFINES

Nat_SET

INCLUDES

Array (max_card, 0 .. max_nat)

VARIABLES

   ctr

INVARIANT

   $ctr \in 0 \mathrel{..} max\_card \;\wedge$
   $nat\_set \;=\; arr\,[1 \mathrel{..} ctr] \;\wedge$
   card $(nat\_set) = ctr$

INITIALISATION

   $ctr := 0$

OPERATIONS

   $nn \longleftarrow howbig =$
      BEGIN
        $nn := ctr$
      END
    ;
   $add\,(nn) =$
     IF
       $nn \in arr\,\;[1 \mathrel{..} ctr]$
     THEN
      $skip$
     ELSE
      $set\,(ctr + 1, nn)\;||$
      $ctr := ctr + 1$
     END
    ;
   $remove\,(nn) =$
     IF
       $nn \in arr\,[1 \mathrel{..} ctr]$
     THEN
       ANY
        ix
       WHERE
        $ix \in \mathbb{N} \;\wedge$
        $ix \leq ctr \;\wedge$
        $arr\,(ix) = nn$
       THEN
        $set\,(ix, arr\,(ctr))\;||$
        $ctr := ctr - 1$
       END
     END
    ;

```
bb ⟵ find (nn) =
   IF
      nn ∈ arr [1 .. ctr]
   THEN
      bb := 1
   ELSE
      bb := 0
   END

END
```

(10.3)

```
IMPLEMENTATION

   Server_ref_imp

REFINES

   Server_refined

SEES

   Bool_TYPE

IMPORTS

   sofar_Nvar (100)

INVARIANT

   sofar_Nvar = sofar

INITIALISATION

   skip

OPERATIONS

   resp, num ⟵ go =
      VAR
         bb
      IN
         bb ⟵ sofar_EQL_NVAR (100) ;
         resp ⟵ NEG_BOOL (bb) ;
         IF
            bb = FALSE
```

```
      THEN
        sofar_INC_NVAR ;
          num ⟵ sofar_VAL_NVAR
      ELSE
          num := 1
      END
    END

      END
```

Figure S10.1 illustrates the dependencies of this implementation.

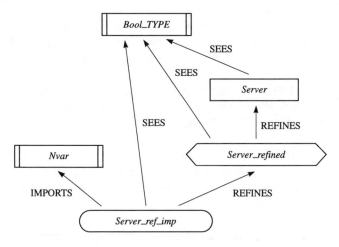

Figure S10.1 Dependencies of the server refinement implementation.

Bibliography

The following annotated list includes all the works referred to in this book. The index item 'References' will lead the reader to the places in the text where a reference is made. It also includes other works about B, and a selection of works on the wider theme of formal methods for software development. For these last two categories, no index entries will be found.

Abrial, J-R. (1989). A formal approach to large software construction. In *Mathematics of Program Construction* (van de Snepscheut, J. L. A., ed.). Springer-Verlag, Berlin.

Abrial, J-R. (1991). A refinement case study. In *Proceedings of the 4th Refinement Workshop* (Morris, J. M. and Shaw, R.C., eds). Workshops in Computing, Springer-Verlag, Berlin.

Abrial, J-R. (1992). On constructing large software systems. In *Algorithms, Software, Architecture* (van Leeuwen, J., ed.). Information Processing 92, Vol. 1. Elsevier Science Publishers B. V. (North Holland), Amsterdam.

Abrial, J-R. (1993). B-Technology technical overview. In B-Core (1994).
An excellent summary of the mathematical foundations of the abstract machine notation. For a fuller account, readers should consult Abrial (1996).

Abrial, J-R. (1996). *The B-book — Assigning Programs to Meanings.* Cambridge University Press, to appear.
An extended account of the mathematical foundations of abstract machine notation and the B-Method.

Abrial, J-R, Lee, M. K. O., Neilson, D., Scharbach, P. and Sorensen, I. H. (1991). The B-Method. In *VDM 91 — Formal Software Development Methods, 4th International Symposium on VDM*, Vol. 2. Springer-Verlag, Berlin.

B-Core (1994). *B-Toolkit.* B-Core (UK) Ltd, Oxford.
The manual for the B-Toolkit. It includes an installation guide, user's manual, summary of the abstract machine notation, summary

of the contents of the reusable library, and operating instructions for the demonstrations distributed with the B-Toolkit.

Bicarregui, J. (1993). Algorithm refinement with read and write frames. In *FME '93 Proceedings*, Lecture Notes in Computer Science 690. Springer-Verlag, Berlin.

Bicarregui, J. and Ritchie, B. (1993) Invariants, frames and postconditions: a comparison of the VDM and B notations. In *FME '93 Proceedings*, Lecture Notes in Computer Science 690. Springer-Verlag, Berlin.

Bicarregui, J. and Matthews, B. (1995) Formal methods in practice: A comparison of two support systems for proof. In *SOFSEM '95: Theory and Practice of Informatics*, (Bartosek, M., Staudek, J. and Wiedermann, J., eds). Springer-Verlag, Berlin.

Bowen, J. and Stavridou, V. (1993). Safety-critical systems, formal methods and standards. In *Software Engineering Journal*, July, pp. 189 – 209.

Chapront, P. (1992). Vital coded processor and safety related software design. In *Safety of Computer Control Systems 1992 (SAFECOMP '92), Computer Systems in Safety Critical Applications* (Frey, H. H., ed.). Proceedings of the IFAC Symposium, Switzerland, 29 – 30 October, 1992, pp. 141 – 5, Pergamon Press.

DaSilva, C., Dehbonei, B. and Mejia, F. (1993). Formal specification in the development of industrial applications: subway speed control system. In *IFIP Transactions, Formal Description Techniques* (Diaz, M. and Groz, R., eds), Vol. C, Part 10. Elsevier Science Publishers B. V. (North Holland), Amsterdam.
   A short account of the B-Method and an example from a safety-critical application.

Dehbonei, B. and Mejia, F. (1995). Formal development of safety-critical software systems in railway signalling. In *Applications of Formal Methods* (Hinchey, M. G. and Bowen, J. P., eds), Prentice-Hall International (UK) Ltd, Hemel Hempstead.

Dijkstra, E. W. (1975). Guarded commands, nondeterminacy and formal derivation of programs. *Communications of the ACM*, **18**(8).
   Proposes the guarded command language as a basis for programming.

Günther, T., Schewe, K-D. and Wetzel, I. (1993). On the derivation of executable database programs from formal specifications. In *FME '93 Proceedings*, Lecture Notes in Computer Science 690. Springer-Verlag, Berlin.

Hammond, J. (1993). *Translation from Z to the Abstract Machine Notation*. Praxis plc, 20 Manvers Street, Bath BA2 1PX, UK.
    This report, issued in the course of DTI IED Project No. 1639, describes how Z specifications can be converted into abstract machines for development using the B-Method.

Hoare, J. P. (1995). Application of the B-Method to CICS. In *Applications of Formal Methods* (Hinchey, M. G. and Bowen, J. P., eds). Prentice-Hall International (UK) Ltd, Hemel Hempstead.

Jones, C. B. (1980). *Software Development − A Rigorous Approach*. Prentice-Hall, Englewood Cliffs, NJ.

Jones, C. B. (1986). *Systematic Software Development Using VDM*. Prentice-Hall, Englewood Cliffs, NJ.

Lano, K. (1996). *The B Language and Method: A Guide to Practical Formal Development*. Springer-Verlag, Berlin.

Lee, M. K. O., Scharbach, P. and Sorensen, I. H. (1993). Engineering real software using formal methods. In *Proceedings of the 4th Refinement Workshop* (Morris, J. M. and Shaw, R.C., eds). Workshops in Computing, Springer-Verlag, Berlin.

Mills, H. D., Linger, R. C. and Hevner, A. R. (1986). *Principles of Information Systems Analysis and Design*. Academic Press Inc., San Diego, California.
    Describes an approach to software specification that uses black boxes (stimulus history and response functions) instead of state machine models.

Morgan, C. C. (1994). *Programming from Specifications*, 2nd edn. Prentice-Hall, Englewood Cliffs, NJ.

Spivey, J. M. (1992). *The Z Notation: A Reference Manual*, 2nd edn. Prentice-Hall, Englewood Cliffs, NJ.

Thomas, M. (1994). The role of formal methods in achieving dependable software. In *Reliability Engineering and System Safety*, **43**, pp. 129 − 34.

Woodcock, J. C. P. and Loomes, M. (1988). *Software Engineering Mathematics*. Pitman Publishing, London.

Wordsworth, J. B. (1992). *Software Development with Z*. Addison-Wesley, Harlow.
Describes the use of the Z specification language for model-based software specification and development.

Glossary

This glossary gives brief definitions of all the technical terms used in this book. For most of the terms listed here, you can consult the book index to get more information. Where a term has more than one meaning, the meanings are numbered. Where such a term is used in the glossary in explaining another, the number of the relevant meaning appears in parentheses after the term, unless the sense is obvious from the context.

abstract machine
>Any one of the three constructs of the B-Method: machine, refinement, implementation.

abstract machine notation (AMN)
>A combination of mathematics and substitutions that is used in specification and design in the B-Method.

abstract object
>In AMN, a value chosen to represent a more complex object.

abstract operations
>Operations on abstract variables.

abstract state
>A set of values of abstract variables.

abstract variables
>In a refinement – the variables of the machine or refinement being refined. In an implementation of a machine – the variables of the machine. In an implementation of a refinement – the variables of the refinement.

algorithm design
>The process of organizing program statements to make operations.

AMN
>See **abstract machine notation**.

analyser
>A tool in the B-Toolkit that checks the syntax and type-correctness of an abstract machine, and establishes its suitability for processing by other tools.

animator
> A tool in the B-Toolkit that allows you to execute an analysed machine.

annotation
> A comment in an abstract machine intended for informal explanation.

annotation change
> A change to the definition of an abstract machine that does not change its meaning.

antecedent
> The proposition on the left of an implication.

API
> See **application programming interface**.

append
> A mathematical operation to add a value to the end of a sequence (1).

application programming interface
> A layer in the layered software model that provides functions used by application programs.

autoprover
> A tool in the B-Toolkit that attempts to discharge proof obligations.

base generator
> A tool in the B-Toolkit that generates two machines and an implementation from a system definition.

bijection
> A function that is an injection and a surjection.

binary relation
> In set theory, a set of ordered pairs.

bound variable
> A variable that is not free. See **free variable**.

cardinality
> For a finite set, the number of members in the set.

Cartesian product
> A mathematical notation that denotes the set of all ordered pairs whose first members are in one set and whose second members are in another (not necessarily different) set.

character

(1) A number in the range 0 to 255.

(2) A graphical representation corresponding to a character (1).

code generator

A tool in the B-Toolkit that produces C code from an analysed implementation.

commit

A tool in the B-Toolkit that registers an abstract machine as part of a development.

component machine

A machine in the component layer of the layered software model. It provides preconditioned operations on its state, and enquiry operations to decide whether the preconditions are true.

composition

An operation to combine two relations.

concatenation

A mathematical operation to join one sequence (1) to the end of another.

concrete operations

Operations on concrete variables.

concrete state

Values of concrete variables.

concrete variables

In a refinement – the variables of the refinement. In an implementation – the variables of the implementation.

conjunct

A predicate that is part of a conjunction.

conjunction

A logical operation corresponding to 'and'.

consequent

The proposition on the right of an implication.

constraints

A predicate about the parameters of a machine. It is used to exercise control over how users of the machine can instantiate it.

context
> A predicate about the sets and constants of a machine.

data design
> The process of choosing program data structures to represent the abstract structures of a specification.

deferred set
> A set of a machine whose value is determined by the implementation.

dependency
> A relation between abstract machines in which the meaning of the first is determined, at least in part, by the mathematical content of the second.

disjunct
> A predicate that is part of a disjunction.

disjunction
> A logical operation corresponding to (inclusive) 'or'.

domain
> The set of first members of the pairs of a relation.

empty set
> A set with no members.

encapsulation
> A software engineering practice that identifies the data to be managed by a software system, and allows it to be viewed or changed only through a defined interface.

enumerated set
> In AMN, a deferred set whose values are given symbolic names in the machine definition.

enumeration
> A set defined by listing its members.

equivalence
> A logical operation corresponding to '... if and only if ...'.

existential quantification
> A predicate that asserts something about at least one member of a set.

existential quantifier
> The symbol that binds variables in an existential quantification.

free variable

> A variable is free in an expression if it is not bound by a quantifier, a set comprehension, a generalized sum, a generalized product, a generalized union, a generalized intersection or a lambda abstraction.

from-set

> A set from which the first members of the pairs of a relation are drawn.

function

> A relation in which no two pairs have the same first member.

generalized substitution

> A representation of a specification as a function from predicates to predicates.

given set

> In set theory, a set introduced to guarantee that other sets can be constructed. In AMN, a parameter, deferred set or enumerated set of a machine.

guard

> A predicate that controls the use of a substitution.

implementation

> The final construct in developing software by the B-Method, from which code can be generated. One of the three types of abstract machine.

implication

> A logical operation corresponding to 'if ... then ...'.

injection

> A function whose inverse is also a function.

instantiation

> The process of defining values for the parameters of a machine.

interface

> In the B-Method, a generated machine that provides a testing interface for another machine.

interface generator

> A tool in the B-Toolkit that generates a sample application for a machine that has an analysed implementation.

interprover
> A tool in the B-Toolkit that allows you to investigate failures in the autoprover and to supply new theory and tactics.

intersection
> A mathematical notation that denotes the set of values common to two sets.

invariant
> (1) A predicate specifying a relation between the values of the variables in a loop that is true every time the while-test is made.
>
> (2) A predicate specifying a relation between the values of the variables of an abstract machine that is established by the initialization and preserved by the operations.

inverse
> A mathematical operation that reverses the pairs of a relation.

lambda abstraction
> A method of defining a function which gives a value expression for each argument.

library machine
> A low-level machine provided as part of the B-Toolkit.

linker
> A tool in the B-Toolkit that combines object modules into executable objects.

local variable
> In AMN, a variable introduced in the ANY-WHERE-THEN-END or VAR-IN-END substitution. In algorithm design, variables that are not part of the concrete state, but are used in algorithms to hold intermediate results.

loop
> In programming languages, a construct in which a group of instructions is repeated as long as a predicate remains true.

loop substitution
> In AMN, a loop is a substitution with a while-test, body, variant and invariant. It formalizes the loop programming construct.

machine

> The specification construct of the B-Method. One of the three types of abstract machine.

markup generator

> A tool in the B-Toolkit that creates formatter input for an analysed construct.

maths change

> A change to the definition of an abstract machine that changes its meaning.

membership

> A relation between a value and a set of which it is a member.

multiple assignment

> A simultaneous replacement in an expression of several free variables by values.

natural numbers

> The whole numbers from 0 upwards.

negation

> A logical operation corresponding to 'not'.

non-determinism

> A method of specifying an operation in which the outcome is not uniquely determined by the inputs and current state.

null set

> Same as empty set.

operation

> (1) An interaction with an abstract machine that changes or enquires upon its state.
>
> (2) A substitution (with inputs and outputs) that preserves the invariant (2) of an abstract machine.

ordered pair

> A mathematical construction from two values that allows them to be distinguished as first and second.

parallel substitution

> A combination of substitutions in which each takes its own effect independent of others.

parameter
> A name in a machine definition whose value is to be supplied by the user of the machine.

partial function
> Same as function.

partial injection
> Same as injection.

powerset
> A mathematical construction from a set that denotes the set of its subsets.

precondition
> A predicate on the inputs of an operation and the current state of an abstract machine that the user of the operation must know to be true before attempting the operation.

predicate
> A mathematical notation that denotes true or false depending on values assigned to its free variables.

prepend
> A mathematical operation to add a value to the front of a sequence (1).

proof obligation generator
> A tool in the B-Toolkit that generates proof obligations for consistency of a machine and correctness of a refinement or implementation.

proof printer
> A tool in the B-Toolkit that prints proof obligations and their proofs.

proper subset
> A relation between sets in which the first is a subset of the second, and the sets are not equal.

proposition
> A variable over true and false.

pseudo-program
> A notation borrowed and extended from programming and used in abstract machine notation to denote a substitution.

quantifier
> See **existential quantifier** and **universal quantifier**.

range
> The set of second members of the pairs of a relation.

refinement
> An intermediary between a machine and an implementation. One of the three types of abstract machine.

relation
> A set of ordered pairs.

remake
> A tool in the B-Toolkit to re-establish the previously existing state of a development after you have committed a maths change to one of its components.

retrieve relation
> A predicate in the invariant (2) of a refinement or implementation that specifies the relation between the abstract and concrete variables.

sequence
> (1) A mathematical formalization of the idea of an ordered collection of values.
>
> (2) A substitution (2) consisting of two substitutions (2) in order.

set
> An unordered collection of values.

set comprehension
> An expression that denotes a set by giving, as a predicate, a property that determines which values are members of the set.

set enumeration
> Same as an enumeration.

simple substitution
> The replacement in an expression of all the free occurrences of a variable by a value.

singleton
> A set with exactly one member.

software design
> The process of choosing a concrete implementation for an abstract specification.

state
> Values in an abstract machine that are changed by the operations, but persist between operations.

string
> (1) A finite sequence (1) of characters (1).
>
> (2) A finite sequence (1) of characters (2).

subordination
> A relation between abstract machines in which the mathematical content of the first determines, at least in part, the meaning of the second. (The subordination relation is the inverse of the dependency relation.)

subset
> A relation between sets in which all the members of the first set are members of the second.

substitution
> (1) The act of replacing a variable of a term or predicate in all its free occurrences by some expression.
>
> (2) A pseudo-program regarded as denoting a substitution (1).

surjection
> A function whose range is the whole of the from-set.

system definition
> An AMN construct used to define complex data structures. It is used as input to the base generator.

term
> A mathematical expression denoting a value from some set.

theory
> Rules used in the autoprover that embody the properties of mathematical notation.

to-set
> A set from which the second members of pairs in a relation are drawn.

total function
> A function whose domain is the whole of the from-set.

total injection
> An injection that is a total function.

truth table
> A table showing how the value of a propositional function depends on the values of its constituent propositions.

type
> A property of variables in AMN. The type of a variable is a set, constructed from given sets, of which the variable is a member.

union
> A mathematical operation to construct a set from the members of two others.

universal quantification
> A predicate that asserts something about all the members of a set.

universal quantifier
> The symbol that binds variables in a universal quantification.

variable

> (1) An undetermined value from some set.

> (2) A named aspect of the state of an abstract machine.

Z
> A specification language invented by J-R. Abrial. Like AMN, it uses set theory and predicate calculus to specify data and operations.

Index of abstract machines

This index lists all the machines, implementations and refinements used in the examples, except library machines. In this index the abstract machines are listed in alphabetical order. For each abstract machine the index shows the page on which it is defined, whether it is a machine (mch), implementation (imp) or refinement (ref), and the pages on which it is used.

Name	Type	Def	Used
Array	mch	260	269 (extended by *Student_array*)
			302 (included by *Nat_SET_refined*)
Birthday_book	mch	273	
CMA	mch	39	169 (imported by *CMA_names_imp*)
			192 (refined by *CMA_refined*)
			289 (refined by *CMA_imp_seq*)
			292 (refined by *CMA_imp_arr*)
			299 (imported by *RCMA_imp*)
CMA_imp_arr	imp	292	
CMA_imp_seq	imp	288	
CMA_names	mch	164	168 (refined by *CMA_names_imp*)
CMA_names_imp	imp	168	
CMA_ref_imp	ref	198	
CMA_refined	ref	192	198 (refined by *CMA_ref_imp*)
FFCMA	mch	87	
Nat_SET	mch	261	302 (refined by *Nat_SET_refined*)
Nat_SET_refined	ref	302	
Owners	mch	51	
Positive	mch	259	
RCMA	mch	297	298 (refined by *RCMA_imp*)
RCMA_imp	imp	298	
RMan	mch	23	66 (included in *RRMan*)
RRMan	mch	64	139 (refined by *RRManI*)
RRManI	imp	139	
RRRMan	mch	157	159 (refined by *RRRManI*)
RRRManI	imp	159	
Server	mch	59	301 (refined by *Server_refined*)
Server_refined	ref	301	304 (refined by *Server_ref_imp*)
Server_ref_imp	imp	304	
Storman	mch	61, 265	294 (refined by *Storman_imp*)
Storman_imp	imp	294	

Name	Type	Def	Used
Student_array	mch	269	287 (refined by *Student_array_imp*)
			292 (imported by *CMA_imp_arr*)
Student_array_imp	imp	287	
Student_record	mch	166	169 (imported by *CMA_names_imp*)

General index

A

abstract machine 8
abstract object 176
abstract operations 131
abstract sets 211
abstract state 95
abstract variables 95
algorithm design 95, 192
analyser 27
animator 27
annotation change 30
antecedent 206
  consolidating 207
ANY-WHERE-THEN-END rule 57
ANY-WHERE-THEN-END substitution 56
  local variable 56
  then-part 57
API 11
API-layer machine 157, 158
  Class manager's assistant 164 – 166,
  297
  Customers 173
  Recoverable resource
  manager 157 – 158
append to a sequence 225
application programming interface 11
arithmetic expressions 204
arithmetic functions 204
arithmetic relations 204
ASSERTIONS clause
  implementation 131
  machine 41
  refinement 193
assignment sign 20
autoprover 29

B

B-Toolkit
  analyser 27
  animator 27
  annotation change 30
  autoprover 29
  base generator 176
  code translator 152

B-Toolkit *(continued)*
  committing 27
  demonstration copy vii
  interface generator 152
  interprover 30
  library machine 39
  linker 152
  markup generator 31
  maths change 30
  proof obligation generator 29
  proof printer 29
  remake 30
backward composition 220
backward composition sign 220
BASE part 175
  MANDATORY section 175
  OPTIONAL section 175
BEGIN-END rule 46
BEGIN-END substitution 46
bijection 222
bijection sign 222
binary relation 218
Birthday book
  full-function machine 273
  informal state machine 92
body of a loop 112
Boolean substitution 68
bound variable 209
braces
  in set comprehension 208
  in set enumeration 208

C

cardinality 216
Cartesian product 218
Cartesian product sign 218
CASE rule 86
CASE substitution 86
  else-part 87
character 164
choice-by-predicate rule 84
choice-by-predicate substitution 84
choice-from-a-set rule 57
choice-from-a-set substitution 57